RHETORICS OF INSECURITY

Rhetorics of Insecurity

BELONGING AND VIOLENCE
IN THE NEOLIBERAL ERA

Edited by Zeynep Gambetti and Marcial Godoy-Anativia

A joint publication of the Social Science Research Council
and New York University Press

NEW YORK UNIVERSITY PRESS

New York and London

www.nyupress.org

Library of Congress Cataloging-in-Publication Data

Rhetorics of insecurity : belonging and violence in the neoliberal era /
edited by Zeynep Gambetti and Marcial Godoy-Anativia.

    pages cm

  "A joint publication of the Social Science Research Council and New
York University Press."

  Includes bibliographical references and index.

  ISBN 978-0-8147-0843-9 (cl : alk. paper)

   1. Security (Psychology) 2. Security, International. 3. Violence.
4. Neoliberalism. I. Gambetti, Zeynep editor of compilation.
II. Godoy-Anativia, Marcial editor of compilation. III. Social Science
Research Council (U.S.)

BF575.S35R36   2013

155.9—dc23

2013001058

New York University Press books are printed on acid-free paper, and their
binding materials are chosen for strength and durability. We strive to use
environmentally responsible suppliers and materials to the greatest extent
possible in publishing our books.

Manufactured in the United States of America

C 10 9 8 7 6 5 4 3 2 1

P 10 9 8 7 6 5 4 3 2 1

References to Internet websites (URLs) were accurate at the time of writing.
Neither the author nor New York University Press is responsible for URLs
that may have expired or changed since the manuscript was prepared.

To Hrant Dink, who dared to speak up in an insecure world

Contents

Acknowledgments

This volume is the long-simmered result of a very interesting conversation that emerged among the regional programs—the Ford Foundation–funded Regional Advisory Panels (RAPS)—at the Social Science Research Council (SSRC) in the late 1990s and early 2000s. At the time, there was a fantastic architecture of area-based regional programs that were profoundly internationalized through the RAPS and the dense networks of scholars, from both North and South, that they brought to the table. This architecture allowed for and encouraged cross-pollinization between area programs, and its program directors consistently sought opportunities to create dialogue and collaboration across these deeply internationalized bodies of regional expertise. The contributions to this volume were initially commissioned for our 2007 workshop entitled "Citizenship, Securitization and Vernacular Violence," which took place at Boğaziçi University Department of Political Science and International Relations, in Istanbul, Turkey, January 26–27, 2007, and which convened a group of scholars drawn from the networks of the Latin America, Middle East/North Africa, South Asia, Southeast Asia, and Africa Programs at the SSRC. The Istanbul workshop was a follow-up to the April 2005 meeting convened by the Regional Programs, "Belonging, the Crisis of Citizenship and the Nation State" in Dakar, Senegal, and on the "Social Inequalities and Conflict" meeting convened later that year in Bogota, Colombia. Each of these convenings sought to focus inquiry on different dimensions of citizenship and belonging in a post–Cold War, neoliberalized planet. In particular, the January 2007 workshop in Istanbul sought to advance the SSRC's work on the relationship between the production of different types of localized conflict and violence, and various processes at the global level.

We are deeply indebted to program directors Seteney Shami, Eric Hershberg, Alcinda Honwana, Itty Abraham, and Ronald Kassimir for their investment in and enthusiasm for this work, as well as to the members of the Regional Advisory Panels and SSRC Regional Programs staff. We are also indebted to Stephen Jackson, then deputy director of the SSRC's Conflict Prevention and Peace Forum, who played a key role in keeping these conversations going at key moments, and would also like to thank Peter Sahlins, then director of Academic Programs at the Council, who was crucial in making the Istanbul workshop a reality. We thank all the contributors to this volume for their intellectual energy, generosity, and patience, but especially Rossana Reguillo and Peter Geschiere for their support and guidance throughout the process. Many thanks are due to the Department of Political Science and International Relations at Boğaziçi University, the Hewlett Foundation, and the Ford Foundation. We are also indebted to Craig Calhoun, Seteney Shami, Alyson Metzger, and Michael Simon of the SSRC for their unswerving faith in the project as well as for their invaluable help in materializing it.

Special thanks also go to Yasemin Ipek Can, who not only contributed a paper to the volume but also shouldered the logistics of the 2007 workshop. Political Science and International Relations Department students whose diligence and generous smiles won the hearts of workshop participants also deserve recognition here: Volkan Yilmaz, Zuleyha Demirok, Lisya Yafet, and Samil Can.

Finally, we would like to honor the memory of Paul Price, former editorial director at the SSRC. Price was enthusiastic about reviving the project after a long slumber and presenting the manuscript to New York University Press in 2011. We were immensely saddened to hear that he passed away before seeing the published volume.

RHETORICS OF INSECURITY

States of (In)security:
Coming to Terms with an Erratic Terrain

Zeynep Gambetti and Marcial Godoy-Anativia

The twenty-first century started off by undoing the promise of a New World Order. Announced by George Bush Sr. in the 1990s, the new order was expected to involve a multipolar world in which human rights, democracy, and peace would prevail. The one that is being delivered instead seems set to undermine the universality of rights and the legitimacy and desirability of popular rule. War, social strife, and structural violence are still haunting the planet. But so are protests that no longer take the visionary paths offered by a century and a half of working-class struggle. Occupy groups and the *indignados* of numerous countries are more anarchic than orderly, more spontaneous and local than any International can encompass. This double movement away from "order" elevates the categories of risk (Beck), control (Deleuze), precarity (Butler), thanatopolitics (Bauman, Mbembe), or state of exception (Agamben) to the level of ordinariness. In line with the dissolution of previous certainties, "security" seems to have become a preoccupying concern. In the words of one of its most vocal theorists, the "ending of the Cold War has created a remarkable fluidity and openness in the whole pattern and quality of international relations" (Buzan 1991: 432). Corresponding to the ambiguity that marks the dissolution of former institutional and material structures, "security" now takes on unexpected twists and instigates novel practices.

The present volume is not so much about how we ended up here as about what it means to be here. It is not, however, a mere extension of so-called security studies in the domain of international relations. We attempt, rather, to explore the ethnographic ramifications of the concern with security in contexts as diverse as mushroom picking in the United States, civil society activism in Turkey, and forms of belonging in Cameroon. The reason why constituting a panorama that spans the globe appears necessary is that "combat cultures" (Tsing) functioning as forms of identification, threat dramaturgies that recruit citizens as vigilantes, and peculiar notions of freedom (freedom as survival, freedom as security) have become integral parts of dissimilar cultures. The essays at hand contend with such questions as how security discourses shape technologies of identity and how novel forms of entrepreneurial or risk-embracing citizenship create exclusion in India, Cameroon, the Democratic Republic of Congo, Turkey, Mexico, the United States, Russia, and the Netherlands. The red thread that runs through the reflections consists of the ways in which violence is inherent to processes of securitization that unequally but persistently affect local cultures and values across the globe.

In analytic terms, the volume is structured around two related binaries that emerge quite clearly from the contributions at hand. The first is an insecurity/security binary that may be derived from Rossana Reguillo's definition of "rhetorics of security," and which, to differing degrees of immanence and elaboration, is present across the texts. In her essay, Reguillo defines "rhetorics of security" as "that set of eloquent arguments that seeks to persuade and provoke emotive responses through tropes (reasonings and judgments) anchored in a principle of generalized insecurity." The second binary is an analysis of the present conjuncture as a moment of articulation between two distinct sociohistorical projects—neoliberalism and neoconservatism. A reflection upon these two elements suggests that the insecurity/security binary may be articulated as a *spatial* dimension that marks the way social practices are ordered on a local or territorial basis, and the neoliberal/neoconservative binary as a *temporal* one that marks a specific moment in the history of (Western) societies, allowing us to speak of our approach as a *space-time* formulation. The underlying concern is to address the question of whether we are facing what might be called a global production of subjectivities of security—and if so, why now, at this particular moment in time.

These two axes enable us to ground one of the fundamental claims of this book: political liberalism is among those discourses that are destabilized through the paradoxical alliance between terms that constitute the very condition of existence of their contradictory "others" in the present era. Faith in the rule of law, in the autonomy of civil society, and in the rational-legal basis of citizenship cannot possibly be sustained under present conditions for a number of reasons: first, paralegal or extralegal processes tend to become the underside of the maintenance of law and order; second, civil society tends to become indistinct from the state; and third, citizenship is no longer a merely legal concept but also an "insider" status whose boundaries are established through discourses and practices of autochthony, volunteerism, and vigilantism, and which share in the formal and informal distribution of globalized benefits. In other words, all of the observations presented in this volume focus on forms of de-institutionalization and disaffiliation, accompanied by a paradoxical re-institutionalization of the dismantled state through various "state effects" and cultures of securitization.

Political liberalism assumes that law is the most effective bulwark against power—the power of the masses as well as the power of the state apparatus. On a minor note, business law is considered to be the condition of possibility of fairness in the economic realm, since it regulates and enforces compliance with contracts, sets boundaries to accumulation so as to thwart the formation of monopolies, and assigns duties and obligations to employers as well as to employees. Law is therefore taken to be the universal that orders particularities in such a way as to allow for fundamental rights and liberties to take effect. The legalist-contractual approach, very much in line with the basic tenets of political liberalism, equates politics to law and democracy to procedure—that is, to a framework that allows for the rights-bearing individual to enjoy sovereignty as far as the decisions concerning his life are concerned. Likewise, problems posed by social and economic inequality are to be "solved" through legal arrangements. More often than not, this approach takes as given certain human capabilities or "powers," as the Rawlsian concept of justice as fairness demonstrates. Individual citizens are free by "virtue of their two moral powers (a capacity for a sense of justice and for a conception of the good) and the powers of reason (of judgment, thought, and inference connected with these powers)" (Rawls 1996: 19). These capacities are thought to be the very ground upon which the public good may be erected and codified through law.

What shatters this seemingly harmonious universe is not, as is often argued, the rise of postmodernism or identity politics. Questions of identity and plurality can conveniently be settled through the Rawlsian notion of an overlapping consensus among reasonable beings. The historical conjuncture that reveals the flipside of law and reason is neoliberalism—the unconcealed acknowledgment of market logic as the sole arbiter of value. On the ideational front, Rawls seems to have been defeated by Nozick and Dworkin on the one side and by Hayek and Friedman on the other. On the practical front, neo-liberalism appears as "the solution at last found" to do away with the tension between political and economic liberalism, public good and private interest, citizen and man, sovereignty and necessity, by subjugating the former terms to the latter. This, we argue, could not have been possible without the two binaries (or alliances) around which the discussions in this volume are constructed.

Neoliberalism/Neoconservatism

The neoliberalism/neoconservatism binary is intended as a temporal marker, as a strategic analytic figure that will enable us to reflect upon why particular forms of affiliation and disaffiliation are emerging at this point in time. The historical confluence of a (more or less) consolidated neoliberal economic project with a neoconservative political program may be, for our purposes, the single most important outcome of the past three decades.

Although the attempt to come up with a standardized definition of neo-liberalism may be futile, the contributors to this volume agree upon some of the basic features of the novel political economy. In this introduction, we outline these so as to bring forth the implicit background consensus upon which the texts are built. The aim is to avoid constructing neoliberalism as a kind of "empty signifier" that explains everything and anything; we wish, rather, to deploy it as a trope that represents practices and subjectivities enabling the generalized outsourcing and individualization of risk.

The regime summarily called "neoliberalism" has inherited from liberalism the faith in the market economy as an eventually self-regulating mechanism of exchange and distribution of goods and services, and also of rights and liberties. The prevailing Chicago school creed considers economic liberty to be the condition of possibility of political liberty. This assumption is based as much on pure hypothetical reasoning as on the claim that any interference with the market would inevitably lead to totalitarianism—a Hayekian proposition taken up uncritically by monetarists such as Milton Friedman. But one need not be a "market fundamentalist" in order to suppose that the retreat of authoritative institutions and clear-cut legalistic boundaries may provide opportunities for a creative reshaping of individual choices. The post–Washington Consensus belief is that a small but responsive state undertaking the function of safeguarding public order will empower citizens in novel ways by transferring unto them the moral (and political) responsibility of constituting their own lives.

This outlook, however, is overshadowed by ways in which neoliberalism is being imposed through a hitherto unparalleled level of orchestration between multinational corporations, intergovernmental organizations, and states. According to scholars who emphasize the disempowering features of global market making, the basis of capital accumulation is being shifted from production to finance, not only owing to the latter's potential for unrestricted expansion but also because financial instruments and institutions allow for the spreading of risks (Harvey 2005: 161–162). The defining impacts of neoliberal globalization are neatly summarized in the following passage:

> 1 [The protection of] the interests of capital and [the expansion of] the process of capital accumulation (if this is viewed as occurring within and because of a structural crisis in capitalism or a long-term economic stagnation, then neoliberal economic globalization is essentially a strategy of crisis management or stabilisation); 2) the tendency towards homogenisation of state policies and even state forms in the direction of protecting capital and expanding the process of capital accumulation, via a new economic orthodoxy, i.e. market ideology (wherein even the state itself becomes subject to marketisation while simultaneously being deployed instrumentally on behalf of capital); 3) the addition and expansion of a layer of transnationalised institutional authority above the states (which has the aim and purpose of penetrating states and rearticulating them to the purposes of global capital accumulation); and 4) the exclusion of dissident social forces from the arena of state policy making (in order to insulate the new neoliberal state forms against the societies over which they preside and in order to facilitate the socialisation of risk on behalf of the interests of capital). (Amoore et al. 1997: 181)

What needs to be underlined here is the fact that state power is the paradoxical instrument of the dismantling of the welfare state. The elimination of the obstacles in the way of marketization (trade union power, social rights, political liberalism, constitutionalism) has called for outright coups in certain parts of the world—Chile was the first laboratory for such an experiment (Harvey 2006)—austerity packages, ethnic wars, or "wars against terrorism" in others.[1] A return to the process of "primitive accumulation" was also required in order to turn hitherto uncommodified areas or resources into marketable entities. This was conspicuously accompanied by the will to suppress protests, allow unemployment to rise, and to deprive local populations of their traditional means of livelihood through a form of structural violence that makes previously self-sufficient peasant communities dependent on the market. To such an inventory, one needs to add the sinister phenomenon of "disaster capitalism" where social turmoil, natural disasters such as Hurricane Katrina, and even stock market crashes become means of transferring capital and property from the stricken to powerful creditors (Klein 2007; Smith 2007).

This short chronicle of violence compels us to probe further into the way neoliberalism ticks at the political and societal levels. Contributors to this volume agree that the prefix "neo-" in neoliberalism represents a new social and political logic that has emerged from the relatively short history of the International Monetary Fund and World Bank–led imposition of the "free market" around the globe.

The structural transformation undergone by the state, the dismantling of welfare regimes, and the replacement of the concept of rights with market-based criteria of performance could not have been achieved without a substantive shift in subjectivities and patterns of belonging. As Maurizio Lazzarato brilliantly demonstrates, financialization is not solely an economic phenomenon. Looking at how pension funds become fiscal resources for both private and public enterprises, he shows how this is an individualizing technique that entraps the wage earner in such a way that the latter is at the mercy of both the employer and the market. Reversing the trend of the socialization of risks (social security schemes and mutual associations), financialization turns the worker into a peculiar type of capital within a "multiplicity of investments (in training, mobility, affectivity) that the individual as 'human capital' must make to optimize performances" (Lazzarato 2009: 121). The wage earner thus turns proactive in ensuring the profitability of capital in general. The paradox lies in that the individualization of risk reconstitutes individuals as the subjects of their own destiny, while subjecting them to a permanent state of insecurity and precarity (Butler 2009).

Seen in this light, celebrating hybridity and deregulation for their liberating potential might be a sign of misplaced optimism, given the renewed power of capital to co-opt resistances through new forms of subjectivation. As Lois McNay asks, "If individual autonomy is not the opposite of or limit to neoliberal governance, but rather lies at the heart of disciplinary control through responsible self-management, what are the possible grounds upon which political resistance can be used?" (2009: 56). Exploring such a prospect is the purpose of the present collection of essays. For instance, how neoliberalism encourages resourcefulness as a survival strategy that transgresses the narrow limits prescribed by law or convention still needs to be mapped out in all its details and detours. Likewise, the relationship between these new entrepreneurial subjectivities and organized crime, lynching and vigilantism, xenophobia and ethnic cleavages, and terrorism or combat cultures calls for closer scrutiny.

It would be misleading, though, to conceive of neoliberalism as the very opposite of conservatism. As Wendy Brown convincingly argues, aversion to the "social" is one of the instances in which neoliberal values and neoconservative ones converge. But reconciling "the Party of Moral Values and the Party of Big Business" or "threats to security" and "threats to humanity" is not a simple feat, and the alliance is an uneasy one (Brown 2006: 698). The neoliberal logic glorifies laissez-faire rationality except when legal measures are needed to ensure capital accumulation and keep opposition at bay; neoconservatives advocate interventions into the private realm to regulate morality, but also press for detaxation so as to benefit the growth of wealth in private hands. Brown sees the one as preparing the ground for the other: "Neoconservatism sewn in the soil prepared by neoliberalism breeds a new political form, a specific modality of governance and citizenship, one whose incompatibility with even formal democratic practices and institutions does not spur a legitimation crisis because of the neoliberal devaluation of these practices and institutions that neoconservatism then consecrates" (702).

David Harvey also argues that neoconservatism is consistent with the neoliberal distrust of democratic institutions. Indeed, "neo-conservatism appears as a mere stripping away of the veil of authoritarianism in which neoliberalism sought to envelop itself" (Harvey 2005: 82). The former tends to resolve some of the contradictions inherent in neoliberal market economy. In response to the chaos that would govern when competitive and acquisitive interests are allowed free reign, "some degree of coercion appears inevitable to restore order" (82). The neoconservative twist to the modern problem of order is to highlight threats and propose militarized solutions to social problems.

In many ways, the neoliberal-neoconservative articulation can answer some of the key questions raised by the power of neoliberalism. It is certainly a useful temporalization of neoliberalism and also quite instrumental to the political imperative to move the debate forward. The point is that the complementarity between neoliberalism and neoconservatism cannot but engender frictions or ambivalences.

Theoretically speaking, Hobbes's *Leviathan* suggests that the conservation of the status quo through repressive sovereignty is the rather paradoxical requirement for sustaining a private sphere of possessive individualism and market exchange. Historically speaking, the edgy complementarity between conservatism and liberalism can be said to have surfaced when, in the eighteenth and nineteenth centuries, the discourse of democratic rights proved too much for the free market to withstand. Revolutions and working-class movements were threatening the formal limits that political liberalism set for itself. Locke's attempt to democratize the sovereign instance while at the same time maintaining the inequalities of property and labor expenditure was backfiring. Indeed, Disraeli's fear of poverty and of the rising power of working-class movements epitomizes the main thrust behind the conservative reaction at the end of the nineteenth century. Historically, conservatism seems to have served as a savior to economic liberalism.

Today, neoliberalism appears to devolve onto civil society the powers initially transferred to the state, thus dissolving the power differential between the state and society. But this, too, carries a price tag: state power may be devolved only on the condition that the second and more fundamental inequality between capital and labor be sustained. Like Locke's ultimately paradoxical attempt to render equality (rights) and inequality (property) compatible, neoliberalism also backfires. Devolving power onto civil society is too much for the "free market" to withstand. The neoliberal agenda of "rolling back the state" cannot but set free alternative social forces—legal and paralegal, of resistance and revolt—that threaten the globalization of a particular model of accumulation. Countersystemic protests ranging from the World Social Forum to today's *indignados* and Occupy movements testify to the presence of new spaces of solidarity that have emerged as a response to the rapid transformation of social bonds.

Whereas nineteenth-century conservatism was a reaction against socialism, twenty-first-century neoconservatism seems to be a reaction against the plurality of forms that civil society takes when the state's unifying institutionality recedes. Given the altered conditions of capital accumulation in the neoliberal era, new foundations must be found for unity and conformity, so as to counterbalance the market imperative that generalizes risk and binds sections of the population together in a struggle to survive its deadly competitiveness. Unity in insecurity can only be sustained under extremely marginal conditions (as depicted in some of the contributions here). A number of strategies and *dispositifs* have been deployed to invent new bonds: war against terrorism, autochthony, self-care, vigilantism, paralegality, neopatrimonialism, xenophobia, militarism, and so forth. Thus, to use Tsing's insights, the articulation of neoliberalism and neoconservatism needs to be examined at its points of "friction." This is, in fact, what De Genova, Gambetti, and Ipek Can attempt to do. These and other essays in this volume seek to demonstrate that neoconservatism is not a trade-off between liberty and security, but the condensation of the complementarity that has emerged between a geopolitics of fear (the globalization of suspicion) and a political economy of societal regulation (the globalization of neoliberal governmentality).

Insecurity/Security

Here we touch upon the second axis around which the contributions in this book evolve: Security is a neoliberal technique of power that operates as a counterpoint to the principle of universality—of law, of the provision of state services to all citizens, and of Enlightenment ideals embodied in the republican version of liberalism—to which all law-abiding states had hitherto paid lip service, at least.

Political science and international relations literature barely does justice to the intricate connection between security and the socioeconomic rationale that seems to underlie it. Writing in 1991, Stephen Walt argued that security was fundamentally about war, but that from the 1980s onward, scholars broadened the scope of the concept to "include topics such as poverty, AIDS, environmental hazards, drug abuse, and the like" (Walt 1991: 213). This was risky, as far as Walt was concerned, since security studies could then expand excessively in such a way that even "pollution, disease, child abuse, or economic recessions could be all viewed as threats to 'security'" (213). The premonition seems to have come true. Buzan, for instance, takes for granted that among the five categories that he defines,[2] "societal security concerns the ability of societies to reproduce their traditional patterns of language, culture, association, and religious and national identity and custom within acceptable conditions for evolution" (Buzan 1991: 433). In other words, what political philosophy and the social sciences called by a variety of other names (entitlement, justice, sovereignty, nationalism, praxis, socialization, political culture, and the like) have now come to be labeled as "security" concerns. The terminological shift points to a practical one as well: the securitization of social praxis frames the issue as one involving "survival." A type of "panic politics" (Buzan 1997: 14) ensues that calls for exceptional measures in realms that were formerly regulated through law and welfare policies. This dramatization of praxis need not be legitimized by an "objective" threat, as in the case of military emergencies. This is why Tarak Barkawi claims that the "proliferation of security politics is . . . a prime instance of what Max Weber called rationalisation, the increasing dominance of means over valued ends in modern culture, science and politics" (Barkawi 2011: 703). Objective ends seem to have given way to vague threat perceptions that need not be verified before deploying various means of security.

It must be remembered, nonetheless, that the insecurity/security binary has a long history. The most fundamental (and the most dubious) relation between liberalism, violence, and insecurity was conceptualized by Hobbes, long before Carl Schmitt took up the task in the twentieth century. In Hobbes, both state and society appear to be founded by a willful pact established with the consent of all. This representation conceals the twofold violence at the very core of the foundation: first, the pact is not a product of the free will, but rather of the fear of violent death. In other words, Hobbes's liberalism does not exchange liberty for security; it replaces the prospect of unexpected and violent death for the security of a regulated death within the legal order. Second, legality can provide security only if there exists a sovereign, that is, an instance that is capable of repression for the sake of order and compliance. The belief that, when institutionalized and legal, violence somehow turns benign (read: predictable and nonarbitrary) cannot undo what Walter Benjamin calls "the ultimate insolubility of all legal problems" (Benjamin 1978: 293), that is, the paradoxical enlisting of violence as a means to settle the boundary between what is legal and what is not.

This is to say that the nature of the order established by the modern liberal state is fundamentally ambivalent. Security seems to hinge upon conformity, since individual freedoms can only be sustained within the boundaries forcefully assigned to each life activity by sovereign power. Rights cannot take effect without securing compliance, that is, without enforcing a set of obligations through sanctions and punishment. Every liberal "right" entails the regulation and supervision of domains of existence. The state is that instance which continually imposes a certain behavior on individuals, correcting those who fail to subordinate themselves to rules and norms. Enforcement, therefore, does not cease to contain an element of violence when it is associated with the seemingly benign term "law."

While these aporias of political liberalism were couched, if not in the language of reason, at least in that of rationality, what appears to have been transformed in the age of neoliberalism is the state's willingness or capacity to provide for such regulation. Schematically speaking, it is logical to expect an effervescence of anarchical forces once the state retreats—protest movements that have emerged since the 1990s testify to this. The millennial neoliberal task is, therefore, to achieve conformity without resorting to the ultimate, form-giving institutionality of the state. The solution that seems to have materialized is the transfer onto "society" of the obligation to provide for security. The emergent societal model is best represented by the figure of Behemoth that results from the fusion of state, economy, and society. This is an amorphous structure marked by the indistinction of public and private, legality and illegality, resistance and subjection, such that an "invisible hand" effectively regulates all spheres of life without resorting to the rigidity of law.

* * *

In keeping with this line of argument, what emerges as a common concern espoused by the texts in this volume is that the practices, rhetorics, and agendas of security are both reactive to and productive of rapidly expanding cartographies of insecurity. This book deploys a variety of methodological, analytic, and empirical approaches to examine both the production of this generalized insecurity and its reproduction through the very practices, tactics, and strategies erected to combat it, that is, discourses of security. The growing mass of disaffiliated, nonaffiliated and para-affiliated subjects discussed by Geschiere, Tsing, Reguillo, Derluguian, and others speak to insecurity as an outcome of social processes that long antecede the attack on the World Trade Center.

Indeed, September 11, 2001, brought to light the neoconservative imperial project based in the United States that adapted itself to the large-scale neoliberal expansion and consolidation that took place during the Clinton administration. That consolidation created previously unimaginable amounts and scales of wealth and power. In the United States, it transformed the university, changed immigration law, and finished with the dismantling of the welfare state. Domestically, the neoconservative project offers moral and social order along with the undoing of all things New Deal. It signals a return to primary forms of "advanced" capitalist accumulation, no doubt perfected in ante- and postbellum America. The Obama regime does not seem to be either able or willing to reverse this trend in the international or national arena. The way it deals with Latin America (Carranza 2010; Shifter 2010) or with police brutality against Occupy movements suggests that it is unrealistic to expect its electoral promises to be fully fulfilled. Elsewhere in the world—in Europe, as well as in Russia, India, Turkey, and Africa—the comeback of xenophobia and militarism is coupled with the newly discovered fantasies of "war against terrorism" and "autochthony." These follow the line of "creative destruction" as outlined by Harvey (2006): they create new agencies and practices while stifling others.

Many of the chapters evoke the idea of indistinction, reversal of terms, ambiguity, and confusion. This might indeed be the sign of the paradoxical alliance between neoliberalism and neoconservatism that needs to be explored in its multiple effects on social and political life. A closer look at what is discussed in each contribution would suffice to reveal the complexity of the mechanisms that go into the sustaining of the two binaries security/insecurity and neoliberalism/neoconservatism.

Peter Geschiere discusses some elements for a genealogy of the related notion of "autochthony." His main contention is that going back to the (contested) roots of this notion in classical Athens is worthwhile for better understanding its highly variegated and even paradoxical expressions in different parts of the present-day world (Africa, Canada, Europe, the Pacific). In Geschiere's account, it is precisely the dispersed history of the concept—and its capacity for taking on such variegated meanings under the guise of apparent self-evidence—that makes "autochthony" a key notion for understanding the quite surprising convergence of a neoliberal ideology and an obsessive preoccupation with local belonging and security in our globalizing world. Turning to funerals in Cameroon to highlight the paradoxes tormenting Dutch society, Geschiere convincingly shows how autochthony's promise of security necessarily breeds practices of insecurity. Often expressed in violent terms, the fight over locality is also one over property, resources, new profit venues, and market shares. The emphasis on "belonging to the soil" not only marks the migrant or "stranger" as *allochton*, but also modifies relatively tolerant societies beyond recognition, such that exclusionism and coerced integration into the dominant culture become "normal" practices.

In a similar vein, Stephen Jackson looks at the politics of authenticity revolving around the concept of *Congolité* in the Democratic Republic of Congo from mid-2006 onward. Having materialized shortly before the country's first democratic elections in more than four decades, *Congolité* dominated discussions of the elections so much that substantive policy debates about postwar reconstruction became unimaginable. The "venomous potency" of *Congolité* was that the discursive exclusion of individuals or groups that did not "fit" turned out to be dangerously vague. Alongside the "non-Congolese" or outright "foreigners," presidential candidates or groups supporting them were included or excluded according to where they belonged in a set of overlapping binaries: western Congolese or eastern, Lingalaphone or Swahiliophone, Francophone or Anglophone. Jackson argues that even though *Congolité* might seem to have emerged from nowhere as a proximate and virulent product of the elections, as a merely tactical politics of authenticity and localness, the elections were, in fact, the catalyst that caused this new discourse to crystallize out of a number of distinct but related preexisting elements. This, he contends, reveals a paradox at the heart of the liberal project of postconflict state building. The process of constructing democratic institutions can in fact electrify discursive forms of violence that are either homegrown or imported.

In his provocative essay, Georgi Derluguian picks up a comparable thread in the former Soviet Union. Asking whether globalization breeds violent anti-Enlightenment reactions, Derluguian opts for a class perspective to analyze the effects of the collapse of the developmentalist state project. The two coping strategies that developed in response to this collapse are neopatrimonialism and mobilization of ethnic and religious solidarities. Contesting the idea that ethnic strife is caused by the urge to defend local cultures against the onslaught of "McWorld," Derluguian seeks instead to show how the delegitimization of the developmental state has opened up an array of profitable alliances and influences that were up for grabs. A new class of enterprising patrons, mainly from bureaucratic backgrounds, became the gatekeepers of access to resources and mobilized support along ethnic and religious patterns of belonging. The simultaneous growth of a subproletarian class willing to seek its means of subsistence in informal and often illegal activities has in fact left the middle class in a structural and moral void. Instead of complying with the neoliberal vision of the creation of a new, property-owning middle class that would enable civil society to flourish in the postcommunist era, middle classes in Russia today have a penchant for "Pinochet rather than Jefferson."

The "civility" of civil society is also questioned by Yasemin Ipek Can, whose chapter probes into volunteer activity in post-1990 Turkey as a particular response to the threat posed by the weakening of the welfare state and the neoliberal restructuring of society. The chapter discusses how the "middle class" and its civil society organizations (CSOs) have started to align themselves with the state to assume the duty of "sharing the state's burden." Field research into the activities of one particular CSO, which took on a prominent role in the provision of educational facilities to "disadvantaged" segments of society, reveals how the most individualizing technologies of the self may be used by CSOs to promote loyalty to Republican modernism and neoliberal market values. Volunteers engaged in bettering the lives of children in urban neighborhoods with a heavy population of rural migrants speak both the official language of the state and neoliberal jargon of individualism. Risk management becomes an everyday practice of the self, an aptitude that school children must begin to acquire. Holding the individual responsible for knowing how to navigate in increasingly treacherous socioeconomic and cultural terrains, the CSO engages in a "discourse of blaming" and reduces every "lack" into a "failure." History and structure fade away into oblivion as children are taught to take care of their selves—they thus become the proactive agents of their own insertion into the market.

The contradictory ways in which history is incorporated into neoliberal ideology is a central concern in two other chapters. In her ethnography of marginal foragers in the US Pacific Northwest, Anna Tsing looks at how the poor and precarious come to endorse market values. Here, through the prism of commercial mushroom pickers of Southeast Asian origin, state militarization seems most present in the form of public memories of the US–Indochina War. Tsing explores how a varied set of subcultures of military memory among Southeast Asian refugees and white Vietnam veterans influences the performance of risk-based entrepreneurship. War continues to shape lives, even many years after the official conflict has ended, via a new political economy: supply-chain capitalism. Arguing that culture is the emergent economic strategy of our times, Tsing describes a set of "cultures of freedom" that are necessary to sustain the supply chain by linking cultural-economic niches throughout the global system. Emerging out of military conflicts, evictions, harassments, and dispossessions, these forms of "popular neoliberalism" enable the dispossessed to recoup their losses and breed new cultures of work that hinge upon modes of insecurity. Violence, Tsing argues, is not only a consequence of privatization but also a condition that allows free-market entrepreneurship to thrive.

The militaristic ideology that pervades Tsing's piece finds an echo in Nicholas De Genova's theoretically profound analysis of the spectacle of security. Elaborating on Guy Debord's theses to demystify US establishment ideology, De Genova reveals how history is buried in culture through discourses of "terrorism," "security," and "consumption." The theme of "regeneration through violence" (Pearl Harbor related to the bombing of the Twin Towers) serves to secure a dehistoricized identity, while the spectacle of security assures the continuation of consumption patterns. The latter is indeed necessary to uphold a system that feeds upon a dutiful and patriotic submission to "business-as-usual"; that is, to securing and superintending egotistic social relations in everyday life. The paradox of refuge into mundane comfort in the face of the spectacle of an omnipresent yet elusive menace conceals the fact that the status quo is the *real* catastrophe.

The discourse on terrorism also becomes an ally of the neoliberal-neoconservative transformation undergone by civil society in Zeynep Gambetti's chapter on societal violence in Turkey. Gambetti argues that 2005 marks a break in civil society's demeanor vis-à-vis the Kurdish question in Turkey. Noting that lynching attempts have been occurring in regular intervals against Kurds, leftists, the Roma, and university students throughout the country since then, Gambetti explores how the criminalization of dissenting identities (all conveniently labeled "terrorists") works in tandem with a shift in the notion of citizenship: from rights-bearing members of civil society, citizens turn into the willing executioners of the state. The dispensation of justice by citizens themselves buttresses the state by aligning civil society and citizens along national and market-based objectives. In civil society, associations armed with national values rush to fill in the gap left by the downsizing of the social state, while citizens take onto themselves the responsibility of policing dissenters and would-be enemies. The figure of the "terrorist," emerging from thirty years of armed conflict with the Kurds, turns out to be a convenient tool in pushing forward new strategies of control as well as the privatization of livelihoods and natural resources.

In another twist that the discourse of "terrorism" can take in the era of neoliberalism, Nandini Sundar looks at what she calls the "industry of insecurity" in India. From 2006 onward, she notes, there has been a peculiar shift in the government's response to the Naxalites (Maoist guerilla fighters). Previously, official pronouncements on the Naxalites located the movement largely in its "socioeconomic" context, with the usual statements about the need to bring development to "tribals" (indigenous peoples). However, this has now changed to an overwhelming focus on military assault in the form of counterinsurgency warfare, thus prompting an armed response from the Naxalites. Perhaps, argues Sundar, it is not coincidental that the shift accompanies a phase of primitive accumulation where a large number of agreements have been signed between the government and private companies to exploit the mineral resources in areas under Naxalite influence. Her chapter explores the ways in which the statistics of killings in the counterinsurgency operations as compiled by the government have constructed the Naxalite "problem" in a particular way. She also looks at the role of the media and censorship, and at state security laws that criminalize dissenting views or human rights activists. The chapter further examines state and Maoist notions of legality and justice as well as the problems involved in any attempt to get justice for the multiple victims of the area.

A common theme in most of the chapters, the issue of the enlargement of zones of paralegality—or, to borrow from Giorgio Agamben, of zones of indistinction—in the neoliberal era, is also central to Rossana Reguillo's piece on drug cartels in Mexico. Reguillo maps out a critical terrain that enables her to analyze the triple relationship between the exhaustion of the institutional order, the intensification of syncopated *violencias*, and the enormous productive power of "paralegality." By the latter, she means a set of strategies and practices that create, institute, and maintain a "text" that is parallel to the legality constituted by contingent agreements and negotiations, and is capable of engendering an order that runs alongside the state and social institutions. Confronted by this parallel order as well as by its own crisis of legitimacy, the state and its associated enclaves of power respond by redoubling their discourses of legality—a process that is most clearly exemplified by what Reguillo calls "rhetorics of security." Thus, paradoxically, the insecurity generated by these *violencias* finds its counternarrative in the security of authoritarianism and zero tolerance.

The essays thus point to how the "frictions" within the binaries security/insecurity and neoliberalism/neoconservatism create contradictory states of being. Today, security becomes the ultimate frontier of privatization, the latest stage of the neoliberal dismantling of the state, which privatizes and redistributes its core functions. The present situation is not characterized by the total transfer of the state's monopoly to the private sector, but rather, as Sundar puts it, by "an expansion of options or greater market choice in the use of violence"— and, it must be added, of boundary setting and law enforcement.

Within this matrix, radicalized senses of belonging—and of othering—accompany the disaffiliation that both market forces and wars against terrorism provoke. The mapping out of the emergent subjectivities would require much more analysis into seemingly disparate techniques of material and symbolic survival across the globe. The developmentalist aspiration toward rights-bearing citizenship and rule of law may indeed become obsolete under conditions that redefine bonds. The insecurity caused by the simultaneity of law and its suspension feeds into what Judith Butler calls *precarity*, "that politically induced condition in which certain populations suffer from failing social and economic networks of support and become differentially exposed to injury, violence, and death" (Butler 2009: 25). Groups or individuals whose lives are rendered precarious are caught up in a dilemma whereby the instance to which they appeal for protection (the state) is at the same time the instance that produces precarity. The question that comes to mind, then, is whether neoliberalism effectively spells the end of political liberalism (as we know it).[3]

Though it has become morally impelling—if not merely fashionable—to conclude by proposing exit strategies and venues of hope, we shall deliberately refrain from doing so. This volume admittedly paints a gloomy picture of the neoliberal horizon. And yet neoliberalism is a highly complex and ambivalent process of capital accumulation, such that it is misleading to construct strict causalities. What appears as a form of resistance might eventually end up reproducing the very mechanisms that the security/insecurity binary feeds upon—or the aggravation of precarity may in time serve to generate the conditions of possibility of a new political economy of agency.

Notes

1 According to Harvey, New York City was the first theater in which the market effects of austerity packages were tested and approved.
2 These are: military, political, economic, societal, and environmental security.
3 This parenthetical is borrowed from the eloquently entitled work by Graham-Gibson (1996).

References

Amoore, Louise, Richard Dodgson, Barry K. Gills, Paul Langley, Don Marshall, and Iain Watson. 1997. "Overturning 'Globalisation': Resisting the Teleological, Reclaiming the 'Political'." *New Political Economy* 2:179–195.
Barkawi, Tarak. 2011. "From War to Security: Security Studies, the Wider Agenda and the Fate of the Study of War." *Millennium: Journal of International Studies* 39:701–716.
Benjamin, Walter. 1978. "Critique of Violence." In *Reflections*. New York: Shocken Books.
Brown, Wendy. 2006. "American Nightmare: Neoliberalism, Neoconservatism, and De-democratization." *Political Theory* 34:690–714.
Butler, Judith. 2009. *Frames of War.* London: Verso.
Buzan, Barry. 1991. "New Patterns of Global Security in the Twenty-First Century." *International Affairs* 67:431–451.
Buzan, Barry. 1997. "Rethinking Security after the Cold War." *Cooperation and Conflict* 32:5–28.
Carranza, Mario E. 2010. "Reality Check: America's Continuing Pursuit of Regional Hegemony." *Contemporary Security Policy* 31:406–440.
Graham-Gibson, J.-K. 1996. *The End of Capitalism (As We Knew It).* Oxford: Blackwell.
Harvey, David. 2005. *A Brief History of Neoliberalism.* New York: Oxford University Press.
———. 2006. "Neo-liberalism as Creative Destruction." *Geografiska Annaler: Series B, Human Geography* 88 B (2):145–158.
Klein, Naomi. 2007. *The Shock Doctrine: The Rise of Disaster Capitalism.* New York: Metropolitan Books.
Lazzarato, Maurizio. 2009. "Neoliberalism in Action: Inequality, Insecurity and the Reconstitution of the Social." *Theory Culture and Society* 26:109–133.

McNay, Lois. 2009. "Self as Enterprise: Dilemmas of Control and Resistance in Foucault's *The Birth of Biopolitics.*" *Theory, Culture and Society* 26:55–77.

Rawls, John. 1996. *Political Liberalism.* New York: Columbia University Press.

Shifter, Michael. 2010. "Obama and Latin America: New Beginnings, Old Frictions." *Current History* 109:67–73.

Smith, Neil. 2007. "Disastrous Accumulation." *South Atlantic Quarterly* 106:769–787.

Walt, Stephen M. 1991. "The Renaissance of Security Studies." *International Studies Quarterly* 35: 211–239.

CHAPTER ONE

Free in the Forest: Popular Neoliberalism and the Aftermath of War in the US Pacific Northwest

Anna Lowenhaupt Tsing

It's simple. Everyone here, Asian and white, wants the same thing: freedom—and money.
—Southeast Asian mushroom entrepreneur in Oregon, 2006

Across the world, *freedom* is in the air. Yet what is this freedom? There is a lot about freedom that might make us want to turn away in horror. First, great powers go to war in freedom's name, creating disaster zones of conquest and mayhem. Second, freedom is the justification of vast schemes of privatization of once-common resources, consolidating global wealth in the hands of elites. The first of these kinds of freedom is "political" freedom; the second is "market" freedom. In the past few decades, these two notions of freedom have become inextricably entangled in the plans of world leaders, ushering in an era of global dislocation and impoverishment. It is difficult to be enthusiastic about such programs for freedom. Still, it is hard to give up completely on freedom's potential; it has also been the source of great hope. To explore both terror and possibility, an ethnographic approach is required. What about freedom makes it possible for poor people to embrace privatization and war? There is hard necessity, and there is enchantment, and these are closely intertwined. This chapter investigates one illuminating margin of these dark times for freedom.[1]

Margins are interconnected. At the bottom of emergent neoliberal social hierarchies, the possibilities for scavenging in the remains have multiplied. Scavenging can be a source of freedom—and even, perhaps, a site to glimpse the possibilities of a rowdy cosmopolitanism of open-ended interactions across difference. But there is nothing utopian about scavenging; it flourishes in the ruins of all the worst kinds of greed and terror. This chapter describes a popular culture of freedom: commercial mushroom picking in the national forests of the US Pacific Northwest. I show how political and entrepreneurial commitments to freedom are productively mixed at one margin of US society. At the heart of my description is the continuing importance of the US–Indochina War, and the conflicts that emerged from it, in shaping contemporary social forms. Most of the pickers are veterans or refugees from that time of war, and they carry landscapes of war wherever they go. I argue that "popular neoliberalism" becomes possible as war dislocations draw people into risky entrepreneurial niches. The perverse political economy of global supply chains depends on the continual mobilization of labor for such niches.

Most war stories focus on the immediate moment of conflict. Yet war shapes lives for many, many years. Raymond Scurfield writes movingly of the soldiers he got to know during and after the US–Indochina War through his position as a psychiatric social worker: "It is a wonder that so many armed forces personnel survive the insanity of repeated exposures to the horrors of war," he writes, describing veterans; "war leaves an indelible imprint on all who participate in it or are exposed to it" (Scurfield 2004: 19, 206). The problem is even broader in those lands from which US veterans return: Whereas many US Americans know war intimately only through the experiences of soldiers, citizens of other countries have not been so fortunate. There are few residents of Laos, Cambodia, and Vietnam whose lives are not shaped directly by the aftermath of war. Those who move to other countries as refugees bring their war experiences with them. One goal of this paper is to show how war continues to shape lives even many years after the official conflict has ended. Every time the United States launches a new war, pundits and policy makers represent it not only as a fresh start but also as a flash in the pan: a quick, clean strike that surely will be over soon. Yet wars have persistent long-term effects. Wars do not evaporate from the landscape easily.

A second goal of this paper is to argue for the importance of an emerging new political economy organized through global supply chains.[2] In this economic form, the commodity chain is not contained in one large corporation but rather consists of links through which entrepreneurs make, convey, and market a product. Supply chains make use of cheap, risky, and illegal labor. Commodities can be produced without secure wages or benefits by drawing on pools of willing labor. War is very good at producing insecure and willing labor. War disrupts ordinary livelihoods and dislocates large populations. Cheap labor is one result; new entrepreneurial niches are another. Dislocated people are often willing to try risky and illegal ways of making a living. Furthermore, in the entrepreneurial niches of supply chains, laborers are mobilized to work because they are willing to *identify* with this niche, not because it promises a guaranteed economic standard. Rather than wage-and-benefit packages, the niches of supply chains beckon to those open to trying their hand at an unusual set of working conditions, a particular "culture" of work. Wars are good at mobilizing work cultures involving privation, mobility, and danger. Wars are not fought just to create potential supply-chain labor; however, supply chains make good use of the availability of such labor. This volume argues that "cultures of insecurity" develop with neoliberal expansion. Perhaps this is not only because privatization often requires violence but also because free-market entrepreneurship thrives on the aftermath of violence.

Finally, the chapter has a third goal: to offer a modest contribution to discussions of Southeast Asian refugees in the United States. This field is dominated by two genres: first, accounts of the terrors of life before coming to the United States; and second, investigations of how refugees are brought into the forms and fora of US politics and culture. Yet between these two lies an important space for reflection: In what ways are war experiences part of the ongoing struggles and dreams of refugees? John Marlovits's (2008) research on the treatment of depression in Seattle describes the institutionalization of silences about just this question. In contrast to white middle-class sufferers from depression, Southeast Asian refugees are counseled to remain quiet about the causes of their troubles, and instead just to take drugs. To speak of old wounds, say the counselors, reopens them. Beyond the mental health implications of this policy, it offers a vivid reminder of what both scholarship and US public culture are missing. How have refugees made landscapes of war part of the US experience?

The setting for my story is the colorful backcountry of Washington, Oregon, and northern California, where thousands of Southeast Asian refugees as well as whites and Latinos gather every fall to pick matsutake, a wild mushroom that earns high prices when sent fresh to Japan. The matsutake harvest offers an unusual situation for personal entrepreneurship: The mushrooms grow wild on national forests, and all one needs is a picking permit, camping equipment, and transportation to join the harvest. Picking mushrooms, however, is beset with risks and dangers. There are times and places in which picking is illegal; the fines are large. Really lucrative picking tends to require transgression of the law. All but the most seasoned jungle fighters and hunters get lost in the forest, where it is possible to freeze in the cold night temperatures. Meanwhile, almost all pickers carry loaded guns—as do deer and elk hunters, in the forest in the same months. Armed altercations are rare, but the danger always exists. Hostilities have marked relations among ethnic groups. When the money is good, gangs arrive to rob pickers. Sometimes there are almost no mushrooms because of the weather, and investments in camping, gas, and food are not returned. The competition is also very keen, and only the most seasoned and aggressive pickers make more than pocket money.

Why do pickers return every year despite these risks and dangers? One Southeast Asian spokesperson gave me an answer the day I arrived: "It's simple. Everyone here, Asian and white, wants the same thing: freedom—and money." As an anthropologist who approaches the "simple" with attitude, I was suspicious. But her answer has turned out to be truer than I imagined. Many pickers told me that they turned to mushroom picking because it offered them freedom. This brings me back to my opening question. What is this *freedom*? How does it ricochet between political ideology and economic strategy? My tentative answer is that the mediation between these two meanings of freedom is accomplished through a war-saturated social and natural landscape. There have been no wars, of late, in central Oregon. The pickers bring a culture of war with them and use it to navigate the landscape. Some carry these meanings through their own war experiences; for others it is an enactment without earlier referent. But even the latter is a form of cultural engagement with war.

Why, I wondered, do so many Lao and Cambodian pickers wear camouflage?[3] Some of them are too young to have been soldiers in Southeast Asian wars; but there is the social memory of war—and the mimicry of war. Pickers dress in camouflage even if they never fought. "These people weren't soldiers," said one wry Lao picker gesturing at a camouflaged group of colleagues, "They're just pretending to be soldiers." But isn't it dangerous to wear camouflage given that the forests are full of rifle-toting deer hunters? The most interesting answer I got when I asked was from a Hmong picker who explained his camouflage as follows: "We wear camouflage so we can hide if we see the hunters first." This, of course, assumes that the hunters might try to kill you. The landscapes of war do not feel far away.

In what follows, I show how these landscapes of war mediate between political endorsements of freedom and the risky personal entrepreneurship also known as freedom. My investigation is thus part of a larger curiosity about what I call popular neoliberalism. Why do poor people endorse entrepreneurship as freedom? To determine the meanings and practices that constitute freedom must be an ethnographic endeavor.[4]

The pickers I spoke with did not all tell versions of the same story; their stories were self-consciously crafted around dilemmas of culture, nationality, and race. The landscapes they showed me varied in relation to their legacies of engagement with war. The stories I retell here are thus divided by the national, ethnic, and racial categories endorsed by their tellers. However, these are not just stories of specificity: Although the stories are different, every group imagined their stories as allegories of human experience in the aftermath of war. I think they were right.

The US–Indochina War changed how many people in the United States, and beyond, imagine war. United States soldiers were not just seen as brave but also as traumatized and enraged; US allies were not just stalwarts but also unfairly commandeered, often unruly, and given, sometimes, to brutality and civil war. If I revisit some of these stories as they have come to live again in Oregon hills, it is not to further stereotype *that terrible war*. More recent wars are just as terrible, and Indochinese images may be useful to remove the destructive sheen of their continuing threats. As damaged people assemble from more recent US wars, their parallel stories mingle with these.

White Vets and Mountain Men

Frontier romanticism still runs high in the mountains and forests of the Pacific Northwest. It is common sense to glorify Native Americans *and* identify with the white settlers who tried to wipe them out. Self-sufficiency, rugged individualism, and the aesthetic force of white masculinity are points of pride. Historian Richard White describes how the Northwest's progressive politicians in the 1930s built from "hardscrabble" resentments against the East, encouraging a "pious, essentially backward-looking rural nostalgia" (1995: 70). Today, neoconservatives have more success in energizing rural sensibilities, and many white mushroom pickers and buyers are fans of US conquest abroad, creationism, and white superiority. Yet the rural Northwest has also gathered hippies, marijuana growers, and other iconoclasts. White veterans of the US–Indochina War bring their war experiences into this self-consciously rough and independent mix, adding a distinctive mixture of resentment and patriotism, trauma and threat.

White veterans contribute to an emergent *culture of freedom* in the backcountry. With the blossoming of the wild mushroom trade in the late 1980s, freedom and money seemed to go hand in hand. War memories are simultaneously disturbing and productive in forming this niche. War is damaging, veterans tell us, but it also makes men. Freedom can be found *in* war as well as *against* war. The following vignettes introduce several ways of being a white veteran in the mushroom forests.

Alan felt lucky when he managed to aggravate a childhood injury enough to be sent home from Indochina. For the next six months he served as a driver on an American base. One day he received orders to return to Vietnam. He drove his jeep to the depot and walked out of the base AWOL. He spent the next four years hiding in the Oregon mountains, where he gained a new goal: to live in the woods and never pay rent. He was captured by the marines, but managed to avoid active duty; as soon as he was free he returned to the forest. When the matsutake rush came, it suited him perfectly. Alan imagines himself as a gentle, dope-smoking hippie who works against the combat culture of other vets. He has had only one "flashback" in which he panicked in a crowd of Asians. Life in the forest is his way of keeping clear of psychological danger.

Not all war experience is so benign. When I first met Geoff I was overjoyed to find an informant with so much knowledge about the forest. Telling me of the pleasures of his childhood in eastern Washington, he described the countryside with a passionate eye for detail. My enthusiasm to work with Geoff was transformed, however, when I talked with Tim, the white picker who had introduced us. Tim said that Geoff had served a long and difficult tour in Vietnam. Once, his group had jumped from a helicopter into an ambush. Many of the men were killed and Geoff was shot through the neck but, miraculously, survived. When Geoff came home he screamed so much at night that he could not stay home, and so he returned to the woods. But his war years were not over. Tim described a time he and Geoff had surprised a group of Cambodian pickers on one of Geoff's mushroom patches. Geoff had opened fire, and the Cambodians had to scramble into the bushes to get away. Once Tim and Geoff had shared a cabin, but Geoff spent the night brooding and sharpening his knife. "Do you know how many men I killed in Vietnam?" he asked Tim. "One more wouldn't make a bit of difference."

The line between truth and fantasy is hard to draw. Robin says he was a Special Forces sharpshooter in Vietnam and Laos. He says he learned Lao, and, indeed, he nods and laughs during Lao conversations at the mushroom buying station where he often hangs out. I don't think, however, that he actually understands; rather, he aims for good relations with Lao pickers, who seem to regard him as a harmless drunk who might sometimes mediate with more offensive whites. Robin says he hates "Viets," because they killed too many of *us*, by which I think he means white Americans. He says there are no Vietnamese in the mushroom forests (basically true) because they know they would get killed if they came. (Most Vietnamese Americans imagine themselves with better things to do than to pick mushrooms.) He also has a bad opinion of "Cambodians," who, he says, come in big groups to clean out the mushrooms. He describes a team that stretched out in a great line across the forest, with machine gunners on each side to shoot anyone who got in their way. In his friendliness to Lao pickers, however, Robin differentiates himself from other white vets, whom he describes as uniformly antagonistic to Asians. He tells the story of the white reaction to the advent of Southeast Asians in the forest: They put up signs along the highway saying, "The Khmer Rouge Lives Here." Many white pickers told me of this incident, with a mixture of horror and glee at the sheer *badness* of it. Robin elaborates: Seven Asian pickers have disappeared in the struggle between white vets and Asians, he says. No one ever found the bodies. Their relatives and friends covered up the disappearances, saying only "He go home." Robin is not a trustworthy informant, but his stories speak to the anxiety, fear, and antagonism many whites feel in a landscape now dominated by Southeast Asian refugees. He also tells of his own bravado: After his Indochina tour, he says, he joined the police but was discharged for shooting a suspect six times. He still wears a sheriff's belt buckle, which, he says, keeps the police from ever bothering him. On both sides of the law, simultaneously, he maneuvers through the armed and racialized landscape.

White pickers imagine themselves not only as violent vets but also as self-sufficient mountain men: loners, tough, and resourceful. One point of connection with those who did not fight is hunting. One white mushroom buyer, too old for Vietnam but a strong supporter of US wars, explained that hunting, like war, builds character. He described the incident in which Vice President Cheney shot a friend in the face while bird hunting as the ordinary experience of hunting, which because of its risks brings men into their own power. Hunting is, then, a form of war, which makes men. Through practices of hunting, even noncombatants can partake in reimagining the forest landscape as a site for making freedom.

Cambodian Survivors

The civil war that followed the US occupation of Iraq was a recent reminder of how imperial intervention can tear up the social landscape, creating the conditions for atrocity. Certainly, this was the case in Cambodia. "Nowhere was the [US–Indochina] war so brutal, so devoid of concern for human life, or so shattering in its impact on a society as in Cambodia" (Hildebrand and Porter 1976: 7). Hundreds of thousands of peasants were forced from their villages by the war and then faced conditions of starvation in the capital city. The Khmer Rouge regime inherited this broken landscape and escalated the terror, destroying the country with further gratuitous violence. Cambodian refugees have had to make up their own histories of freedom in the United States. Such histories are guided not only by Cambodian atrocities but also by their moment of entry: the shutting down of the US welfare state and the end of expectations of full standard employment in the 1980s. No one offered Cambodians stable jobs with benefits. Like other Southeast Asian refugees, they had to make something from what they had—including their war experiences. With the matsutake boom of the late 1980s, forest foraging, with its opportunities for making money through sheer intrepidness, became one appealing option. Cambodian refugees joined a wave of Lao, Hmong, and Mien refugees from California cities in making the mushroom harvest a time of freedom—in its many guises.[5]

What is this freedom? One white buyer, exalting the pleasures of war, suggested I speak with Ven, a Cambodian who, the buyer said, would show me that even Asians love imperial war. Since Ven spoke to me with this introduction, I was not surprised by his endorsement of American freedom as a military quest. Yet our conversation took turns that I don't imagine that buyer would have expected, and yet corresponded to what I learned from other Cambodians in the forest. First, in the confusions of the Cambodian civil war, it was never quite clear on which side one was fighting. Where white vets imagined freedom on a starkly divided racial landscape, Cambodians told stories in which war bounced a person from one political bloc to another, and often unexpectedly, and without understanding the field. Second, where white vets took to the hills to recover the freedom of war, Cambodians offered a more optimistic vision of recovery *from* war in the forests of American freedom.

At the age of thirteen, Ven left his village to join an armed struggle. His goal was to repel Vietnamese invaders. He says he did not know enough about

Cambodian politics to identify the national affiliations of his group; he later found it to be a Khmer Rouge affiliate. Because of his youth, the commander befriended him and he was kept safe, close to the leaders. Later, however, the commander fell out of favor, and Ven, as a close associate, became a political detainee. At one point, his group of detainees was sent to a jungle area to fend for themselves. By chance, this turned out to be an area Ven knew from his jungle fighting days. Where others saw empty jungle, he knew the concealed paths and forest resources. At this point in the story, I expected him to say that he escaped, especially since he was beaming with pride about his jungle knowledge. But no: He showed the group a hidden spring, without which they would not have had fresh water. Perhaps there was something communally empowering about this forest detention—even in its coercions. Returning to the forest draws from this spark.

Ven's life, however, must have deteriorated. When he tried to continue his story, he became too choked up to speak. We quickly moved back to the pleasures of American freedom, and Ven recovered himself in paeans to the safety of American life, in which he could raise a family in a peace maintained through the might of American military hegemony. The continuing advance of US conquest creates the conditions, he explained, for American freedom and well-being.

Other Cambodians spoke about mushroom foraging as healing from war. One woman described how weak she was when she first came to the United States; her legs were so thin and frail that she could hardly walk. Mushroom foraging has brought her back to health. The matsutake itself is a tonic, she said; she eats the mushrooms and hikes across the mountains, and in those activities she has regained her health.

Even young people echoed these themes. The teenage daughter of a Cambodian war veteran told me quite a confused history of the war, including the fact that Pol Pot was a Vietnamese slave raider. She hardly knew about the war; and yet it shaped her life. She said she had accompanied her father to pick mushrooms because it was the only way she could stay away from gang violence in the California city in which she was raised. Landscapes of war continue to be potent in the United States as long as many refugees continue to experience warlike conditions in communities torn by violence. New generations are trained in taking sides for survival. Mushroom picking, for this young woman too, was a healing process from confusing and confused wars.

One of her father's friends, Heng, a handsome man in his prime, told me about his experiences as a member of an armed militia in Cambodia. He became the leader of a group of twenty men, and he was proud of his leadership skills. But while patrolling one day he stepped on a land mine, which blew off his leg. He begged his comrades to shoot him, since the life of a one-legged man in Cambodia was beyond what he imagined as human. He imagined himself begging on the streets; he would never have a family. Through luck, however, he was picked up by a UN mission and transported to Thailand. In the United States he gets along well on his artificial leg. Still, when he first told his relatives that he would pick mushrooms in the forest, they scoffed. They refused to take him with them, since, they said, he would never be able to keep up. Finally, an aunt dropped him off at the base of a mountain, telling him to find his own way. He found mushrooms! Ever since, the matsutake harvest has been an affirmation of his health and ability to survive. Another of his buddies, meanwhile, is missing the other leg, and he jokes that together in the mountains, they are "complete."

The Oregon mountains are both a cure for and a connection to his old habits and dreams. I was startled into this conclusion one day when I asked Heng about hunters. I had been mushroom picking by myself that afternoon and was absorbed in the work when suddenly shots rang out nearby. I was terrified. I couldn't tell where the shots came from; I didn't know which way to run. I asked Heng about it later. "Don't run!" he said. "To run shows that you are afraid. I would never run. That's why I am a leader of men." The woods are still full of war, and hunting is its reminder.

Almost all the hunters are white, and they tend to be unhappy about the presence of Asian Americans. (The next day a hunter in his truck tried to run me off the road.) This tense situation makes parallels to war yet more apparent. This theme was especially consequential for Hmong, who, unlike most Cambodians, identify as hunters as well as hunted. Hmong know the forest through hunting—and through war. To hike in the forest evokes both simultaneously.

Hmong Hunters in Familiar Hills

During the US–Indochina War, Hmong became the front line of the US military presence in Laos. Recruited by Hmong general Vang Pao, whole villages gave up agriculture to subsist on US Army airdrops of food. The men called in US bombers, putting their bodies on the line so that Americans could destroy the country from the skies. Although some Hmong also fought for the Pathet Lao, it is not surprising that US policy singled out Hmong as particular enemies of Lao liberation. Hmong refugees have done relatively well in the United States. Hmong communities hold out against assimilation, however, and allow war memories to run strong. The landscapes of wartime Laos are very much alive for Hmong in the United States, and this shapes both the politics of freedom and freedom's everyday activities.[6]

Consider the case of Hmong hunter and US army sharpshooter Chai Soua Vang. In November 2004, he climbed into a deer blind in a Wisconsin forest just as the white landowners were touring the property. The landowners confronted him, telling him to leave. Perhaps they shouted racial epithets; perhaps someone shot at him. In any case, he shot eight of them with his semiautomatic rifle, killing six.

The story was news, and the main tenor in which it was told was outrage. A report on CBS News quoted local deputy Tim Zeigle, who said Vang was "chasing after [the white landowners] and killing them. He hunted them down."[7] The violation of property was prominent in local white commentary. Fox News quoted Jim Arneberg, owner of the Haugen Inn in nearby Haugen: "It's pathetic. They let all these foreigners in here, and they walk all over everybody's property."[8] Hmong community spokesmen immediately took their distance from Vang and focused on saving the reputation of the Hmong people. Some commentators brought up racism in both the original confrontation and the ensuing trial.[9] (Native Americans in the area were perhaps the most sympathetic to Vang.)[10] But no one publicly suggested any reason why Vang might have assumed a sharpshooter's stance to eliminate his adversaries.

The Hmong I spoke with in California and Oregon all seemed to know, and to empathize. What Vang did appeared utterly familiar. He could have been a brother or a father; he was neither pathological nor evil. Although Vang was too young to have participated in the US–Indochina War, his actions showed them how well he was socialized in the landscapes of that war. There every man who was not a comrade was an enemy, and the goal of war was to eliminate every enemy. For those on the ground, it was kill or be killed. The elder men of the Hmong community still live very much in the world of these battles; at Hmong gatherings, the logistics of particular battles—the topography, the timing, the surprises—are the subject of men's conversations. One Hmong elder whom I had asked about his life used the opportunity to tell me about how to throw back grenades and what to do if you are shot. The logistics of wartime survival were the substance of his life.

Hunting recalls the familiarity of Laos for Hmong in the United States. The Hmong elder explained his coming of age in Laos: as a boy, he longed for his own knife; then he wanted a bow and arrow; then he longed for a muzzle-loader (all of these for hunting); finally, he longed for a semiautomatic. He joined the army. The skills he had honed in hunting served him well in jungle fighting. Now in the United States, he teaches his sons how to hunt. In hunting, he shares with them his Laotian war-honed manhood; he trains them in survival skills. His son told me that hunting is one of the few times his father talks to him about his life. His US education is in the hands of public schools; but his Hmong education requires hunting. Hunting brings Hmong men into a world of landscape tracking, war survival, and manhood.

Hmong mushroom pickers are comfortable in the forest because of hunting. Unlike other pickers, Hmong rarely get lost; they use the forest-navigation skills they know from hunting. The forest landscape reminds older men of Laos: Although the climate and the trees are different, there are wild hills and valleys and the necessity of keeping your wits about you. Such familiarity in itself brings the older generation back to pick each year; like hunting, this is a chance to remember forest landscapes. Without the sounds and smells of the forest, the elder told me, a man dwindles.

Tou and his son Ger kindly took my assistant Lue and me for many a matsutake hunt. Ger was an exuberant hiker and teacher, but Tou, while clearly more knowledgeable, was a quiet elder. As a result, I valued each of the things he said all the more. One afternoon after a particularly long and pleasurable mushroom hike, Tou collapsed into the front seat of the car with a sigh. Lue translated from Hmong. "It's just like Laos," Tou said, telling us of the hills and valleys of his original home. His next sentence seemed to me a non sequitur: "But it's important to have bought insurance." It took me the next half hour to figure out what he meant. He offered a story: A relative of his had gone back to Laos for a visit, and the hills and valleys had so drawn him that he left one of his souls behind when he returned to the United States. He soon died as a result. Nostalgia can cause death, and then it's important to have bought life insurance, because only that allows the family to buy the oxen and other materials for a proper funeral. Tou was experiencing the nostalgia of a landscape made familiar by hiking and foraging. This is also the landscape of hunting—and of war.

Frontiers of the Lao Diaspora

As Buddhists, lowland Lao pickers tend to object to hunting.[11] Instead, Lao are the businessmen of the mushroom camps. Most Southeast Asian mushroom buyers are Lao. In the campgrounds, Lao have opened noodle tents, karaoke, and barbeque shops; they run the gambling, and, according to popular report, the drugs and prostitution. Many of the Lao pickers I met originated from or were displaced to Laotian cities. They find it easy to get lost in the woods. But they enjoy the risks of mushroom picking and explain it as an entrepreneurial sport.

I first started thinking about cultural engagements with war when I was hanging out with Lao pickers and buyers. Camouflage is particularly popular among Lao men. Most are further covered by protective tattoos—some gained in the army, some in gangs, and some in martial arts. Lao rowdiness is the justification for US Forest Service rules that disallow gunfire in the campgrounds. Most homicides in the mushroom camps involve domestic violence between Lao couples. Compared to the groups I have just described, the Lao I met seemed, on the one hand, less wounded by the actual moment of war, and, on the other, more involved in its simulation in the forest.

But what is a wound? Bombing by the United States in Laos displaced 25 percent of the rural population, forcing fleeing refugees into cities—and, when possible, abroad.[12] If Lao refugees in the United States have some of the characteristics of camp followers, is this not also a wound?

Some Lao pickers grew up in army families. Sam's father served in the Royal Lao army; he was set to follow in his father's footsteps by enrolling in the US army. The fall before his enrollment he joined some friends for a last hurrah—picking mushrooms. He made so much money that he called off his army plans. He even brought his parents to pick with him. He also discovered the pleasures of illegal picking one season when he made three thousand dollars in one day by trespassing on national park lands. Ever since, he has sought out the most inaccessible spots, legal and illegal. Meanwhile, he has learned the skills of buying. Staying independent, he has refused to give his loyalty to a particular company, instead making his own strategies for gain.

Like white pickers, the Lao I knew looked for the out-of-bounds and hidden places where one might find a completely undisturbed mushroom patch. (In contrast, Cambodian, Hmong, and Mien pickers often used careful observation in well-known common spots.) Lao pickers also—again like whites—took pleasure in boasting of their forays outside the law and their ability to get out of scrapes. (Other pickers went outside the law more quietly.) As entrepreneurs, Lao were mediators, with all the pleasures and dangers of mediation. In my own inexperience, I found the entrepreneurial grasp of combat readiness a confusing set of juxtapositions. Yet I could tell it somehow worked as advocacy for high-risk accumulation.

Thong, a strong young man in his mid-thirties, seemed to me a man of contradictions: a fighter; a fine dancer; a reflective thinker; a judgmental critic. Because of his strength, Thong picks high, inaccessible places. He told of his encounter with a policeman who stopped him for speeding one night more than forty miles from the mushroom camp. He told the policeman to go ahead and impound his car; he would walk through the frozen night. The policeman gave in, he said, and let him go. When Thong said that mushroom pickers are in the forest to escape warrants, I thought he might be speaking for himself. Then, too, until quite recently he was married; in the process of getting a divorce, he quit a well-paying job to pick mushrooms. At the least, I believe he aimed to escape the obligations of child support. Yet he is contemptuous of pickers who, he said, abandon their children for the forest. He is not in touch with his own children.

Meta thinks a lot about Buddhism. Meta spent two years as a monk in a monastery in California; returned to the world, he works to renounce material things. Mushroom picking is a way for him to do this work of renunciation. Most of his belongings are in his car. The money comes to him easily but disappears just as easily. He does not mire himself in possession. This does not mean he is ascetic in a Western sense. When he is drunk, he sings a tender tenor karaoke. And now he would like to get enough money to visit his family in Laos. He urges me to correspond with an entrepreneurial brother in Laos even as he shows me a Buddhist manual on nonattachment.

The grey-zone entrepreneurship enacted in Lao communities extends cultural economies of wartime survival from one generation to the next. Even young people who did not know war in Laos endorse combat culture in the Oregon forests. Among Lao pickers, children of mushroom pickers sometimes became mushroom pickers, too, building from and extending their parents' wartime bravado. Paula first went picking with her parents, who have now moved to Alaska. But she maintains her parents' social networks in the Oregon mushroom forests, thus earning the status and room for maneuver of much more seasoned pickers. Paula is daring. She and her husband arrived ready to pick ten days before the US Forest Service opened the season. When the police caught them with mushrooms in their truck, her husband pretended that he couldn't speak English, while Paula berated the policeman and Forest Service officials. Paula is cute and looks like a teenager; she can get away with more sass than others. Still, I was surprised at the chutzpah she claimed. In her story, she dared the police to interfere with her activities. They asked her where she found the mushrooms, she recalled. "Under green trees," she said. Where were these green trees? "All trees are green trees," she insisted. Then she pulled out her cell phone and started calling her supporters.

What Is Freedom?

United States immigration policy differentiates "political refugees" from "economic refugees," granting asylum only to the former. This requires potential immigrants to endorse "freedom" as a condition of their entry. Southeast Asian Americans had the opportunity to learn such endorsements in refugee camps in Thailand, where many spent years preparing themselves for US immigration. One Lao buyer explained why he moved to the United States rather than France: "In France they have two kinds, freedom and communist. In the US they just have one kind: freedom." He went on to explain that he prefers mushroom picking to a steady job with a good income—he has been a welder—because of the "freedom."

Lao strategies for enacting freedom—or at least talking about it to me—contrast sharply with those of the other picker group that vies for the title "most harassed by the law": Latinos. Latino pickers tend to be undocumented migrants who fit mushroom foraging into a year-round schedule of outdoor work. During mushroom season many are said to live hidden in the forest instead of in the legally required industrial camps and motels where identification and picking permits might be checked. Those I knew had multiple names, addresses, and papers. Mushroom arrests could lead not just to fines but also to loss of vehicles (for faulty papers) and deportation. Instead of sassing the law, Latinos I knew tried to stay out of the way, and, if caught, juggle papers and sources of legitimation and support. In contrast, most Lao pickers are citizens, and, embracing freedom, hustle for more room. Yet only white citizens feel empowered to call the US Forest Service to task for racial profiling and other public issues.[13]

Contrasts such as these have motivated my search to understand the cultural engagements with war that shape forest landscapes and forms of freedom practiced by white veterans and Cambodian, Hmong, and Lao refugees. I am arguing that veterans and refugees negotiate American citizenship through endorsing and practicing "freedom." In this practice, militarism is internalized; it infuses the landscape; it inspires strategies of foraging and entrepreneurship.

Several kinds of political economic developments make these niches analytically significant. First, global capitalism promotes forms of subcontracting in which self-consciously independent entrepreneurs become linked through globe-spanning commodity chains. Matsutake commerce is one such chain; it links these obscure freedom fighters to gourmet restaurants and high-end perks in Japan. The "cultures of freedom" I describe here make commodity production possible in this chain; they also stand as icons of the cultural entrepreneurship involved in global supply chains more generally. Once, the standardized structure of the corporation seemed to tell us the most about capitalism. Today, however, it is the linking of cultural-economic niches.

Indeed, I risk a generalization: *Culture is the emergent economic strategy of our times.* For much of the twentieth century, powerful institutions worked to segregate culture and economy. Culture was understood as the glue of soon-to-be-archaic communities; economy would be the forward-looking universalism of the modern world. International organizations and regimes of knowledge worked hard to institute these definitions. The development states of the global south and the welfare states of the global north put these definitions into the organization of national economies. The standardized labor imagined for the "cultureless" economy seemed particularly real in the wage and benefits packages of big corporations; such packages became the basis of so-called standard employment. Since the 1990s, however, such arrangements have been falling apart. National economies are no longer the goal; standard employment has disappeared in many places. The ideology of separate spheres for culture and economy is stronger than ever. But the mobilization of labor and capital is increasingly bound to forms of entrepreneurship that use the vocabulary of culture. Homebound women sew our clothes in culturally organized sweatshops; techie subcultures call in investors; indigenous people market themselves; cultural "branding" is the product on everyone's minds. Culturally self-conscious economic strategies are not always what Hardt and Negri (2000) call "immaterial labor"; very material forms of labor, such as mushroom picking, are part of this story. The change I am describing is not a new universal value formation, but rather a heterogeneous patchwork of value forms, held together—but not homogenized—by global chains of capital and commodity. The commitments to "freedom" I have described here make one such chain possible.

Second, such cultural-economic niches emerge out of military conflicts, evictions, harassments, and dispossessions. David Harvey (2005) has usefully argued that neoliberalism needs to be understood in relation to *accumulation by dispossession*. "Popular neoliberalism" is one response to accumulation by dispossession. Through their entrepreneurial strategies, the dispossessed attempt to survive despite their losses. Commercial mushroom picking is a form of entrepreneurship for those not only without capital but also without the privilege of safe ancestral homes. Its conflations of political and market freedom are central, too, to other strategies that allow people to survive disruption, dislocation, and war.

Such niches build new modes of citizenship. Modernization—with its standardization of the "cultureless economy"—was a powerful dream for homogenized citizenship. As modernization dreams thin out, so too do assimilation projects. Yet the rowdy cosmopolitanism of postassimilation public space threatens the nation's cultural hierarchies. In the United States, one compromise has been to require every national subculture to endorse "freedom." This endorsement differentiates insiders from outsiders, and the loyal from the subversive. In this vision, *American multiculturalism is a coalition of cultures of freedom.*

Refugees and soldiers are key players in this drama. Yet when veterans and refugees literalize agendas of freedom, the results are not always what authorities would like. Veterans who use their freedom for spousal abuse or illegal drug use are referred to psychologists; refugees whose freedom moves them toward gangs or smuggling are arrested as criminals. Meanwhile, it seems possible to explore these imagined deviations as emergent features of cultures of freedom, that is, public and communal means for navigating American citizenship.

My study thus also addresses the making of culture and identity. Social scientists have known for a long time that culture is not an enclosed and static formation. Yet in times of war, "culture" is easy to mobilize as an essential characteristic of the enemy. In the United States, as I write this, Islam represents such a threatening other that many people's brains close down in considering its possibilities. Imagined differences in culture become an excuse for discrimination. Thinking through the residues of old wars is useful to work against this conceptualization of culture. Nothing I learned in Oregon's forests suggested to me that essential cultural characteristics of either whites or Southeast Asians had anything to do with their common embrace of war and freedom. Instead, the forms of culture I learned about were emergent with political and economic histories in the making. Powerful algorithms of identity arose in immigration policy. Memories of war drew out legacies of self-reliance and danger, exciting entrepreneurship in, and beyond, the forests. Landscapes in which war memories come to life thus *make* culture by bringing violence, survival, and livelihood inside the mix called freedom.

Notes

1   *Free in the Forest* is the title of a classic account of the political actions of Vietnamese Montagnards during the US–Indochina War (Hickey 1982). Hickey was an advocate for the "freedom" of the Montagnards, but he was also a part of the US effort to recruit hill peoples for US war efforts. Indeed, anthropological renderings of "freedom" helped stimulate CIA mobilization of hill peoples across Southeast Asia. (See Salemink 2003 for a useful review of the ties between anthropology and imperial rule in this area.) This chapter is based on fieldwork in Oregon during matsutake seasons between 2004 and 2008. In 2005, David Pheng contributed to the research and translated from Khmer. In 2006 and 2007, Lue Vang patiently worked with me through most of the season, interviewing and translating from Hmong. In 2005 and 2007, Hjorleiffur Jonsson was an ideal collaborator, offering insights and translating from both Lao and Mien. I am deeply grateful for their enthusiasm, perspicacity, and hard work. The research is part of a study of global economic and scientific connections involving matsutake mushrooms. The Matsutake Research Group, whose collaborations constitute that research, includes Shiho Satsuka, Lieba Faier, Michael Hathaway, Timothy Choy, and Miyako Inoue, as well as myself. All personal names of the pickers in this essay are pseudonyms. This chapter was written for a 2007 conference on "Citizenship, Rhetorics of Security, and Neoliberal Violence," and I am grateful to the conference organizers and participants for pushing my thoughts this far. I am also grateful to Gail Hershatter for helping me to revise

that paper for this volume. Earlier versions were presented at the University of Washington and the University of Michigan, where colleagues and students were wonderful interlocutors.

2   See Tsing 2009 for a fuller exposition of this form.

3   I follow local convention in speaking of pickers and buyers of Southeast Asian origins as Lao, Cambodian, Hmong, and Mien, without the qualifier "American." All, however, are residents of the United States. Because they arrived with refugee status, almost all are US citizens.

4   I owe this insight to conversations with Megan Moodie. See Moodie 2006.

5   The majority of Southeast Asian mushroom pickers and buyers live in California cities—and, to a lesser extent, Oregon and Washington cities—and come to the forests of the Pacific Northwest for specific mushroom picking seasons. Some, however, follow year-round circuits of mushroom picking across the western states. For an excellent discussion of the mushroom circuit, focusing on Oregon's white pickers, see McClain 2000.

6   See Tsing 2013 for a fuller attempt to think about Hmong American political dilemmas, including their sense of betrayal by US withdrawal from Laos.

7   CBS News, "Deer Hunter Charged with Murder," November 29, 2004, http://www.cbsnews.com/stories/2004/11/30/national/main658296.shtml.

8   Foxnews.com, "Arrest Made in Wisconsin Hunting Massacre," November 22, 2004, http://www.foxnews.com/story/0,2933,139239,00.html.

9   Wameng Moua, "Coaltion Observations: Trial Was Bias," *Hmong Today*, November 3, 2005, http://www.hmongtoday.com/displaynews.asp?ID=2059.

10   "American Indian Neighbors React to Hmong Shooter in Minnesota," News from Indian Country, Commentary, Paul DeMain, posted October 3, 2005, New American Media, http://news.newamericamedia.org/news/view_article.html?article_id=0e52014d2d74ceaf0eba8db7e540c48a.

11   Following local custom, I use the unmodified term "Lao" to refer to the US diaspora of lowland (or "ethnic") Lao (*Lao Loum*).

12   For some tentative figures, see *A Country Study: Laos*, "The Refugee Population," http://lcweb2.loc.gov/frd/cs/latoc.html#la0065.

13   In October 2006, the white owner of a pickers' campground brought in an advocacy group to call the US Forest Service to task for slapping preseason fines only on Southeast Asians and Latinos.

References

Hardt, Michael, and Antonio Negri. 2000. *Empire*. Cambridge: Harvard University Press.

Harvey, David. 2005. *A Brief History of Neoliberalism*. Oxford: Oxford University Press.

Hickey, Gerald. 1982. *Free in the Forest*. New Haven: Yale University Press.

Hildebrand, George, and Gareth Porter, 1976. *Cambodia: Starvation and Revolution*. New York: Monthly Review Press

Marlovits, John. 2008. "Fugues of Depression: An Ethnography of Affect and Mental Illness in Seattle." PhD dissertation, University of California, Santa Cruz.

McClain, Rebecca. 2000. "Controlling the Forest Understory: Wild Mushroom Politics in Central Oregon." PhD dissertation, University of Washington.

Moodie, Megan. 2006. "Culture or Freedom? The Gendered Intimacies of Modernization in Rajasthan, India." PhD dissertation, University of California, Santa Cruz.

Salemink, Oscar. 2003. *The Ethnography of Vietnam's Central Highlanders, 1850–1990*. Honolulu: University of Hawaii Press.

Scurfield, Raymond. 2004. *A Vietnam Trilogy: Veterans and PostTraumatic Stress*. New York: Algora.

Tsing, Anna Lowenhaupt. 2009. "Supply Chains and the Human Condition." *Rethinking Marxism* 21(2):148–176.

———. 2013. "Subcontracting Sovereignty: The Afterlife of Proxy War." In Sigal R. Ben-Porath and Rogers Smith, eds., *Varieties of Sovereignty and Citizenship*, 58–74. Philadelphia: University of Pennsylvania Press.

White, Richard. 1995. *The Organic Machine: The Remaking of the Columbia River*. New York: Hill and Wang.

CHAPTER TWO

Autochthony, Citizenship, and (In)security: New Turns in the Politics of Belonging in Africa and Elsewhere

Peter Geschiere

For Africa, the 1990s seemed to become the decade of democratization.[1] In retrospect, however, it rather seems to have been marked by an upsurge of struggles over belonging and "autochthony"—over who is "in," but especially over who can be excluded as a "stranger." Of course, these struggles were clearly linked to democratization. In many areas, "autochthony" became a powerful political slogan for local groups who feared they would be outvoted by more numerous immigrants when, after a long period of stifling authoritarianism, elections once more acquired real political meaning. Other aspects of the neoliberal tide unleashed by the Washington Consensus had similar effects, notably the new emphasis in the policies of the major development agencies on "by-passing the state," and decentralization—again, after a long period of statist development policies that stressed nation building as a main condition for achieving development.

Like democratization, decentralization inevitably raised the thorny question of belonging: who can claim to belong to a certain region or locality, and have access to the new circuits of development funding; and who can be excluded as a "stranger," an *allogène*? Citizenship thus became a bone of contention. Instead of the heavy ideological emphasis on forging one national citizenship, uniting all local groups into one nation, which marked the period of forceful nation building during the first decades after independence (the 1960s up to well into the 1980s), the dominant preoccupation in the 1990s became to purify the nation and exclude foreigners (Ivory Coast became a stark example of this), or to distinguish between citizens who "really" belong in certain areas and others who do not belong there, even if they are citizens of the same state (Cameroon, Nigeria, Congo).

My aim in this contribution is to explore a few more general implications of this upsurge of belonging. The African continent—and especially the parts that are deeply marked by the development circuits—is marked in an especially direct way by the neoliberal tide. In many respects, the continent is still the favorite laboratory for development economists and other development experts for trying out new forms of social engineering. So it is probably one of the areas in the world that was most directly affected by the new approach to global issues promoted by the Washington Consensus, with its strong accent on giving free scope to "the" market and lifting all institutional barriers for this. Elsewhere, nation-states may have had more clout to withstand the abrupt application of these ideas. African examples may therefore highlight particularly strongly the paradox that the neoliberal tide—here especially exemplified by democratization and decentralization, as some sort of unhappy twin—came to promote a true obsession with belonging and closure, often expressed in quite violent terms.

It is important to emphasize, however, that Africa is certainly not exceptional in this. Autochthony and other forms of belonging may have triggered particularly violent confrontations here. Yet throughout the globe the New World Order, announced by Bush Sr. at the end of the Cold War, seemed to usher in a world marked by communal conflicts and an obsession with cultural difference, rather than by the free circulation of sophisticated cosmopolitans. The Canadian anthropologist Tanya Murray Li (2002) speaks of a "deep conjuncture of belonging" for Southeast Asia, but this may have global dimensions. I think the term "conjuncture" is particularly well chosen here. Murray Li uses this term to point out that all sorts of apparently unconnected trends seem to converge in quite unexpected ways in a preoccupation with local belonging. In her studies of "indigenous peoples" in Southeast Asia, she focuses on global ecological concerns with biodiversity, but also on the equally global worry about "disappearing cultures." For Africa, as mentioned, it is rather democratization and decentralization that play a crucial role. For Europe, it might be the popular fear of ever more numerous immigrants from the South and the East that has center stage. Yet, disparate as these trends may be, they meet in a growing concern about locality and belonging as some sort of flip side to globalization and neoliberal ideals of liberating "the" market.

The global character of this "conjuncture of belonging" makes it all the more interesting to explore what these discourses on belonging have in common and how they can have such mobilizing force in widely different corners of the globe. In this respect autochthony—the claim to come from the soil itself—is of particular interest. In some senses it is an ultimate form of belonging: how can one belong more than when one is "born from the soil?" The aim of this text—in close connection with the contribution in this collection on similar issues by Stephen Jackson on eastern Congo—is to show that autochthony, as a particularly pregnant form of belonging, sharply highlights certain contradictions that seem to be given with the notion of belonging itself.

First there is the point, already mentioned, that the upsurge of autochthony is certainly not special to Africa. It is may now be a very powerful idea, notably in Francophone Africa, but lately the notion has proven to have great appeal also in very different parts of the world.[2] In Flanders and the Netherlands, it has become a powerful term for the self-identification of the nationals, and especially the supporters of the New Right, notably in contrast to Arab and Turkish immigrants. In Italy, Umberto Bosi is playing with the term to define the "Other" of his Lega Norte. It is becoming current in Quebec and the Pacific—be it in a quite different sense (see Geschiere 2009, chapter 5). Clearly our time provides a propitious setting for such a notion. All the more reason to try and compare its different trajectories and implications in various parts of the world.

Two other points that seem to be given with the notion as such might be of special interest in the context of this collection on citizenship and the growing obsession with (in)security. One is the surprising paradox between autochthony's promise of a basic security and its practice of haunting insecurity. In all the examples below, autochthony seems to have a peculiar receding quality. At first sight it seems to be self-evident who is autochthonous and who is not; and indeed, its protagonists always present autochthony as something that is self-evident, or even "natural."[3] Yet in practice, these identities are always severally contested. The general tendency toward purification—who is the "real" autochthon?—makes identification draw ever closer circles, excluding ever more people as "not really" belonging. Below, we will discuss a Cameroonian example in which people tended even to redefine their own relatives as *allogène,* in order to be able to exclude them from a development project. It is precisely this receding quality that gives autochthony discourse such an insecure trend—Stephen Jackson (2006) speaks rightly of "nervous languages."

In general terms, this is quite unexpected. What could give more security than the fact that one belongs to the earth? Yet there is always the nagging fear that others are more autochthonous, or worse, that one can be denounced as a fake autochthon. There are many examples of precisely this obsession with "traitors" from within, who have to be unmasked, that give autochthony discourse such violent overtones—recall the horrible diatribes of *Radio Mille Collines* in Rwanda against the *cancrelats* (cockroaches) "among us." Closing the group may seem to promise security, but it is the concomitant need to purify the group from strange elements that may hide "inside" that triggers deep feelings of insecurity.[4]

This has to be related to a last point, similarly paradoxical and probably equally of broad relevance: that is the way in which the local and the global are intertwined in an often implicit way in autochthony discourse. Again, there is a basic contradiction here. The very notion of autochthony seems to suggest an obsession with the local. But as AbdelMaliq Simone (2001: 25) has put it so eloquently for present-day Africa: "the fight is not so much over the terms of territorial encompassment or closure, but rather over maintaining a sense of 'open-endedness'" (cf. also Mbembe 2002: 7). Autochthony movements may celebrate the local against foreigners and immigrants, but they do so in order to defend special access for so-called "autochthons" to the modern global flows.

In the rest of this chapter I propose to include a few short vignettes that can illustrate these tendencies in particular contexts in Africa, notably in Cameroon, and Europe.[5] Then I discuss a few elements of the history of this notion, again both in Africa and Europe, that can further highlight the points above.

The Funeral as a Final Test of Belonging

A striking aspect of the upsurge of autochthony in Cameroon—but also elsewhere in Africa—is the central role of the funeral in debates over belonging; this is accompanied by a spectacular proliferation of all sort of "traditional" (often rather "neotraditional") funeral ritual. Thus, the funeral "at home"—that is, in the village of origin, also for people whose families have lived for generations in the city—becomes a true celebration of belonging.

The Cameroonian economist Celestin Monga (1995) speaks of une *mauvaise gestion de la mort* (bad management of death). This is, of course, quite strong language. As an economist, Monga is clearly worried by the rapidly growing and ever more ostentatious spending at such occasions. But he is even more worried that such a private occasion becomes so highly politicized, precisely because "belonging" has become such an overriding criterion in democratic politics.

Indeed, when we began to study—together with a number of Cameroonian colleagues (Francis Nyamnjoh, Cyprian Fisiy, Antoine Socpa, and Basile Ndjio)—the rapidly increasing role of autochthony in everyday life in Cameroon, we hardly suspected that the funeral would take center stage in our research.[6] Instead we focused on the direct link between democratization and autochthony. A rapid overview of Cameroonian politics in the 1990s may give some background to the increasing political significance of the funeral "at home."

The 1990s in Cameroon were marked by the sometimes quite desperate struggle of President Paul Biya, the leader of the former one-party state, to remain in power despite democratization and multipartyism. Only toward the end of 1990 did Biya—probably under direct pressure from François Mitterrand, then president of France—permit freedom of association, which immediately brought a proliferation of opposition parties. However, the regime's stubborn refusal to meet the popular demand for a National Conference inspired the opposition to launch "Operation Ghost Town," blocking public life in the major cities for more than a year. Biya refused to give in, and after 1992 the operation petered out. The crucial presidential elections of 1992 became a scandal, since it was quite clear that Biya obtained his narrow victory over his main rival (John Fru Ndi)—38 percent against 35 percent—due to massive rigging. However, in subsequent years Biya held out against all pressure, his party won all subsequent elections, and the presidential election in October 2004 brought a landslide victory (more than 70 percent) over his main rival (still Fru Ndi, who now obtained only 17 percent).

Biya's capacity for political survival is, indeed, impressive—all the more since this took place in the midst of a deep economic crisis. The regime is generally counted among the most worrying examples of the "criminalization" of the state (cf. Bayart et al. 1999); indeed, under Biya Cameroon rapidly rose to the first position on the list of the world's most corrupt countries. Biya's personal charisma is almost nil, and he has become increasingly invisible to the population, spending much of his time abroad and limiting his public appearances to a minimum. This begs the question how he and his team have nonetheless succeeded in completely outmaneuvering the opposition, which seemed to be in such a promising position in the early 1990s. For the authors quoted above, an obvious answer is the regime's success in playing the autochthony card, which proved an ideal weapon to divide the opposition by fomenting local conflicts over belonging. The consequence was that, already toward the end of the 1990s, all opposition parties had lost their national profile and had become bogged down in all sorts of local conflicts. Only Biya's party, the RDPC, could claim with some justice to be present throughout the country.

It is important to emphasize the incisiveness of this change, which formed a true reversal of the ruling clique's policies. Until far into the 1980s Biya remained faithful to the overriding ideological emphasis of his predecessor, President Ahidjo, on national unity and the strengthening of national citizenship. Reality was, of course, different: Ahidjo's famous policy of "regional balance" was in reality a clever way of playing off the various ethnic blocs against each other. Yet formally, no autonomous form of organization was allowed outside the one-party structure, since this was viewed as an attempt to divide the national citizens who, on the contrary, should stand united behind the president. Around 1990, however, the same regime quickly abandoned the idea of nation building and national citizenship, defending instead its support for autochthony movements in various parts of the country against immigrants, by invoking the new constitution—which, indeed, obliges the government to protect "minorities" and "indigenous peoples."[7]

It is in this constellation that debates about belonging have become part of everyday life, and that bringing back the body of a deceased person to the village, to be buried there, has become a major political event—especially when the dead is a prestigious member of the urban elite. That this idea of the funeral "at home" as a celebration of belonging had complications of its own in the new political configuration became clear to me during a visit to Mamfe (South West Cameroon) in 1996, when people were still talking excitedly about the funeral of the wife of a general from the region, a few months earlier. On the map, Mamfe, situated close to the border with Nigeria, does not seem to be very far away from Cameroon's main city and economic center, Douala. Yet throughout the country, Mamfe is considered to be a really far out place because of the condition of the road that leads there. Indeed, the

Mamfe road has become proverbial in Cameroon for the misery of traveling under adverse circumstances, especially during the wet season.

I arrived in Mamfe toward the end of the rainy season and the road did, indeed, live up to its reputation. However, people still regaled me with stories that a few months earlier, when the general wanted to bury his wife in the village, the road had been much worse. Of course, on this occasion all members of the urban elite had to come down to Mamfe and, of course, they all got stuck on the road. People kept coming back to this, with true Schadenfreude. It served the elites right to be stuck in the mud, since they had always neglected their own area; now they at least found out for themselves what a misery this road was. Indeed, there had been so much rain that it seemed that the whole funeral could not take place. But finally the general took a drastic decision. He "chartered" several helicopters from the army and had his wife's body flown in from Yaounde, together with the main guests.

People talked about all this as if the whole exercise was more or less self-evident: of course, urbanites—and certainly as prestigious a person as the general's wife—had to be brought back to be buried in the village; so it was only logical that the general went to such great lengths. Older informants had other stories to tell, however. Indeed, to them this whole emphasis on burying "at home" seemed to be new. The Banyangi (the people of the Mamfe area) have a long history of migration: the women, especially, travel around the world and are famous for their readiness to engage in trade of all kinds (or to put it in less diplomatic terms: Cameroonians and others will often associate them with prostitution). In earlier days—already during the 1930s—Banyangi elders had sent delegations to the coast, in order to persuade the women to come back and marry at home, in most cases without much success.[8] So it had always been an issue how to bring women back "home." But the elders could not remember this strong emphasis on bringing back the bodies of deceased kin.

In many parts of Africa, people insist now that this emphasis on burying "at home"—that is, in the village—has been a traditional custom, which has existed since time immemorial. And, indeed, in cities like Yaounde or Douala, there are still hardly any cemeteries: to be buried in the city is now seen as a sign of social disgrace. But on closer inspection it seems that for many groups this "custom" is quite new—probably copied from groups who have done this much longer.[9]

It is clear also that, especially in recent times, this burying at home acquired great political significance. In a recent interview, Samuel Eboua, an eminence grise of Cameroonian politics, explained, for instance: "Every Cameroonian is an *allogène* anywhere else in the country . . . than where his ancestors lived and where his mortal remains will be buried. Everybody knows that only under exceptional circumstances a Cameroonian will be buried elsewhere."[10] This is, indeed, powerful language: any idea of the equality of all Cameroonian citizens, that was—at least formally—so dear to Cameroon's first president, Ahidjo, seems to have disappeared here.

Yet, it is quite clear that Eboua voices a current opinion. This emphasis on "burying at home" is also the argument for protagonists of autochthony to justify their insistence that immigrants—these *allogènes*—should go "home" and vote there; and even more that they should stand candidate there, and not in their new surroundings where they are only "guests." The argument is that, since the latter still want to be buried in the village, they clearly consider their home to be there. So if they want to join in politics they should do this there, rather than to try and prevail over their "hosts." After all, a "guest" should never try to dominate his "host" in his own house.[11]

The consequences of all this is a rather macabre traffic of bodies in order to confirm contested claims of belonging. In the contributions cited above (see note 6) we discuss at greater length cases of people digging up their father's body and reburying it elsewhere in order to prove a "belonging" that seemed politically more opportune. An even more complicated case took place in 1999 in Buea (also in South West Cameroon), when gendarmes disturbed a funeral to "arrest" the body in order to have it buried elsewhere. Clearly they acted on behalf of a politically more influential faction among the deceased's kin who wanted to prove a different kind of belonging. Of course, all this is not completely new: the funeral was always important as a mark of belonging. Yet is it quite clear that with democratization and the return of real politics, this emphasis on belonging received new impetus, turning the funeral into a crucial and often fiercely contested moment in the politics of belonging. The direct involvement of the national political leadership in such struggles is also striking. When the funeral concerns an important person, even the president himself may be involved—and, indeed, in all the cases we have, invariably on the side of the *autochtons*, defending their "belonging" against "strangers." Thus the funeral has become an important moment in the politics of autochthony that over the last decade has proved to be so effective for maintaining the Biya regime in the saddle.

Striking in this example is the complicated mixing of local and global elements. The funeral "at home" may seem to be a celebration of the local: the body of the deceased is brought back to where he or she belongs.[12] Yet, most urbanites—especially elite figures who are accustomed to a certain degree of comfort—abhor the idea of really living in the village. Most want to celebrate their "belonging" to the village from a safe distance. In the new political constellation, it may be vital for ambitious politicians—and indeed for anyone—to prove their belonging to a certain locality. Yet this is especially urgent in order to defend one's position in the country's centers, and more and more—think of the growing importance of NGOs—to claim a special access to global circuits of opportunity and support.[13]

The New Forest Law: Autochthony in an Almost Empty Area

In Cameroon, it is particularly the more developed coastal areas, like the South West Province or the city of Douala, that are hotbeds of autochthony struggles. This is hardly surprising. These are quite densely populated areas whose economic dynamism attracted numerous immigrants.

My second example, however, shows that even in the forest area of Southeast Cameroon—generally seen as one of the most backward parts of the country, very thinly populated (only a few inhabitants per square mile) and hardly attracting any immigrants—the language of autochthony and exclusion of *allogènes* can emerge with surprising force. But here the background is not so much the new style of politics since democratization, but rather the new approach of the global development establishment, mentioned above, with its emphasis on decentralization and local autonomy.

This example can illustrate another aspect of autochthony discourse, highlighted above: its "receding," or even "segmentary" nature. The "other," the "stranger," can be constantly redefined, and at ever-closer range. There is never an end to debates about who "really" belongs. Even your own kin can be redefined as *allogènes* or outsiders. And, again, the parallels with the equally volatile ways in which this language is used elsewhere—for instance in present-day Europe—are striking.

A few years ago, I did a brief study of the effects of the new forest law in East Cameroon (where I have done fieldwork since 1971).[14] The new Cameroonian forest law of 1994 is generally seen as a major breakthrough in the struggle to save the rain forest. Over the last decade this struggle has become a most confusing tangle of divergent interests: of the global ecological movement, the Cameroonian state, expatriate logging companies, development projects, the local population, and many more. Moreover, this knot is complicated by surprising alliances. For instance, ecologists and logging companies—surprised to find themselves in agreement—often seem to agree that the first thing to be done is to empty the forest of its population by forced resettlement.

The 1994 law is deeply imbued with ecological considerations.[15] It was almost literally forced down the throat of the Cameroonian parliamentarians by the World Bank. Only under very heavy pressure of financial sanctions did the Parliament pass the law. Indeed, it is striking how strongly "ecological" the Bank has become—at least where the Cameroonian rain forest is concerned. A major advance of the law is that ecological concerns are coupled with attention to the rights of the local population. Indeed—and this might be quite new in the ecological movement—the initiators of the law seem to have understood that in these sparsely populated areas conservation of the forest is only possible with the participation of the locals. Consequently, there is now less emphasis on emptying the forest by resettling the population. Instead, the local communities are recognized as major stakeholders in managing the forest resources: they acquire the right to create their own "community forests" and exploit these themselves. Moreover, they are supposed to receive a major share of the profits on logging by others. Indeed, the law takes the new ideal of financial decentralization very seriously: 50 percent of the taxes on logging are supposed to remain in the area and to go to the municipality or even the village concerned.

As said, Cameroon's East province, where the main remaining forest resources are to be found, has long been the most neglected part of the country, so some guarantee that at least part of the logging revenues will be invested locally is most welcome. Nonetheless, one can not help wondering whether the ideal of financial decentralization is not applied here in an all too simplistic sense. On paper, the new law would imply that huge sums of tax money would go to municipalities of a few thousand inhabitants. Of course, the extremely centralist traditions of the Cameroonian administration guarantee that all this money will never get there. The official calculations raise high expectations, however, and these immediately trigger fierce struggles over belonging in what were highly fluid societies.

The same applies to the role attributed to "the local community." What is striking is that the law is careful not to define this notion more closely—no doubt for good reasons: the forms of social organization prevailing in the forest area were (and are) extremely segmentary. These used to be very open societies, with constant splitting and fusing of segments, and without fixed positions of authority.[16] In such a context, a logical consequence of proclaiming "the local community" (without further specification) as a major stakeholder in the management of the forest is, again, intense fighting over belonging and exclusion: Who will be allowed to profit from the new "community forest"? And who can be excluded as ultimately an *allogène?* Such questions become all the harder to solve since, in the segmentary logic of these societies, the "stranger" can be constantly redefined, at ever closer range. In the case studies I have of the few villages who had their "community forest" already formally attributed, the first struggles over exclusion were directed against a few persons who had, indeed, come in quite recently from outside. But subsequently accusations of not "really" belonging were directed against people closer by: for instance, against relatives who—at least according to some— did not "really" fit into the patrilineal order (even though they had lived for generations in the village).

Most language groups in the East have a special term for a child that does not live in the village of its biological father—it may be born from a love affair, and the mother may have left it with her own family when she left the village for her marriage elsewhere; or the mother may have brought it along to the village of her new husband. The Maka, for instance, call such people (preferably behind their backs) *kwa*—a term that is now often translated as "slave." The term is a heavy insult; normally it is brought up only during very serious confrontations, and this will trigger fierce debates about people's descent and the claims they derive from it. Yet nowadays such accusations that so-and-so is "really" a *kwa*—and therefore does not fully belong—crop up regularly in discussions among the villagers about the new opportunities offered by the new forest law. The implication is clear: such "strangers" should not fully share in the benefits of a community forest or in the taxes paid by logging companies. Promoting a not clearly defined local community as stakeholder of the forest resources gives a new edge to older—and generally disregarded—forms of social exclusion.

Indeed, the rapidity with which the forest law triggered such struggles over belonging even in the very thinly populated East Province, shows the elasticity of the autochthony discourse. As said, in the Cameroonian context it was to be expected that belonging would be an issue in the quite densely populated coastal zones where there is a real pressure on land. But my second example shows that there is no end to autochthony, precisely because it is such an empty term. It means no more than "I was here earlier," and that can become a claim toward the exclusion of "the other" in any circumstance. As my friend from Yaounde (but born in Bamileke land) remarked: "nothing is impossible in autochthony."[17]

Autochthony, Dutch Style: A Canon as a Beacon for "Integration"?

As said, the upsurge of autochthony is certainly not limited to Africa. So it might be apposite to balance the two preceding examples with a very brief example from Europe, where—also since the 1990s—autochthony discourse has undergone a similar renaissance, be it under very different circumstances. The Dutch case is of special interest here, not only because here (as in neighboring Flanders) the same terminology of *autochtonen* versus *allochtonen* is used but also because the switch from a more open society, with at least formally some respect for cultural differences, to a stern emphasis on integration into the dominant autochtonen culture took place surprisingly rapidly. Key events in this transition where two shocking events that drew a lot of attention abroad: the murder of populist politician Pim Fortuyn by a radical ecologist in 2002; and the even more gruesome murder of filmmaker Theo van Gogh by "Mohammed B.," an Islamic fundamentalist in 2004.[18]

However, much more important that these murders was the fact that Fortuyn in his short but stormy career as politician showed how deep the popular resentment was of the current policies, which tried to contain dissatisfaction about rising numbers of immigrants. To put it more bluntly, Fortuyn showed how many votes could be gained—within a few months he rose to 40 percent in the polls, and many observers believe he would have been the next prime minister if he had not been murdered—by playing the anti-immigration card. This had a considerable effect on the policies of all established parties. The new cabinet, elected just after the murder of Fortuyn, immediately announced a complete change, especially regarding the immigration issue: drastic curtailing of immigration, speedy extradition of "illegals," and a new policy toward the remaining *allochtonen* aiming at their forceful "integration," especially in cultural respects. The new view was that it was not their socioeconomic marginalization but rather their "refusal" to be culturally integrated that was at the heart of the whole *immigranten* problem.

In retrospect, the change was, of course, not as abrupt as it seemed to be at the time. Protagonists of the rights of the *autochtone* population and of the need for forceful *integratie* of the immigrants tended to paint the preceding decades as a long period of "soft" multiculturalism. Yet it remains to be seen where the policies were, indeed, so one-sided during those years. The reaction came in any case already before Fortuyn's meteoric rise in Dutch politics. Already in 2000, Paul Scheffer—a Dutch journalist who in subsequent years became a leading opinion maker—published his milestone article in *NRC/Handelsblad* (the Dutch "quality" newspaper) with the telling title "The Multicultural Drama." That article and all his subsequent ones are a strong protest against the "cosmopolitan illusion" among many Dutch and their tendency to view "national confidence" as "disposable." These would be basic ingredients of sloppy "multiculturalism" that only led to "segregation." For Scheffer it was high time for a drastic change: the Dutch "should take their own language, culture, and history much more seriously." Scheffer recalls with some nostalgia the time that the political elite still felt it had a "civilizing mission": Dutch bashfulness about their cultural heritage was a serious obstacle to real integration of *allochtonen* (Scheffer 2000a: 2). "If the Netherlands finally recognizes that it is an 'immigration-country' it should at last do what any immigration country has done—that is, emphasize the transfer of language, historical consciousness, and law-culture" (Scheffer 2000b: 3). Scheffer asked urgently for much more reflection on how to give shape to a "modern citizenship" that could be shared by immigrants. Notably, a better knowledge of the landmarks of Dutch history could provide a common basis for this shared citizenship. One solution would be, therefore, the formulation of a "canon"—that is "a core of historical and literary basic texts" (and apparently Scheffer has only Dutch texts in mind here)—that would provide "general points of reference" (Scheffer 2006: 31). This canon had to be central in education so that immigrants' children would internalize it in their youth. But it should provide also a basis for *inburgeringscursussen* (lit. courses to "citizenize"), which immigrants-to-be and also immigrants who were already in the Netherlands would have to attend—if necessary under some coercion.[19]

Precisely because "culture" and "history" are so central in Scheffer's interpretation, it might be useful to emphasize that he—like so many protagonists of *integratie* and belonging in general—has a rather fixed view of both. Of course, when one defends forceful *integratie* there is some urgency to define into what exactly the *allochtonen* will have to integrate. But here Scheffer seems to loose firm ground—or rather, his search for firm ground seems to force him to oversimplify. Striking, for instance, is the facility with which he opposes "traditional" to "modern" culture (2006: 23–24 and 30). Such rigid oppositions are certainly not conducive to promote integration—unless integration is seen as a painful process, some sort of all-or-nothing battle. Even more striking is his invoking of one national history as a precondition for integration. Especially for the Dutch case, this is problematic in view of the powerful tradition of "pillarization" which for so long dominated Dutch politics and which—as Lijphart (1986) showed so well—was based on the maintenance of deep cultural and historical rifts between the different "pillars" (Protestant, Catholic, liberal, and later socialist). The whole appeal of Scheffer to one national culture and history smacks of an artificial return to the nineteenth century (and even then, Dutch nationalism was more pedagogic than emotional).[20]

Such considerations suggest that Scheffer's high expectations of a canon—this was one of the few concrete solutions he proposed—might have been somewhat rash. Especially the premise, presented as some sort of self-evident truth, that common points of reference in culture and history would be preconditions for the integration of newcomers might need further reflection. Yet the idea of a canon was and is shared by many others, and not only in the Netherlands. One can wonder whether the recent drive to formulate national canons in various European countries stems from worries about the nonintegration of immigrants, or rather from the fear of a loss of national identity with ongoing European unification. In any case, it is striking that two smaller countries took the lead. Denmark was the first to publish its canon in the spring of 2006. But the Dutch one followed in the same year. It was also clear that in both cases the government launched the project with expectations similar to those Scheffer had in mind in his articles. The Dutch minister of education, culture and science, Maria van der Hoeven, explicitly asked the committee in her installation letter for a canon that would promote integration and *burgerschapsvorming* (citizen training), especially among the younger generations (Canon van Nederland 2006: 96).

However, in its final report, the committee and its chairman, Frits van Oostrom (a prominent expert of medieval literature in the Netherlands), were much more careful. The report warned against exaggerated expectations: a canon could certainly not be imposed; if coupled with national pride, it would easily lead to blinkers; and therefore it should certainly not be equated with a Dutch identity (Canon van Nederland 2006: 19–23). The committee even expressed its doubts concerning the notion of a "national identity" as such. A canon might be associated with *inburgering* (learning to be a citizen), but even here the committee was prudent: this should certainly not be seen as the main motive behind its canon (24). Its main aim had rather been to formulate a canon "of the country in which we live together . . . offering society a common framework of reference for mutual communication and for operating as a Dutch person in the world. Thus, the canon for Boulahrouz and Beatrix."[21] Clearly, the committee was very conscious of the risk that a canon might imply a fixing of something (culture?) that is always in flux. It proposed a quite original solution for this by constructing its canon from a series of "windows," rather than from specific events or facts. Each of its fifty "windows" opens up to a ramification of stories and links with related topics and aspects. Thus, the committee hoped to have provided a common but open framework for teaching history at school, which could constantly be adapted to changing circumstances.

The reactions were, of course, highly diverse. The most critical ones came from the press that is usually equated with the right. From this side the committee was, for instance, reproached for having missed its chance by not daring to couple history to national identity in a time when there was a dire need for this in view of general individualization and adaptation problems of immigrants.[22] Laudatory comments came from the leftist press, where the committee was praised for refusing to link history and national identity.[23] But even *NRC/Handelsblad* (middle of the road to rightist) complimented the committee for not having followed the minister's instructions to link the canon directly to the integration issue (October 16, 2006: 1). Clearly the Dutch committee succeeded in maintaining a prudent distance from the political aims behind its installation. The very idea of taking "windows" as building blocks also showed a keen sense of the fluidity of culture and history, which would make any use of them in the service of clear-cut political aims a highly complicated affair—much more so than many protagonists in the Dutch immigration debate seemed to hope for.

It is clear also that the committee, with a prudence that might be wise, seemed intent on not taking a clear stand on two major issues. The first is that none of the fifty windows referred explicitly to the historical heritage immigrants brought along when settling in the Netherlands.[24] This left open the question to what extent a canon should provide space for groups who insist on their right to "differ" (not only immigrants, but also groups who claim a minority status in another sense). A second and related issue, of even broader impact, concerns the question, already raised above, as to whether a common core of values and historical knowledge is indeed a precondition for living together in one country. The committee seemed to hesitate here. It clearly hoped that its fifty windows would provide a common framework of knowledge that could strengthen citizenship. But it was as clearly concerned that a canon might serve efforts to fix and impose a core identity—which in practice might rather reinforce splits. The overall lesson of this nuanced effort to launch a common canon seemed to be that the Dutch identity, so easily assumed by *autochtonen* when they oppose themselves to *allochtonen,* was much less self-evident when it had to be given more concrete form.

In the Dutch case, the uncertainty that marked the autochthony discourse, despite its apparent self-evidence, seems to take a different form again. It is rather a basic uncertainty about what constitutes autochthony. The call for forceful *integratie* of newcomers makes it highly urgent to define what they have to integrate into: Dutch "culture" and "history"? A problem is clearly that when these have to be grasped, they assume the receding quality we met in the earlier examples of autochthony discourse.

Elements of a Genealogy: Classical Athens and French Sudan

It might be worthwhile to make a brief excursion back into time. In historical perspective as well, autochthony's trajectories prove to have been very different from one another; but again the same tensions and paradoxes emerge that are apparently given with this seemingly basic notion.

This is particularly clear in the very origin of the term itself, classical Athens.[25] Indeed, for the Athenian citizens of the fifth century bce—the city's Golden Age, the time of Pericles and so many other famous men—*autochthonia* became a crucial point of identification. For them, it was Athenian autochthony—the claim that its citizens "were born from the soil"—which made the city exceptional among all Greek *poleis.* All other cities had histories of having been founded by immigrants. Only the Athenians were truly *autochthonoi*: this was the very sign of their city's excellence and, most important, also of their special propensity for *demokratia.*

The classical texts—Euripides, Plato, Demosthenes—are surprisingly vivid on this aspect. To the present-day reader, it might come as a shock to read in the text of these venerated classical authors the same language that is now so brutally propagated by Africa's protagonists of autochthony or Europe's prophets of the New Right. Here I can only give a few rapid examples.

In "Erechtheus," at the time one of Euripides's most popular tragedies, the great tragedian makes Praxithea, queen of Athens, deliver the following speech at the moment she is ready to offer her daughter for sacrifice in order to save the city: "I could not find any city better than this. To begin with we are an autochthonous people, not introduced from elsewhere; other communities are imported, different ones from different places. Now someone who settles in one city from another is like a peg ill-fitted in a piece of wood—a citizen in name but not in his actions."[26] One can almost imagine the audience cheering after such a heroic declamation—all the more so since the first performance of the play must have been staged in 422, when the city was at the height of its naval power but already locked in mortal combat with its archrival Sparta.

In "Menexenes," Plato makes Socrates celebrate Athenian uniqueness in similar terms: "the forefathers of these men were not of immigrant stock, nor were their sons declared by their origin to be strangers in the land sprung from immigrants; but natives sprung from the soil living and dwelling in their own true fatherland."[27] An even more telling example of the force of autochthony thinking in the Athenian context comes from Plato's *Politeia*, the most imaginative of his writings. Even for this model city he deemed it essential that the founder (who necessarily must have come from elsewhere to found his "new" city) had to acquire a certain aura of autochthony in order to create an effective myth of belonging. Plato describes this as "a beautiful lie," which will serve as the basis for the civic instruction of the city's newly settled citizens.[28]

It is noteworthy that all this celebration of autochthony emerged only one century after the high period of the famous Greek colonization—the founding of new cities throughout the Mediterranean—which was to form the basis of the Greeks' Golden Age. Indeed, the author who is still seen as the most genial historian of Athens, Thucydides, gives a completely different view. He seems determined to completely ignore this preoccupation with autochthony—even though he must have lived right in the middle of it—and consistently avoids the very word *autochthon*, probably because he distrusted its rhetorical use. Instead he went to the opposite by explaining the preeminence of Athens by its success in attracting immigrants from all over Greece.

Thucydides sees it rather as a sign of the city's greatness that it even allowed at least some of these immigrants to become citizen (Loraux 1996: 94).

Indeed, modern historians see the upsurge of autochthony in fifth-century Athens as a new phenomenon in a city in which these immigrants—the *metoikoi* who in principle were, indeed, not citizens—were becoming ever more numerous; moreover, at least some of them became considerably richer than the average citizen (see Rosivach 1987). The fierceness of Athens's autochthony—which comes to the fore most graphically from the ways in which Euripides tunes in to his audience—might have a lot to do with the jealousy of ordinary citizen of the wealth these immigrants were accumulating in the territory of their "hosts." There is a strong reminder here of the first Cameroonian example above.

The relevance of these classical examples for present-day struggles did not escape protagonists of autochthony in the modern world. On May 2, 1990, a member of parliament in the French Assemblée nationale, a certain Marie-France Stirbois, member for Le Pen's Front national, surprised her colleagues by delivering a passionate speech about classical Athens and the way in which Euripides, Plato, and even Socrates himself defended the case of autochthony. Apparently her colleague *deputés* were somewhat surprised, since until then Mme Stirbois's interventions had not betrayed such an in-depth interest in the classics (or for that matter in any academic subject). Clearly another sympathiser of Le Front national—probably a professor at the Sorbonne—had written her speech for her (Loraux 1996: 204). However, a good thing came of it: Stirbois's audacious intervention inspired two leading French classicists—Nicole Loraux (1996) and Marcel Detienne (2003)—to produce two incisive studies of Athenian autochthony. Both try to show that classical perceptions of autochthony can hardly be invoked to justify the positions of protagonists of the New Right in present-day Europe, like Le Pen's Front national. Detienne emphasizes especially Plato's irony in the words he puts in Socrates's mouth; Loraux rather stresses the absence of racism in the Athenian context.

There is no doubt that there are indeed important differences from present-day autochthony discourse, notably concerning Plato's version of the link between *autochthonia* and *demokratia*. However, both Loraux and Detienne are more convincing where they point out certain implicit contradictions, which seem to be inherent to the autochthony notion in both its classical manifestations and in its present-day versions. In particular, Loraux's highly sophisticated argument is relevant for our topic of the ambiguities of belonging and securitization. She characterizes the insistence on having remained on the same spot—in Athenian autochthony as in its subsequent variants—as basically a denial of history. After all, history is always about movement. Thus, autochthony is a kind of negative history which always needs an Other—a migrant or rather a "stranger," who does move—in order to define itself.

In Athens, this implied in practice, especially for its aristocratic families, a guilty denial of founding histories emphasizing their foreign origins. They used to be proud of these origins as some sort of aristocratic charter, but with autochthony's rise in the fifth century bce, this became a guilty secret—a skeleton in the cupboard which could be exposed any time by an informer. Thus, a basic incompatibility arises from Loraux's sharp analysis of the classical texts on autochthony. She shows most convincingly that in many ways history—that is, movement and the traces of it—is constantly undermining autochthony's rigidly closed memory. In practice autochthony—or any kind of belonging—sits most uneasily with history.

Thus Loraux's interpretation—like Detienne's analysis of parallel classical texts—rejoins the basic paradox, mentioned above, in autochthony discourse between apparent security and a practice of basic insecurity. In Athens, as well, a person's citizenship (that is, his *autochthonia)* was hardly ever secure. If a man was slandered by someone who put into doubt his citizenship, he could take the slanderer to court. However, this was a risky business: if the slanderer were proven right, his victim would lose not only his citizenship but also his freedom—he could be sold as a slave (Loraux 1996: 195).[29]

The history of autochthony notions on the African continent is much briefer and highlights other ambiguities. Here the term has a clear colonial background—it was introduced by the French colonials in the Sudan at the end of the nineteenth century, in their desperate efforts to try and create some administrative order in the multitude of ethnic groups, chieftaincies, and other social formations in the extensive territories they had conquered so quickly in the context of the "scramble for Africa." The notion of "autochthony" was to play a special role in *la politique des races*, which can be seen as the French equivalent of indirect rule, the better-known British solution for how to administer these vast colonial territories.[30]

The idea of the *politique des races* was especially promoted in West Africa by Governor General William Ponty around 1910. It required the administrators to search for the truly local power holders, rooted in the local groups, and build the new administration on them—thus bypassing the warlike aristocracies, which the French tended to depict as invaders from elsewhere who had subjected the locals to some sort of imperial authority. The consequence was a determined search for truly local groups who had to be protected against their foreign rulers. It was in this context that the term *autochtone* was introduced on the African continent, where it soon would prove to have a history as chequered and tortuous as anywhere else.

A central figure in this new policy was Maurice Delafosse, the great French ethnographer-administrator. Delafosse's huge, three-volume book *Haut-Sénégal-Niger* (from 1912—but based on research in the 1890s) can be read as a determined search for sorting out the autochthonous groups among the kaleidoscope of tribal groups, chieftaincies, and larger state formations that the French had to confront in their newly conquered territories. Indeed, a leitmotiv in the book was that "some *indigènes* are *autochthones*, whereas others are definitely not" (Delafosse [1912] 1972: 280; cf. also Arnaut 2004: 207). Therefore, a vital question in his encyclopaedic description of the various groupings in this area was whether a certain group was, or was not, autochthonous.

Despite his determined search for autochthony, Delafosse was clearly much more interested in migrating groups. Invariably, once he finally found an autochthonous group, it got only a short description in a somewhat condescending language (they are qualified as *malheureux*, poor and backward). In contrast, Delafosse devotes more than forty pages to, for instance, the Peul/Dyula ethnic conglomerate, since he was clearly fascinated by their peregrinations throughout West Africa and their reputation as born empire builders.

There is a paradox here that seems to be general to all colonial rule. The very idea of indirect rule, for instance, implied a similar reliance on local structures as the French *politique des races*. In indirect rule as well, the main task of local chiefs was to keep the population in its place. The distrust of mobile people, which according to James Scott (1998) marks all modern states, was extremely strong in most colonial states: one of the first tasks of the new colonial administration was apparently to fix mobile populations so that taxes could be levied and labor could be recruited.[31] Yet despite this heavy emphasis on fixing—that is, localizing—the population, nearly everywhere the colonials depicted these locals (as Delafosse did for his "autochthons") in quite negative ways: slow-witted, resistant to change, and so on. And this was in marked contrast to migrants, seen as more enterprising, active, and open to change. Indeed, in practice, and despite their ideological commitment to keeping people in their place, colonial administrators seemed invariably to favor migrants. Thus, Delafosse's version of la *politique des races* is a good example of what seems to be in general a surprising tension in colonial rule: a formal betting on locals that was in practice contradicted by an unswerving preference for migrants.

One of the reasons that the term *autochtone* and its fixed counterpart, *allogène* or *allochtone*—after being introduced by the French into the Sudan in their search for the real locals—did flourish in this new setting was that it easily articulated with distinctions already existing locally, although these often had a quite different tenor. Especially in the interior of the West African Sudan, local patterns of organization were built around some sort of complementary opposition between "people of the land" and "ruling" groups; the latter were (and are) often proud to have come in from elsewhere. Thus, "the chief of the land" formed (and still forms) a ritual counterpoint to the chief of the ruling dynasty.[32] To the French ethnologists, "autochthony" was an obvious term to describe this counterpoint position.

A good example is the vast literature on the Mossi, the largest group in present-day Burkina Faso. For generations of researchers, this opposition between what they termed *autochtones* and "rulers" became the central issue inspiring highly sophisticated, structuralist studies (see the studies by Zahan 1961, Izard 1985, and Luning 1997). In this context, the notion of autochthony took on somewhat primitivist overtones. Sabine Luning, for instance, points out how in the prevailing discourse of the Mossi Maana, the *tengabiise* (a term now currently translated, also among the people themselves, as *les autochtones)*, were characterized as some sort of "pre-social," "terrestrial" beings, who were only fully humanized—that is included into a society—by the coming of the *naam*, their foreign rulers. In practice, *naam* power was limited in all sorts of ways by the *tengabiise*. Nonetheless, the *naam* as foreign rulers were formally at the apex of the prestige scale, decidedly above *les autochtones.*

This was certainly not the meaning Delafosse had in mind in his search for *autochtones* for *la politique des races*. It was also not the meaning that came to the fore with so much force in the 1990s with democratization in this part of Africa. One of the main targets of the upsurge of autochthony in neighboring Ivory Coast, under Houphouët-Boigny's successors—first Bedié and now

Gbagbo—are precisely these Mossi immigrants who are supposed to have taken the land of the "autochthons" of the rich cocoa belt in southern Ivory Coast. In this version—as in the version propagated by Delafosse and *la politique des races*—autochthonous is certainly not subordinate; on the contrary it implies a claim to priority and the right to exclude strangers.

Again, there is a striking tension between autochthony's "naturalness" and history. Even from the short history the term has on African soil, it is clear that this apparently self-evident term can take on highly different meanings in quite rapid succession.

* * *

The above explorations into the variations in space and time that are hidden behind apparently similar discourses on autochthony can help to highlight the ambiguities involved in "the global conjuncture of belonging" that marks the present-day world. It seems, indeed, urgent to try and look behind the self-evident naturalness with which autochthony and similar forms of belonging present themselves. Especially the "receding" quality of these notions creates a deep tension between the promise of a basic security (as coming from the soil itself) and a practice of a haunting insecurity (because of the preoccupation with purity and hence the need to unmask "fake" autochthons). Such deep contradictions may help to understand how the neoliberal tide and the renewed belief in the liberating impact of the market can lead to an obsessive preoccupation with borders, closure, and (in)security.

Notes

1   With many thanks for the spirited comments by Zeynep Gambetti, Marcial Godoy, and all the other participants to the SSRC Workshop on Citizenship, Securitization, and Vernacular Violence (Istanbul, January 2007). See for a more elaborate version of some of the arguments developed in this text Geschiere 2009.

2   On Francophone areas, see Jackson on eastern Congo in this volume; see also McGovern 2011 and Arnaut 2004 on Ivory Coast. However, the notion is now also spreading into Anglophone areas (northern Ghana, Southwest and Northwest Cameroon); moreover issues of belonging and the exclusion of "strangers" seem to dominate politics since democratization everywhere in the continent (see Geschiere and Jackson 2006).

3   See Jean and John Comaroff 2001 on the "naturalizing" tenor of autochthony discourse.

4   Compare the reference in the introduction to this volume to Hobbes's Leviathan as a figure who has to create security for the citizens, but at the same time thrives on their feelings of insecurity. Apparently local forms of autochthony (see examples below) do not need the state to get ensnared in this spiral of security breeding insecurity breeding a search for more security, and so on.

5   Since Jackson discusses parallel developments in Congo (see also Jackson 2003), and there is extensive literature on developments in Ivory Coast (for instance, McGovern 2011, Banégas 2006, Marshall 2007), I limit myself here to two examples from Cameroon.

6   See Fisiy 1999, Geschiere and Nyamnjoh 2000, Socpa 2003, Ndjio 2006; see also Bayart, Geschiere and Nyamnjoh 2001.

7   Even the use of these very terms in the new constitution of 1996 is a striking innovation; in the time of nation building it would have been impossible to use them, since this would imply making formal distinctions within the national citizenry (see Geschiere and Nymanjoh 2000).

8   See also Malcolm Ruell (1969).

9   Cf. also the famous case of the funeral of SM in Kenya (see Cohen and Odhiambo 1992). The funeral of SM, the nickname of a famous lawyer in Nairobi, led to a fierce fight—finally decided in the national Court of Appeal—between his Luo clan and his Kikuyu widow over where the corpse should be buried. The widow wanted to bury SM at their sumptuous farm in Nairobi and, together with her lawyers, emphasized SM's identity as a modern Kenyan citizen. But the representatives of his clan insisted that whether a modern person or not, SM was foremost a Luo and a Luo should be buried "at home." Strikingly enough, his clan members finally won in the Court of Appeal—according to strong rumors, after a direct intervention by President Arap Moi himself (who thus clearly gave precedence to ethnic forms of belonging over the idea of modern Kenyan citizenship). But it was at least as surprising, in view of all this emphasis on custom, that Oginga Odinga, the grand old man of Luo politics, sided with the widow. He declared that all this stress on burying at home was new. According to him, the Luo as an expansionist group rather used to bury their dead in newly conquered areas in order to confirm new claims.

10   Translation mine. Interview with Eboua, *Impact-TribUne* 5 (1995): 14.

11   See Socpa (2003) on the way this notion of "guests" who should not try to rule in the *terroir* of their "hosts" is used by Beti "autochthons" against Bamileke "strangers" in conflicts over land in Yaounde, the country's capital.

12   See, for instance, the emphasis Luc Mebenga puts on this aspect in his 1991 thesis on *Les funérailles chez les Ewondo*. He sees a direct relation to the practice of burying the umbilical cord of a baby near the house where it is born; later, when he or she dies, the body should be brought back and be buried there (one can only wonder how this "traditional" idea fits with the high degree of mobility of these seminomadic forest groups up to the colonial conquest, around 1900).

13   Particular graphic examples of this can be found among the Young Patriots, who played such a violent role in the defense of President Gbagbo's autochthony policies in Ivory Coast. Many Young Patriots used the regime's support in order to claim back part of their "ancestral lands" in the southern cocoa belt, which had been appropriated by "immigrants" (often Burkinabe). However, there are now also many stories of how these Patriots became quickly disenchanted with working on their own cocoa farms, and decided to sell them again to "immigrants" in order to have enough money to buy a ticket to France (oral communication, Ruth Marshall).

14   See Geschiere 1982 and 2004.

15   Karsenty 1999.

16   See Laburthe-Tolra 1981 and Geschiere 1982.

17   Cf. Detienne (2003: 59), who makes exactly the same remark in his discussion of "autochthony" in classical Athens—see below.

18   Surprisingly enough, a much more shocking event received much less international attention: the horrible death of eleven "illegal" immigrants who, in 2005, were burned alive when their provisionally erected prison near Schiphol airport (where they were waiting to be extradited) caught fire. This was an inevitable consequence of the firm decision of minister Rita Verdonk, one of the pillars of the new and firmer policy against immigrants, who promised to have 26,000 "illegals" extradited within two years—a policy which, apart from its human aspects, heavily overtaxed the capacity of the bureaucratic services involved and therefore had to lead to detainment under completely unacceptable circumstances (for years several hundred "illegals" were still detained on the so-called *bajesboten* [prison-boats] in the harbor of Rotterdam despite continuous protests—even from the EU—about a completely unacceptable regime).

19   A striking aspect of Scheffer's interpretations is his tendency—like Fortuyn or, for instance, van den Brink (2006)—to explain the problems with immigrants in the Netherlands as a logical outcome of unfortunate policy choices of successive Dutch governments and, thus, as a typical Dutch way of mismanaging the issue. One almost gets the impression that this is a special problem for the Netherlands and not a worldwide problem that affects all richer nation-states in one way or another. It is

also striking that these authors invariably take the American model as an example —apparently still believing that "the melting pot" ideology leads indeed in practice to cultural homogeneity (cf. Bloemraad 2006 about the problematic implication of the American model for integration). In reality protagonists of *integratie* and respect for the *autochtonen cultuur* (like Scheffer, Fortuyn, and Verdonk) follow rather the French assimilation model. But no Dutch politician would ever acknowledge this.

20 See further Geschiere 2009. In his 2007 book—based also on extensive discussions with immigrants—Scheffer is much more prudent; there he even asks for more scope for difference. Unfortunately this book has never had as much impact in public debate in the Netherlands as his blunt 2000 articles.

21 A soccer player of Moroccan descent and the Dutch queen, respectively (Canon van Nederland 2006:24).

22 Robert Stiphout in the weekly *Elsevier*, October 21, 2006, 14.

23 Hubert Smeets in *De Groene Amsterdammer*, October 20, 2006, 12.

24 Of course "Window" 47—"Multi-colored Netherlands after 1945: The multi-cultural society"—provides an opening for this. Still, the inclusion of this window does not answer the basic question as to how to deal with a well-defined historical heritage that stems from elsewhere, but is taken along to the Netherlands by specific groups of migrants.

25 The classical Greek term is *autochthonia* from *autos* (self) and *chtonos* (soil). See Ceuppens and Geschiere 2006 for the semantic correspondences with the parallel Greek notion of *endogenos* (indigenous) and the strikingly different trajectories of both notions in the modern world.

26 Collard, Crop, and Lee 1995: 159–180; cf. also Detienne 2003: 36–39.

27 Bury 2005: 330.

28 Loraux 1996: 176; Detienne 2003: 56.

29 It would be interesting to pursue further the European history of the notion of autochthony and the different ways in which it became articulated with citizenship in this continent. In this respect, the eighteenth century in Western Europe is of special interest, as a crucial period in the crystallization of ideas of national citizenship as a supreme form of belonging; see, for a seminal contribution, Peter Sahlins's *Unnatural French* (2004).

30 More recent authors (for instance, Crowder 1964; Geschiere 1993) emphasized that all the binary oppositions that in those days were used to contrast French with British colonial rule are highly tenuous: *politique des races* as the oppositie of indirect rule, as much as *assimilation* versus association. Especially during the first decades of colonial rule, French officers often had a free hand in imposing highly variable

arrangements at the local or regional level. And, as military men, many of them were as impressed as the British protagonists of indirect rule by African chiefs and their often theatrical display of power. Still, it is true that French colonials—maybe more than their British colleagues—learned to be distrustful of the powerful chiefs, such as Samory (or earlier Omar Tall) who opposed them so fiercely in the Sahelian region.

31 See Roitman (2005) on the French administrators' obsession with *la population flot-tante* in N. Cameroon and elsewhere.

32 Of course, this is far from an exceptional pattern. Similar configurations existed, for instance, in the Ottoman Empire.

References

Arnaut, K. 2004. "Performing Displacements and Rephrasing Attachments: Ethnographic Explorations of Space, Mobility in Art, Ritual, Media and Politics." PhD dissertation, Ghent University.

Banégas, R. 2006. "Côte d'Ivoire: Patriotism, Ethnonationalism and Other African Modes of Self-Writing."*AfricAN Affairs* vol. 105 (421):535-52

Bayart, J.-F., P. Geschiere, and F. Nyamnjoh, eds. 1999. "Autochtonie, démocratie et citoyenneté en Afrique." *Critique Internationale* 10, special issue "'J'etais là avant': Problématiques politiques de l'autochtonie."

Bloemraad, I. 2006. *Becoming a Citizen: Incorporating Immigrants and Refugees in the United States and Canada.* Berkeley: University of California Press.

Bury, R. G., ed. [1929] 2005. *Plato IX.* Loeb Classical Library. Cambridge: Harvard University Press.

Canon van Nederland. 2006. *En Toen Nu—Rapport van de Commissie Ontwikkeling Nederlandse Canon.* The Hague: Ministry of Education.

Ceuppens, B., and P. Geschiere. 2005. "Autochthony, Local or Global? New Modes in the Struggle over Citizenship and Belonging in Africa and Europe." *Annual Review of Anthropology* 34:385–409.

Cohen, D. W., and A. S. Atieno Odhiambo. 1992. *Burying SM: The Politics of Knowledge and the Sociology of Power in Africa.* London: Heinemann/Currey.

Collard, C., M. J. Cropp, and K. H. Lee. 1995. *Euripides, Selected Fragmentary Plays*, vol. 1. Warminster: Aris and Philps.

Comaroff, J., and J. Comaroff. 2001. "Naturing the Nation: Aliens, Apocalypse and the Postcolonial State." *Journal of Southern African Studies* 27(3):627–651.

Crowder, M. 1964. "Indirect Rule, French and British Style." *Africa* 33(4):293–306.

Delafosse, M. [1912] 1972. *Haut-Sénégal-Niger.* Paris: Maisonneuve.

Detienne, M. 2003. *Comment être autochtone? Du pur Athénien au Français raciné.* Paris: Seuil.

Fisiy, C. 1999. "Discourses of Autochthony: Regimes of Citizenship and the Control of Assets in Côte d'Ivoire." Paper presented at African Studies Association meeting, Philadelphia, November 1999.

Geschiere, P. 1982. *Village Communites and the State—Changing Relations of Authority among the Maka, S.E. Cameroon.* London: Kegan Paul International.

———. 1993. "Chiefs and Colonial Rule in Cameroon: Inventing Chieftainy, French and British Style." *Africa* 63(2):151–176.

———. 2004. "Ecology, Belonging and Xenophobia: The 1994 Forest Law in Cameroon and the Issue of 'Community'." In H. Englund and F.Nyamnjoh, eds., *Rights and the Politics of Recognition in Africa.* London: Zed.

———. 2009. *Perils of Belonging: Autochthony, Citizenship and Exclusion in Africa and Europe.* Chicago: University of Chicago Press.

Geschiere, P., and S. Jackson, eds. 2006. *Autochthony and the Crisis of Citizenship. African Studies Review* 49(2), special issue.

Geschiere, P. and F. B. Nyamnjoh. 2000. "Capitalism and Autochthony: The Seesaw of Mobility and Belonging." *Public Culture* 12(2):423–453 (special issue "Millennial Capitalism and the Culture of Neoliberalism," edited by J. Comaroff and J. Comaroff).

Izard, M. 1985. *Gens du pouvoir, gens de la terre: Les institutions politiques de l'ancien royaume du Yatenga (Bassin de la Volta blanche).* Cambridge: Cambridge University Press.

Jackson, S. 2003. "War Making: Uncertainty, Improvization and Involution in the Kivu Provinces, DR Congo, 1997–2002." PhD dissertation, Princeton University.

———. 2006. "Sons of Which Soil? The Language and Politics of Autochthony in Eastern D.R. Congo." *African Studies Review* 49(2):95–122.

Karsenty, A. 1999. "Vers la fin de l'état forestier: Appropriation des espaces de la rente forestière au Cameroun." *Politique Africaine* 75:147–162.

Laburthe-Tolra, P. 1981. *Les seigneurs de la forêt: Essai sur le passé historique, l'organisation sociale et les normes éthiques des anciens Beti du Cameroun.* Paris: Karthala.

Lijphart, A. 1986. *The Politics of Accommodation : Pluralism and Democracy in the Netherlands*. Berkeley: University of California Press.

Loraux, N. 1996. *Né de la terre: Mythe et politique à Athènes*. Paris: Le Seuil.

Luning, S. 1997. "Het Binnenhalen van de Oogst: Ritueel en Samenleving in Maane, Burkina Faso." PhD dissertation, University of Leiden.

Marshall-Fratani, R. 2007. " The War of 'Who is Who': Autochthony, Nationalism and Citizenship in the Ivorian Crisis." *African Studies Review* 49(2): 9–43.

Mbembe, A. 2002. "Les nouveaux Africains: Entre nativisme et cosmopolitanisme." *Esprit* 10: 1–10.

McGovern, M. 2011. *Making War in Côte d'Ivoire*. Chicago: Chicago University Press.

Mebenga, L. T. 1991. "Les funérailles chez les Ewondo: Changements socio-culturels, changements économiques et évaluation de l'esprit de solidarité." Thesis (3rd cycle), University of Yaounde I.

Monga, C. 1995. "Cercueils, orgies et sublimation: Le coût d'une mauvaise gestion de la mort." *Afrique 2000* 21:63–67.

Murray Li, T. 2002, "Ethnic Cleansing, Recurcive Knowledge, and the Dilemmas of Sedentarism," *International Social Science Journal* 173:361–371.

Ndjio, B. 2006. *"Feymania*: New Wealth, Magic Money and Power in Contemporary Cameroon." PhD dissertation, University of Amsterdam.

Roitman, J. 2005. *Fiscal Disobedience: An Anthropology of Economic Regulation in Central Africa*. Princeton: Princeton University Press.

Rosivac, V. J. 1987. "Autochthony and the Athenians." *Classical Quarterly New Series* 37(2):294–306.

Ruell, M. *Leopards and Leaders: Constitutional Politics among a Cross River People*. London: Tavistock.

Sahlins, P. 2004. *Unnatural French*. Ithaca: Cornell University Press.

Scheffer, P. 2000a. "Het Multiculturele Drama.'" *NRC/Handelsblad*, January 29, 2000.

———. 2000b. "Het Multiculturele Drama: Een Repliek." *NRC/Handelsblad*, March 25, 2000.

———. 2006. "Terug naar de Tuinstad, Binnen en Buiten de Ringweg van Amsterdam." Inaugural lecture, University of Amsterdam (Vossiuspers)

———. 2007. *Het Land van Aaankomst*. Amsterdam: De Bezige Bij.

Scott, J. 1998. *Seeing Like a State: How Certain Schemes to Improve the Human Condition Have Failed*. New Haven: Yale University Press.

Simone, AM. 2001. "On the Worlding of African Cities." *African Studies Review* 44(2):15–43.

Socpa, A. 2003. *Démocratisation et autochtonie au Cameroun: Variations régionales divergentes*. Munster: LIT.

Van den Brink, G. 2006. *Culturele Contrasten: Het Verhaal van de Migranten in Rotterdam*. Amsterdam: Bert Bakker.

Zahan, D. 1961. "Pour une histoire des Mossi du Yatenga." *L'Homme* 1(2):5–22.

CHAPTER THREE

Congolité: Elections and the Politics of Autochthony in the Democratic Republic of the Congo

Stephen Jackson

Congolité

In mid-2006, as the Democratic Republic of the Congo (DRC—formerly Zaire) emerged unsteadily from a decade of war and approached its first democratic elections in more than four decades, the Haute Autorité des Médias (or HAM), an official media watchdog of the DRC's transition, handed down a string of sanctions for incitement to discrimination, hatred, or violence.[1] These were connected to the dramatic upsurge of *Congolité*—best translated as "Congoleseness"—that had suddenly emerged as a powerful electoral discourse, in currency on the airwaves, in newsprint, and in political discourse, and encapsulating an exclusionary definition of national authenticity.[2]

As campaigning got underway, the incumbent transition president, Joseph Kabila, was attacked from all sides as a "non-Congolese," a "Tanzanian" or "Rwandan," a "foreigner," someone who could "barely speak French or Lingala," the "foreign candidate" that further foreigners—Belgium, France, the United Kingdom, the United States, and the United Nations—intended to "impose" through "trumped up elections" on an unwary Congolese people, "a migratory bird" (*un oiseau migratoire*) who had only recently and opportunistically nested in the DRC. His parentage was relentlessly questioned—his mother was Rwandan, his father was not even Laurent-Désiré Kabila (the assassinated former president). Putative half-brothers were interviewed on TV channels controlled by Kabila's principal electoral rival, the transition vice president Jean-Pierre Bemba, to prove the point.

"*Mwana Mboka* [Son of the Soil] Jean-Pierre Bemba." Presidential Elections Campaign Banner, Rond-point FORESCOM, Kinshasa, 23 October 2006. Photo by the author.

The Kabila camp, incensed, responded with accusations that Bemba was half-Portuguese. Bemba's camp was outraged: "Tracts have been circulated in the different communes of Kinshasa [alleging that] Jean-Pierre Bemba . . . is not of Congolese origin. May the true *Kinois* [Kinshasans] and Congolese not permit these detractors to destabilize the MLC [Bemba's party]!"[3]

Congolité might appear nothing more than a virulent by-product of the elections, a merely tactical, violent vernacular. But in fact, the elections were a moment of important political conjuncture, in which two related sets of factors converged and caused *Congolité* to crystallize out of a number of preexisting currents.

The first were relatively short-run, self-interested decisions made from the early 1990s to the present by both domestic and international political actors: the Congolese (or formerly Zairean) government and leadership, domestic political parties, and powerful international actors (including the UN and Western governments). These decisions coincided with key moments in the DRC's political trajectory: the thwarted democratization of the early 1990s, the two full-scale wars that affected the DRC from 1996 to 2002, crucial moments in the peace process, the run-up to the 2006 elections, and the elections themselves.

The second factors concern longer-run, eddying currents of xenophobia in the DRC and across the continent. Amongst these were: an older, widely prevalent, and slippery Congolese discourse of authenticity and "autochthony" (a slippery term invoking a direct and inalienable connection between land and identity; Jackson 2006); the persistent political reflex in the DRC and elsewhere (such as Zambia and Côte d'Ivoire) to smear political opponents as "foreigners"; President Mobutu's *Zairianisation* campaign in 1970s, which combined the nationalization of economic assets with cultural purification; and a long-standing vein of Congolese suspicion of and resentment against foreign influence. All of these together engendered a violently exclusionist discourse that preyed upon identity anxieties, indexing a paranoid obsession with the securitization of the body politic from foreign infiltration and pollution.

The 2006 elections, then, become the mechanism through which these two sets of factors converged. This article discusses each in turn, before concluding that postconflict election processes all too frequently give rise to such dangerous moments of conjuncture, threatening still-fragile peace.

Centripetal and Centrifugal Identity Politics from Independence to the 2006 Elections

The Democratic Republic of the Congo is a giant, the twelfth-largest country on the planet, with an estimated 60 million people and as many as 250 distinct ethnic groups. Its vast endowment of natural resources (tropical hardwoods, diamonds, gold, uranium, and much more) fired colonial rapine, fed postcolonial excess and corruption, and has fueled two recent wars, the violent aftershocks of which continue to the present.

Notwithstanding occasional claims of an underlying "Bantu" unity binding the DRC's peoples together (Ndaywel e Nziem 1997: 50), a unitary form of Congolese nationalism emerged only in reaction to Belgian colonialism. At independence in 1960, splits in the nationalist movement reflected an anxious and unresolved question over the DRC's nationhood: "unitarists" (epitomized by the country's first prime minister, Patrice Lumumba), favoring a strongly centralized and nonaligned state, versus "federalists" (Nzongola-Ntalaja 2002: 96–97). To counter Lumumba and his pan-Africanist progressives, Cold Warriors stoked secessionism in the southern, mineral-rich Katanga province, provoking civil war. Once Lumumba had been murdered (with the apparent connivance of Western intelligence organizations), however, international support for Katangan secession evaporated and, after protracted violence (and a huge UN peacekeeping operation, ONUC), a firmly pro-Western centralist, Joseph Mobutu, emerged as the Congo's Cold War strong man, a dictator for more than three decades.

Mobutu changed the country's name to Zaire and strove to forge a common national identity through *Zaïrianisation*. But the contradictions between centripetal political nationalism and centrifugal ethnic regionalism remained unresolved. Indeed, they continued periodically to metastasize—in Katanga, but also in the eastern Kivu provinces, around the bloody animosity between ethnic groups considering themselves "autochthon" (literally "sons of the soil" or authentic first-dwellers) and those of Rwandan descent (Rwandophones). Mobutu cynically manipulated the issue of Rwandophone nationality, alternately bestowing and then confiscating Congolese citizenship on Rwandophones (Jackson 2007). Compounded by the aftershocks of the 1994 genocide in next-door Rwanda, this animosity tipped into rebellion, and finally led to Mobutu's overthrow in 1997 and the installation of a hitherto minor anti-Mobutiste, Laurent-Désiré Kabila, as president.

A year later, after a growing rift with Kabila, his former allies—Rwanda, Uganda, and the Congolese Rwandophone community together—invented a new "liberation movement," the Rassemblement congolais pour la démocratie (or RCD). When other African nations (Angola and Zimbabwe foremost) intervened militarily to defend Kabila, "Africa's First World War" ensued (1998–2002), claiming almost four million lives (International Rescue Committee 2004). In 1999, rivalry between Rwanda and Uganda split the RCD and engendered another rebel bloc, the Mouvement pour la libération du Congo (MLC), led by Jean-Pierre Bemba, son of a prominent Mobutiste.

Intensive international mediation produced little progress at first—though an initial peace agreement in 1999 led to the deployment of UN liaison officers, laying the foundations for the largest UN peacekeeping operation in history, MONUC (Mission des nations unies en RD Congo). Then, in January 2001, Kabila was assassinated by his bodyguard (in circumstances that remain murky) and was quickly replaced by his son Joseph. The latter proved more convinced of the need to make peace and, in December 2002, signed a power-sharing deal with the major factions. A transition government would rule until new elections, in an unwieldy structure known as the "1+4": Joseph

Kabila as transition president and four vice presidents, including Bemba (representing the MLC) and Azarias Ruberwa (RCD).

Congolese attitudes to Kabila almost immediately began to polarize. For Congolese in the east, bitterly resentful of the "occupation" by RCD "foreigners," Kabila was the nationalist cynosure who had prevented the territorial dismemberment of the DRC, and who could now deliver peace. In the west, where Kabila had control, he was suspect, a foreign imposition, lacking democratic legitimacy, someone whose very nationality was doubtful. Political opponents nourished these suspicions, dubbing him the offspring of the elder Kabila's liaison with a Rwandan woman, or worse, whispering that he was the son of a Rwandan Tutsi man, and that his claim of relationship to the late president was fraudulent.

By early 2006, planning for the first democratic elections in four decades was underway. Between 1999 and 2006, the DRC thus followed a now conventional international template for lifting a country out of conflict: multiple rounds of mediation, resulting in peace agreements that gradually bind in an expanding circle of belligerents; adoption of a transition constitution and installation of a transition administration, watched over by a peacekeeping operation (usually under UN auspices); the adoption of a new and more permanent constitution, fresh elections, and the installation of a new, "postconflict" government, marking the end of the "transition" (in the epistemology of postconflict state building, at least).

Democratic elections, in particular, have become the emblematic means through which the international community welcomes delinquent states back to international statehood, a machine for the production of governments with popular legitimacy. While elections cannot resolve underlying conflicts, the underlying international assumption has been that after a peace agreement they can provide a peaceful mechanism through which the social cleavages that drove the war can be channeled and managed.

By comparison with this template, the DRC differed only in terms of scale. The UN peacekeeping operation was the largest ever mounted, with—at its height—more than 22,000 international military, police, and civilian peacekeepers. The elections were the most massive the UN had ever supported: almost one hundred UN aircraft flew round-the-clock missions delivering ballot papers, salaries for elections workers, cohorts of international and national election observers, police and military (to provide electoral security), and journalists. The fully tally of ballot papers for the first round vote alone weighed approximately 1,500 metric tons. More than 50,000 polling stations were opened across the country—many reachable only by helicopter or pirogue. The total UN budget for the electoral process alone weighed in at approximately US$500 million, while the annual cost of MONUC's peacekeeping mounted to approximately US$1 billion.

Crucially, the electoral system set forward under the constitution for the DRC's presidency was the two-round "runoff" majority vote system. There would be no limit on the number of candidates who could run for president, and if no candidate were to win an absolute majority (50 percent plus one vote) in the poll, a second-round runoff would take place between the two highest-scoring candidates from the first round. Used in France, Austria, Brazil, Finland, Portugal, and elsewhere, this had become the favored electoral system for postconflict countries in Africa—such as Liberia's elections of 2011. In theory, it encourages candidates to appeal to a broad cross section of voters, since winning in the second round means garnering the support of a "coalition" of voters whose first-round candidates have been eliminated. Given the vastness and complexity of the DRC, it was hoped this system would help knit together a society riven by war and by long-standing regional and ethnic rivalries, catalyzing the centralizing political tendency that had been questionable for the previous forty years (then to be counterbalanced with newly decentralized provincial-level political administrations).

A blow was struck to these hopes, however, when the veteran opposition figure Etienne Tshisekedi declared he would boycott the elections. Tshisekedi had been Mobutu's interior minister, but then broke away to lead the incipient democracy movement (Nzongola-Ntalaja 2002: 185). Through the 1990s, many Congolese saw Tshisekedi as the Moses who would "lead his people out from under the slavery they experienced in the Zaire of the Pharaoh Mobutu" (de Villers 1998: 83–84). But Tshisekedi had backed himself into a corner: during the peace negotiations, he aligned himself with the hated RCD. Then, when the "1+4" was being composed, he wagered that this shaky transition structure would not survive and refused to consider a position within it. Finally, to the irritation of his supporters, in 2006 he decided to boycott what he deemed would be an irredeemably flawed electoral process and refused to stand for the presidency he had sought so long. Tshisekedi's decision fundamentally altered the electoral equation, clearing the way for a second-round contest between Kabila and Bemba, two former belligerents: elections as the continuation of war by other political means.

As the elections approached, campaigning by all thirty-three presidential candidates reached fever pitch and was almost entirely devoid of detailed visions for the reconstruction of the country. Instead, many of the campaigns revolved around accusations and counteraccusations of inauthenticity. Candidates played up their *Congolité* and the "foreignness" of others in a "xenophobic fever" (Ayad 2006). One candidate—Joseph Olenghankoy, a former Kabila ally who would become campaign manager for Bemba in the second round—repeated allegations first made in January 2005 after his dismissal from the transition government that Kabila was a "foreigner," in "collusion with the forces of aggression" (a thin nationalist code for Rwanda and Uganda), and possessing a "private militia" consisting of Rwandan elements. Bemba—as well as another candidate, Roger Lumbala—had banners put up in Kinshasa proclaiming himself as a *mwana mboka*, Lingala for a "son of the country" or "autochthon," obliquely suggesting that Kabila was neither of the above.

Those supporting Kabila also turned to xenophobic threats. Despite (or because of?) the innuendos that Kabila was really a Tutsi, his transition vice president, Abdoulaye Yerodia, menaced Tutsi at a May 2006 campaign rally, saying: "If you don't want to go back to where you came from, we will put sticks into your backsides to make sure you go back" (Human Rights Watch 2006—"sending you back to where you came from" was a tragically familiar anti-Tutsi trope during the 1994 genocide in Rwanda).

As the July 2006 elections approached, the Kabila camp remained confident of an outright first-round victory. His campaign slogan—"the Artisan of Peace"—evoked his having supported his father's driving out of Mobutu, his having been a principal catalyst for the peaceful conclusion of the war, and his stewardship of the country through the transition. But beyond Kabila, at least five candidates threatened a runoff: Bemba, the rebel leader and businessman, from the northwestern *Mobutiste* heartland of Equateur; Antoine Gizenga, an eighty-year-old veteran opposition figure (and Lumumba's deputy prime minister) from the western province of Bandundu; Oscar Kashala, a long-time émigré and Harvard-educated doctor from the pivotal, central Kasai provinces; Nzanga Mobutu, son of the former dictator, also from Equateur; and Pierre Pay-Pay, a former Central Bank governor and businessman, from the Kivus. Against any of the last four, the contrast with Kabila would have been different: youth versus experience (against Gizenga); belligerent against a "new broom" (Kashala); between the sons of two powerful leaders (Nzanga Mobutu versus the son of the man who overthrew Mobutu); or between two "Easterners," one a warrior (Kabila), the other a businessman (Pay-Pay).

But when the results were declared on August 20, 2006, Kabila had narrowly missed a first-round knockout and it was Bemba he would face in the runoff. Kabila had scored 44.81 percent—impressive, but not enough. He had resoundingly won the east, garnering an almost unbelievable 94.64 percent of the vote in South Kivu, for example.[4] But in the west, his score was greatly less: in Kinshasa, he had polled a disappointing 14.7 percent. Bemba's position was exactly the reverse: coming second with 20.03 percent overall, he had polled strongly in the west (49 percent in Kinshasa, 63.67 percent in his home province of Equateur to Kabila's 1.85 percent) while polling weakly in the east (with less than 1 percent of the vote in South Kivu—Bemba's actions during the war years were remembered with no fondness in the east). Gizenga, the veteran, had pulled in a respectable 13.06 percent, but the remaining candidates had imploded: Nzanga Mobutu and Kashala each captured just 4 percent nationally, the remaining stream of candidates picking up 1 percent or less each.

Kabila would face Bemba in a runoff, therefore. Both men were comparatively young, both had risen to prominence through force of arms, both had served in the transition executive. But for ordinary Congolese, and for the campaign managers that now engaged with ferocity for the second round, the strongest contrast between them was that Bemba was from the Lingala-speaking west, Kabila from the Swahili-speaking east, or, to his detractors, from Rwanda or Tanzania, not Congolese at all. Each had dominated the vote in his half of the country while failing to capture significant support in the other. The runoff was always likely, therefore, to be polarized and venomous, all the more so when violence between forces loyal to both men erupted on the streets of Kinshasa around the announcement of the first-round results. Kabila's Republican Guard advanced with heavy weaponry toward Bemba's compound, vowing to "disarm" Bemba's forces. Bemba became convinced that Kabila was trying to kill him, and was provided UN protection for the remainder of the electoral period.

Security concerns prevented either man from holding large-scale rallies in the second round. Instead, Bemba's camp used his considerable array of TV and radio stations to place *Congolité* at the heart of his campaign.

Controversial and pugnacious Bemba allies—such as Olenghankoy and Pasteur Théodore Ngoy—were ubiquitous. Ngoy used a religious broadcast to rail that "they want to impose on us a chief of their choice . . . it's a question of nationality!"[5] The "they" was kept usefully vague—the international community? Or Rwanda and Uganda, the DRC's neighbors? Bemba's supporters, jostling outside his campaign headquarters in Kinshasa, echoed Ngoy's refrain: "'He's a son of the country' said a youth. 'The other one, we have no idea where he comes from,' said a woman. 'He's done nothing here, and he has said that he doesn't like us, nor has he made any effort to learn Lingala, our language.' . . . 'We, we are ready to die for the unity of our country' explained a youth. 'As for the Whites, let them leave the choice to us'" (Flipo 2006).

Campaign songs and banners rehearsed the same themes: Kabila was an impostor, a non-*Congolais*, being thrust on the DRC through an elaborate charade, a sham, a fraudulent democratic process imposed by unscrupulous international interests.

Congolité and Long-Standing Currents of Xenophobia

The circumstances of the second round, then, laid the basis for a xenophobic polarization around *Congolité*. The specific term was new; but as already argued, it was able to draw its energy from a number of long-run ingredients. The first is the politics of autochthony, all too familiar from the Congolese political climate and from elsewhere on the continent (Geschiere and Nyamnjoh 2001, Geschiere and Ceuppens 2005, Geschiere and Jackson 2006, Jackson 2006, Marshall-Fratani 2006). To be "autochthon" is to be taken as a "son of the soil," someone with a supposedly indisputable historical link to a particular territory. Autochthony (from the Greek, combining *auto-* meaning "self" with *khthon*, meaning "soil" or "land"), and its antonym, allochthony (from *allo-*, implying otherness), have long provided a ready and violent vernacular anchored in binary claims over locality versus foreignness. The term—arriving first in Africa through French colonial discourse (Geschiere and Ceuppens 2005)—has by now reached wide employment across countries as disparate as Cameroon and Côte d'Ivoire. Discourse about autochthony had been key to violent political ructions in the DRC over several decades. During that time, it operated at multiple scales—local, provincial, national, regional—with an imprecision and slipperiness that was, paradoxically, part of its political attractiveness, offering demagogues a politically useful vagueness and multivalence (Jackson 2006). Individuals or groups could be labeled as "not of the soil" because, variously, they were imputed to belong to the wrong village, wrong territory, province, ethnic group, or nationality.

Indeed, the venomous potency of this exclusion lay precisely in the fact that the level at which the individual or group did not "fit" could be left discursively vague. As an example, consider one of the many anonymous tracts issued by the Mayi-Mayi resistance to the RCD during the war, which argued that "by contrast with the other Congolese, in the pay of the Imperialists, the Mayi Mayi forces are dependent on the autochthon population which created them. And that's all. Despite the temptations of poverty, hunger, and all the other misfortunes that continuously strike these ideologically determined combatants, the Mayi Mayi forces still remain proud of their character and their dignity in the defense of their ANCESTRAL LANDS."[6]

The ringing declarations of pride in the "ancestral lands" and the "autochthon population" distract attention from the fact that no specific territory or population is actually being indexed. The discursive drift, rather, allows multiple groups, and their supporters—whatever their ethnicities and local allegiances—to feel included under one banner, the defense of the autochthon territory, however that territory be understood. Just as easily, at other historical moments—during an intensified struggle for control of customary chieftainships within North Kivu, say—the degree of inclusiveness of autochthony slips, so that suddenly the "ancestral lands" being defended are indexed at a smaller, more local scale and populations formerly "in" are now "out"—allies become enemies, brothers become others. Autochthony, in short, offers a slippery political discourse that is as potent as it is unstable—indeed, its instability is its strength, allowing it to be endlessly worked and reworked, invoked and revoked (Jackson 2006).

These general points about autochthony's discursive indeterminacy granted, over a number of years there have been discernible shifts in whether autochthony discourse seemed to focus more at one scale of identity or another. One impact of Rwanda's domination of the Kivus through the RCD rebellion was to skew popular discourse toward the national scale, and toward accusations of "allochthony" against Congolese of Rwandan descent—popularly asserted to be RCD supporters. Without any popular base, the RCD was all but eliminated at the 2006 polls. With the second round pitting two former belligerents, Jean-Pierre Bemba and Kabila, against one another, *Congolité* provided the vernacular through which the underlying resentments concerning autochthony could be appropriated and skewed once more, this time toward a different facet of the national context: an almost existential struggle for the country's soul between eastern and western Congo.

In building on and appropriating the preexisting discourse of autochthony, the electoral sloganeering around *Congolité* indexed a related historical precedent: the long-standing reflex of slurring the parentage and nationality of key Congolese politicians. Almost every key figure, from President Kasa-Vubu to Mobutu himself, at one time or another faced such accusations, being dubbed a "quarteroon," "son of a coolie," "Rwandan," or at least accused of having a Rwandan, Angolan, or other foreign-born wife (Djungu-Simba, cited in de Villers 1998).

Political transitions on the African continent have all too frequently provided the trigger for such slurs. As it transitioned to multiparty democracy in the 1990s, Zambia witnessed a backlash against President Kenneth Kaunda, leader of Zambia from its independence in 1964, but whose parents had migrated from neighboring Malawi prior to his birth. Kaunda's successor, Frederick Chiluba, used this as the basis for attempts to exile Kaunda altogether and to push through an amendment to the Zambian constitution stipulating that both parents of potential presidential candidates must have been born in the country.[7] On March 31, 1999, a Zambian High Court denationalized the former president altogether, ruling: "Dr. Kenneth Kaunda is a stateless person who should be treated as such by all concerned authorities" (Clarke n.d.).

But it was another major francophone nation on the African continent—Côte d'Ivoire—that provided the nadir of this politics of national disqualification. There, for more than a decade, the parallel term has been *Ivoirité*, Ivorianness. *Ivoirité* was, first, the project of a pseudoacademic circuit of advisers to President Henri Konan Bédié, who had come to power in 1993: CURDIPHE, or the Cellule universitaire de recherche et de diffusion des idées et action politique du Président Henri Konan Bédié. *Ivoirité* crystallized around the 1995 elections, and shared with *Congolité* the same animus against "foreigners [who] occupy a dominant, sometimes hegemonic situation in the . . . economy" (Loucou, cited in Akindès 2003), against immigrants whose presence was deemed to be impacting adversely the livelihoods of the "native born," and on foreign domination in political life. As the discourse developed, Akindès argues, it became more and more centered on a vision of authentic "Ivorianness" inscribed in regional, ethnic, and religious identities. This incendiary mixture was merely waiting for a spark to explode. Bédié was deposed by army General Robert Gueï in 1999, and a popular candidate, Alassane Ouattara, was prevented from standing for the 2000 elections by a new law which, as in Zambia, required both parents of a candidate to be native born.[8] In 2002, the country descended into civil war. As Marshall-Fratani mordantly notes, "far from allowing Ivoirians to know, 'once and for all, who is who' the war only made the question more acute and terrifying" (Marshall-Fratani 2006). Long-delayed presidential elections in 2010 saw Gbagbo defeated by Ouattara, who was finally permitted to stand after enormous international pressure. Gbagbo refused to accept the results, and was finally driven from power by a controversial joint UN/French military operation.

Congolité has—mercifully—never yet been saddled with the kind of pseudoacademic imprimatur with which *Ivoirité* was cursed from the beginning. But it seems probable that Congolese ideologues around the 2006 elections, keenly aware of political machinations elsewhere on the continent, drew inspiration for *Congolité* from the ways in which the discourse permitted Ivorian political actors to channel a popular xenophobia in service of their narrow political self-interests. For while autochthony discourse and parentage slurs had a long tradition in Congolese politicking, *Congolité* as a term was a recent arrival.

Congolité also discursively piggybacked on memories of Mobutu's late 1970s campaign for *Zaïrianisation*. As de Villers describes it, this "ideology of 'authenticity', the official ideology of the Second Republic, intended that the development and modernization of the country should be founded upon a return to the tradition of the ancestors" (de Villers, 1998: 87). Mobutu's first move was to purify the very name of the nation, abolishing the colonially imposed "Congo" and instating, instead, a more "authentic" name of his own choosing: Zaire. In the name of building the state, he asserted the centrality of Zairean cultural tradition and political order. Zaireans were supposed to drop the use of "Christian" first names in favor of more authentic appellations, and new, supposedly non-Western, forms of dress were preferred; industries and agricultural concerns still held by foreigners were "nationalized"; and so on, all in the name of a "cultural atavism."

"Nationalization" amounted to little more than a transfer of ownership from colonial to postcolonial elites—predominantly Mobutu's cronies, whose mismanagement led to the fiscal crises of the 1980s, and thus, eventually, to the collapse of *Mobutisme* altogether. But *Zaïrianisation* had some success in building a unitary national identity in the aftermath of the secessionist crisis that had followed independence (Dunn 2003). By contrast with *Congolité's* emphasis on exclusion, as a general rule *Zaïrianisation* can be read as a typically Congolese, half-serious, half-ironized variant of the inclusive African nation-building ideologies characteristic of the period. But the incomplete forging of a unitary Zairean national identity in the face of still prevalent centrifugal regionalisms can, nonetheless, be argued to have prepared the ground for the hypersensitivity over *Congolité*. During the 1998 war, certain international analysts were advocating that the DRC was among a number of essentially unviable states in Central Africa, created by artificial colonial borders; postcolonial attempts to hold them together having failed, it might be best to allow them to "break up" (Ottaway 1999). These arguments were met with outrage by Congolese activists intent on asserting the inviolability of the DRC's borders and territories. But underneath this resurgent nationalism, one could detect a strong undercurrent of anxiety, even of paranoia. This was very much on display, for example, in a variety of anonymous tracts circulating in the Kivus in the 1990s that railed against the Congolese leadership's treachery toward the nation, asserting that "the traditional chiefs have been purchased," "handsomely paid by Rwanda," while Congolese leaders had "taken more than US$500,000 from the Tutsi for the sale of Kivu" (Jackson 2003). That paranoia was, as Žižek has argued for the parallel case of Eastern Europe, precisely a result of the lingering contingency of national identity: "The mechanism at work here is of course that of paranoia. . . . We could perhaps sustain the thesis that Eastern Europe's national paranoia stems precisely from the fact that Eastern Europe's nations are not yet fully constituted as 'authentic states': it is as if the failed, foreclosed state's symbolic authority 'returns in the real' in the shape of the Other, the 'thief of enjoyment'" (Žižek 1990: 55n).

Fourth and finally, *Congolité* tapped into a deep reserve of mistrust of the international community. The roots of this extend back to the slave trade, the colonial period, and the internationally supported and sanctioned murder of Lumumba after independence. The resentment grew during the years of war, when Western powers persistently refused to credit accusations that Rwanda and Uganda were supporting the RCD against Kabila. But during the transition, the animus against internationals switched to Western support *for* Kabila—at the 2003 peace talks in Sun City, South Africa, the one subject that Kabila's international backers had ensured was never opened for debate was that anybody else might preside over the transition executive. Bemba's MLC, unsurprisingly, pressed for a rotating presidency (International Crisis Group 2002: 2), but Western governments insisted on Kabila, privileging stability over inclusiveness. Their reasons, no doubt, varied. Some international players may genuinely have believed Kabila provided the best hope of the transition's success. For others, their interest may have including protecting lucrative mineral concessions concluded with Kabila (or his father). For others still, post-9/11 security imperatives may have influenced their calculus, following a widely read December 2001 *Washington Post* article which asserted that militant Islamic groups—including Hezbollah and possibly al-Qaeda—were exploiting "the corruption and chaos endemic to Congo to tap into the diamond trade and funnel millions of dollars to their organizations back home" (Farah 2001).

Kabila's position as transition president meant he embarked on his election campaign with the considerable advantage of incumbency. Although the elections that would follow in 2006 would be deemed largely "disciplined, peaceful, free and fair" by international observers such as the Carter Center (Gettleman 2006), it is in this narrower but still key sense that detractors would argue Kabila was being "imposed" on the DRC by the international community. The resentment against this was further exacerbated by the deployment of MONUC, resented in some quarters as a form of neocolonialism; and with the deployment to Kinshasa of a special EU military expeditionary force for security (EUFOR) around the elections.

Congolité in the Mass Media and on the Streets

By mid-2006, *Congolité* was everywhere: dominating newspaper columns, radio and TV airtime, and casual conversations. It drew infuriated responses from Kabila and his camp, and punitive sanctions from the HAM—including bans from public broadcast for several key Bemba partisans (including Olenghankoy) of between fifteen and sixty days. And it fascinated and repelled in equal measure the international media covering the Congolese elections, engendering headlines about "the poison of *Congolité*" (Hugeux 2006), a "detestable" campaign climate (Tuquoi 2006), and comparisons with the war of *Ivoirité* in Côte d'Ivoire.

Through Bemba's radio, TV, and print holdings, his supporters were able to whip this antipathy toward frenzy, using a coded mix of political, cultural, and religious references. "We have . . . two candidates: the candidate of the foreigners on one side, the candidate of the Congolese on the other," fumed Olenghankoy on national TV.⁹ "I'm going to give the order to all of my supporters to vote for *Congolité*," declaimed another party leader throwing in his lot with Bemba.¹⁰ "He's a son of the soil, he cares for the country, why would he sell the country?"¹¹

Religious motifs were a useful source of venom. The Congolese were depicted as Israelites, struggling to escape from "slavery" under the "Egyptians."¹² Egpytian, in this context, carried a particular additional valence, since depicting the Tutsi as "Nilotic" invaders who had displaced or enslaved the rightful autochthons of Central Africa has a long xenophobic history in the greater subregion (Jackson 2003; Miles 2000). The ostensibly religious "Thought for the Day" broadcast on CCTV on September 11, 2006, came from Deuteronomy 17:11—"Thou shalt in any wise set him King over thee whom the LORD thy God shall choose: one from among thy brethren shalt thou set King over thee: thou mayest not set a stranger over thee, which is not thy brother." Purported proverbs were enlisted: "In all of this, 'it's better the bad son in the house than the one that they send from far away'. . . Let everyone do their 'diplomacy' in those countries over there so that the 'bird' flies away" (building on the now well-established anti-Kabila trope of him as a "migratory bird").¹³ A campaign song, subsequently banned by the HAM, tied all these various themes together:

> Foreigners are starting to prevail in Congo,
> Those who've come from elsewhere have grown fat while we die of hunger,
> Those who've come from elsewhere have grown fat; let them leave the country to its owners!
> His [Bemba's] father and his mother are known to you,
> But those who've come from elsewhere, where did they grow up?
> The father of Bemba, you know him and his mother as well,
> But those who've come from elsewhere, from where did they come?
> With Bemba, the foreigners will go back where they came from!
> With Jesus, the foreigners will flee!¹⁴

In a final, ironic fling against the international community, Bemba unveiled a new cross-party political platform designed to support his candidacy in the second round: the Union pour la Nation or "UN" for short! This nationalist "UN" seemed purpose-built to contrast Bemba with the other, internationalist UN's alleged attempts to impose Kabila on an unwilling DRC.

Incensed, the Kabila camp did not remain silent—or blameless. Aside from smearing Bemba with their own attacks questioning his *Congolité*, they used the government-controlled RTNC-TV and other channels to try to tar this son of Mobutu's former ally: "reflect on the danger which menaces the DRC faced by the return of the *Mobutiste* dictatorship!"[15] "Every time the toads croak, it is because they are asking God to send them a king. Don't vote for the snake, because he will eat you, the snake always remains a snake."[16] Meanwhile, when the HAM sometimes failed to act quickly enough to silence Kabila's enemies, his Republican Guard took on the task itself, frequently—and entirely illegally—shutting down Bemba's transmitters for protracted periods.

Throughout the electoral period, the UN's distinctive white Land Cruisers were frequent targets of stoning by street youths known as *shégués*, while EUFOR's pilotless drone surveillance aircraft were deeply suspected of playing some hidden role in forcing the populace to vote for Kabila.[17] In an elevated climate of hostility, the UN and much of the diplomatic community quietly evacuated their families and nonessential staff.

Congolité, Insecurity, and Political Conjuncture

As I have argued, then, the 2006 presidential elections were a moment of extreme political conjuncture, permitting various violent or exclusionary discourses to merge in politically potent ways. As has been reviewed, the factors were a mix of historical and structural, deep-rooted and conjunctural. Historically, the DRC emerged from ten years of bloody war, forty years of dictatorship, and seventy-five years of colonization as a weary and fractured postcolonial polity, its trenchant nationalism seemingly in direct proportion to its political incoherence. Its territorial integrity had barely survived a secessionist rebellion shortly after independence. New war in 1998 once again threatened the country's breakup (tellingly depicted in popular tracts as the "violent dismembering" of the Congolese body politic; Jackson 2003). The DRC thus approached the 2006 elections in an anxious climate suffused with an extraordinary availability of heightened discourses of exclusion, whose popular energies could be relentlessly magnified by political manipulation.

Structurally (and inadvertently) the newly chosen electoral system provided both the mechanism and the incentive for these anxieties to become crystallized around *Congolité*. The voter shorthand for the French-style, two-round system for electing an executive presidency is: "First round: vote for the one you like. Second round: vote against the one you hate." As voter options were reduced to a straight runoff between two candidates, so the campaign became the means through which popular insecurities intensified and focused on a reductionist, binary reading of the DRC's political trajectory.

But I emphasize that it would be too easy to write *Congolité* off as the proximate product of all too familiar ethnopolitical manipulation by candidates at election time. Although it crystallized at the moment of the 2006 elections, *Congolité* clearly drew from deep wells of anxiety and resentment within the Congolese populace. It represented, rather, one more node in a lengthy and varying sequence of expressions of apprehension about the "pollution" of the Congolese body politic. The definition of that body politic continues to fluctuate in its scale. At one moment, the object under threat is the national unit, the next moment the village. But the structure of the underlying metaphor remains the same: the solidarity and purity of the group is menaced from the outside. Infiltrators, traitors, Trojan horses smuggle the threat from the outside to inside the group. Key actors are not what they claim to be, those who have no right to be citizens pretend to be citizens, those who have no right to leadership lay claim upon it. These are Žižek's "thieves of enjoyment" (Žižek 1990), hidden and masked protagonists who intrude to prevent the fulfilment of the prelapsarian identity-fantasy of communal unity.

With this understood, the 2006 presidential elections are revealed in their proper role: as precipitant rather than reactant. Describing another rather different "structure of the conjuncture" (the apotheosis of Captain James Cook on his arrival in the Hawaiian islands in 1779), Marshall Sahlins provocatively reverses the conventional formula: *plus c'est la même chose, plus ça change* (Sahlins 1981: 7). His point: to meet new exigencies at moments of conjuncture, preexisting cultural forms are frantically reworked, and "at the extreme, what began as reproduction ends as transformation" (61). The elections did not create a Congolese politics of resentment and othering, but they caused it to be radically adapted and ideologically redeployed in new ways.

After some weeks, during which thousands of tons of ballots were painstakingly collected and compiled, the Independent Electoral Commission finally confirmed on November 15, 2006, that Kabila had won, with 58.05

percent of the national vote to Bemba's 41.95 percent. Although Bemba disputed the result, he did so in the Supreme Court of Justice rather than the streets; the court rejected his appeal, and on December 5, Kabila was inaugurated as the first democratically elected leader of the DRC in more than forty years.

The Migratory Bird Flies On

The much-anticipated explosion of popular anger in the streets of Kinshasa did not materialize. A heavy security deployment by MONUC and EUFOR played a role, as did the assertive actions of Kabila's Garde républicaine (arresting Bemba figures associated with the legal appeal, for example), and the combination of intense pressure and inducement placed before Bemba by key Western states. In the end, Kabila's second-round victory was met with weary acceptance by the population of Kinshasa and the western provinces more generally—they had always expected, after all, that a powerful international conspiracy would see to it that the election was "stolen." Meanwhile, in the eastern provinces, celebrations of the victory continued for days.

But then, in March 2007, violence between Kabila's and Bemba's security forces exploded again. For two days, central Kinshasa was wracked by heavy gunfire, Kabila determined to disarm his opponent, who had continued to retain more than 500 troops under his command for his "personal protection." Bemba took refuge in the South African embassy, and after some weeks, was escorted to Portugal on "humanitarian grounds."

And then, as might have been predicted, the electric energies of autochthony and exclusion that had briefly converged around *Congolité* migrated again. Simultaneously with the second-round runoff, elections to eleven new provincial assemblies had been held. These assemblies then elected the powerful provincial governors, who enjoyed substantial political and fiscal autonomy under the new constitution. The contests for the governorships were also largely conducted through the language of ethnic and regional autochthony—*Congolité* repackaged, as it were, at the provincial level. In an incendiary development, several governorship races were subsequently delayed by Supreme Court cases in which it was alleged that candidates should be barred because they held foreign passports, "automatically" invalidating their *Congolité*, their Congolese nationality, and thus their right to stand for election under the provisions of the constitution.

Five years later, in parallel with the finalization of this chapter for publication, the clock established under the DRC's constitution chimed once more and the country organized presidential elections on November 28, 2011. Much changed, and much remained the same. Of the changes, there were two with radical impact. The first was the May 28, 2008, arrest of Jean-Pierre Bemba by the International Criminal Court in The Hague on three counts of crimes against humanity and five counts of war crimes. His trial began in November 2010, and he remained in The Hague, obviously preventing his participation in the 2011 elections—something that, once again, his most fervent supporters chalk up to another instance of nefarious "international influence."

The second was a radical change to the mechanics of the elections: in June 2011, the Congolese National Assembly approved a revised electoral law, making election to the presidency, as well as to the assembly, a single-round vote by a simple majority in a direct universal suffrage. It was popularly considered that the Kabila administration had effected this change so as to fend off a strong challenge from Tshisekedi, who had this time decided to run. The logic was presumed to be that without a second-round runoff in which disparate opposition forces would be obliged to unite under one candidate, the incumbent would have the luxury of competing against a fractured opposition. So, indeed, it proved: Kabila faced off against ten candidates. And on December 9, after several delays, the Electoral Commission, or CENI, announced that he had won with almost 49 percent, despite massive procedural flaws that international and national observers strongly denounced; the UN noted with "deep concern the findings of . . . observer missions relating to the significant irregularities in the management of the results process, in particular the counting and tabulation of the votes" (MONUSCO 2011).

But placing the defections of the electoral process to one side, it was notable that the 2011 presidential elections passed off without the marked use of xenophobic appeals to *Congolité* that had marred 2006.[18] Only a small number of instances were reported: the Kabila camp, for example, complained about a speech of Tshisekedi on November 18, 2011, at the Place de l'Indépendence, in which he purportedly referred to Kabila as a "Rwandan," and alleged that Tshisekedi's party had been spreading songs and text messages exhorting voters to expel Tutsi from the country. If the explanatory theory of this essay holds true, this would imply that the xenophobic energies that drove *Congolité* have not disappeared; rather, because of the change from two rounds to one round of presidential voting, the electoral process did not provide them with a lens through which to focus on the contrast between two starkly opposing kinds of candidate.

Elections: Miracles and Paranoia

"Is it a miracle?" asked a BBC correspondent, back in 2006, of the apparently peaceful conclusion to one of the largest and most complex electoral processes the world had ever seen, supposedly closing more than a decade of war (Doyle 2006). In one sense, the DRC's elections might seem the textbook example of what the international order can accomplish in postconflict peacebuilding, one part of the standard package to restore security and the "national order of things" (Malkki 1995) in a nervous, insecure, and fragmented world. But the DRC also reveals a paradox at the heart of the liberal project of postconflict state building: in the long run, elections are emblematic moments for democratic teleologies concerning the construction of Weberian ideal-type states on still-smoldering postcolonial or postconflict ruins (Comaroff and Comaroff 2006: vii). In the short run, however, they can be risky conjunctures—as a recent World Bank/UN study has admitted.[19]

To draw an analogy from physics, if you place a soft iron core inside a wire coil and apply an electric current to that coil, the magnetic domains in the soft iron, normally not aligned in any particular direction, will all quickly align themselves with the magnetic field generated and will strengthen the resulting magnetic field. In the same fashion, the conduct of elections can electrify multiple insecurities, expressed through contesting, even mutually contradictory, discursive violences—homegrown and vernacularized imports—causing them to realign in dangerously polarized fashion. And when the current is switched off, the magnetic alignment lingers—a phenomenon all too appropriately known in physics as "hysteresis."[20] Electoral processes—designed to consolidate security through democracy—can risk reenergizing a lingering hysteria about nationhood instead.

Notes

1   Stephen Jackson is currently chief of staff of the United Nations Office in Burundi. He contributed this essay in a personal capacity, and the views expressed do not necessarily represent the official position of the United Nations.

2   This essay has benefitted greatly from the comments of a variety of colleagues, including a number of anonymous reviewers. It was presented in an earlier form at the conference "Politics and Citizen in the Postcolony" at Emory University, April 14–16, 2011, and my thanks are particularly due to the organizers and participants for their feedback.

3   Thomas Luhaka, national executive secretary of the MLC, on Bemba's TV station CCTV, September 12, 2006.

4   In some senses, literally unbelievable. In a few constituencies, turnouts in the high 90 percent range were reported, casting a little doubt on the full reliability of the proceedings. But observers generally confirmed that Kabila had received genuinely massive approval in the East.

5   Broadcast on CCTV's "Emission chrétienne pour la répentence de la nation," broadcast on October 1, 2006, in Kinshasa.

6   Intriguingly entitled *Mawe Mawe ou antifada Mai Mai au Kivu*, it argues for a parallel between the nationalist resistance of the Palestinian people in the Intifada and that of the Congolese in the Mai Mai.

7   A similar stipulation had been a feature of earlier constitutions of the DRC, but has not been reproduced in the new constitution adopted in 2006.

8   Though Ouattara continues to maintain that both his parents were born in Côte d'Ivoire.

9   On CCTV's *Edition spéciale*, broadcast on September 23, 2006, in Kinshasa.

10   Christian Badibanga, president of the Union socialiste congolaise, speaking on Molière-TV's *Rien que la vérité*, broadcast on September 22, 2006, in Kinshasa.

11   The theatre troupe "Cocinaf" on Horizon 33 TV, broadcast on September 4, 2006, in Kinshasa.

12   Gabriel Mokia, president of the Mouvement des démocrates congolais, October 2, 2006, on *Journal télévisé*, RLTV, Kinshasa.

13   Joseph Olenghankoy speaking on CCTV's *Edition spéciale*, broadcast on September 23, 2006, in Kinshasa.

14   Campaign song, broadcast October 14, 2006, on CANAL KIN in Kinshasa.

15   Shé Okitundu, Kabila's chef de cabinet, *Journal télévisé*, broadcast on Horizon 33, Kinshasa, August 31, 2006.

16   Senator Hubert Kingombe, on the variety show *Top gaïeté*, RTNC-TV, September 8, 2006. RTNC-TV was sanctioned by the HAM for this broadcast.

17   Particularly after one of them crashed in a crowded suburb of Kinshasa, killing a bystander.

18   The use of discourse about autochthony and *Congolité* as a political weapon in local and provincial electoral contests was more noticeable.

19   "Post-conflict elections shift the risk [of the resumption of conflict] between years. Specifically, an election reduces risk substantially in the year of the election, but increases it even more substantially in the year following the election. Thus, the net effect is not risk-reducing" (Collier et al., 2006).

20   Deriving from the Greek term for "deficiency," and sharing a common etymology with the psychological notion of "hysteria."

References

Akindès, Francis. 2003. "Côte d'Ivoire: Socio-Political Crises, '*Ivoirité*' and the Course of History." *African Sociological Review* 7(2):73–95.

Ayad, Christophe. 2006. "Fièvre xenophobe au Congo-Kinshasa." *Libération*, June 23.

Clarke, Roy. N.d. "Denationalisation and Deportation as Political Weapons in Zambia." Unpublished paper.

Collier, Paul, Anke Hoeffler, and Måns Söderbom. 2006. "Post-Conflict Risks." CSAE Working Paper Series, Centre for the Study of African Economies, Department of Economics, University of Oxford/United Nations Department of Peacekeeping Operations/World Bank.

Comaroff, John, and Jean Comaroff. 2006. "Law and Disorder in the Postcolony: An Introduction." In Jean Comaroff and John Comaroff, eds., *Law and Disorder in the Postcolony,*. Chicago: University of Chicago Press.

De Villers, Gauthier. 1998. "Identifications et mobilisations politiques au Congo-Kinshasa." *Politique africaine* 72:81–97.

Doyle, Mark. 2006. "DR Congo—Is It a Miracle?" BBC News, November 30, http://news.bbc.co.uk/2/hi/africa/6159139.stm.

Dunn, Kevin. 2003. *Imagining the Congo: The International Relations of Identity*. New York: Palgrave Macmillan.

Farah, Douglas. 2001. "Digging up Congo's Dirty Gems." *Washington Post*, December 30.

Flipo, Blandine. 2006. "Bemba, ici, c'est un phénomène populaire." *Libération*, October 28.

Geschiere, Peter, and Bambi Ceuppens. 2005. "Autochthony: Global or Local?" *Annual Review of Anthropology* 34:385–407.

Geschiere, Peter, and Stephen Jackson. 2006. "Autochthony and the Crisis of Citizenship: Democratization, Decentralization, and the Politics of Belonging." *African Studies Review* 49(2): 1–14.

Geschiere, Peter, and Francis Nyamnjoh. 2001. "Capitalism and Autochthony: The Seesaw of Mobility and Belonging." In J. Comaroff and J. Comaroff, eds., *Millennial Capitalism and the Culture of Neoliberalism*. Durham: Duke University Press.

Gettleman, Jeffrey. 2006. "Observers Deem Congo Runoff Fair, but Vote Tally Isn't Final." *New York Times*, November 2.

Hugeux, Vincent. 2006. "Le poison de la 'Congolité.'" *L'Express*, June 30.

Human Rights Watch. 2006. "D.R. Congo: Halt Growing Violence Ahead of Elections." October 25, http://www.hrw.org/news/2006/10/24/dr-congo-halt-growing-violence-ahead-elections.

International Crisis Group. 2002. *Storm Clouds over Sun City: The Urgent Need to Recast the Congolese Peace Process*. ICG Africa Report Number 44, May 14. Brussels/Nairobi: International Crisis Group.

International Rescue Committee. 2004. *Mortality in the Democratic Republic of Congo: Results from a Nationwide Survey (Conducted April–July 2004)*. Bukavu and New York: International Rescue Committee.

Jackson, Stephen. 2003. "War Making: Uncertainty, Improvisation and Involution in the Kivu Provinces, DR Congo, 1997–2002." PhD dissertation, Princeton University.

———. 2006. "Sons of Which Soil? The Language and Politics of Autochthony in Eastern D.R. Congo." *African Studies Review* 49(2):95–123.

———. 2007. "Of 'Doubtful Nationality': Political Manipulation of Citizenship in the D.R. Congo." *Citizenship Studies* 11(5):481–500.

Malkki, Liisa. 1995. *Purity and Exile: Violence, Memory, and National Cosmology among Hutu Refugees in Tanzania*. Chicago: University of Chicago Press.

Marshall-Fratani, Ruth. 2006. "The War of 'Who Is Who': Autochthony, Nationalism, and Citizenship in the Ivoirian Crisis." *African Studies Review* 49(2):9–43.

Miles, William. 2000. "Hamites and Hebrews: Problems in 'Judaizing' the Rwandan Genocide." *Journal of Genocide Research* 2(1):107–115.

MONUSCO 2011. "MONUSCO calls on INEC to Address Electoral Observer Missions' Concerns." Press statement, Kinshasa, December 12, http://monusco.unmissions.org/Default.aspx?tabid=10847&ctl=Details&mid=13648&ItemID=13602&language=en-US.

Ndaywel e Nziem, I. 1997. *Histoire générale du Congo: De l'héritage ancien à la République démocratique.* Louvain-la-Neuve: Duculot.

Nzongola-Ntalaja, Georges. 2002. *The Congo, from Leopold to Kabila.* London: Zed.

Ottaway, Marina. 1999. "Testimony Prepared for the Hearings on 'Conflicts in Central Africa,'" Subcommittee on Africa, United States Senate. Washington, D.C., June 8.

Sahlins, Marshall. 1981. *Historical Metaphors and Mythical Realities: Structure in the Early History of the Sandwich Islands Kingdom.* Ann Arbor: University of Michigan Press.

Tuquoi, Jean-Pierre. 2006. "Au Congo-Kinshasa, la campagne électorale débute dans un climat détestable." *Le Monde,* May 26.

Žižek, Slavoj. 1990. "Eastern Europe's Republics of Gilead." *New Left Review* 183 (October):50–63.

CHAPTER FOUR

Securing "Security" amid Neoliberal Restructuring: Civil Society and Volunteerism in Post-1990 Turkey

Yasemin Ipek Can

The 1980s and 1990s have generally been considered to mark the beginning of a new period of extensive restructuring, which inaugurated intense economic, political, and sociocultural transformations in many countries across the globe. It is widely held that these transformations fundamentally entailed elements of "liberalization"—a range of "neoliberal" policies that promoted fast-forward privatization of the public sector, relatively sustained dissemination of market structures, and the retreat of the state apparatus from the provision of "public services" (Clarke 1991, 2004). Notwithstanding the glorification of this restructuring, the "retreat" of the state and the ensuing "liberalization" have also been associated with a range of "vested fragilities" that emerged alongside: increased unemployment, widespread social and economic inequality, and a structural inadequacy in meeting the needs of disadvantaged groups in many societies. Diverse civil initiatives have been promoted to fill the gaps that threatened socioeconomic integrity in various countries. Sometimes overtly and sometimes through more ingenious ways, civil society has been called in as a stakeholder to manage and govern these vested fragilities in the new spaces of intervention that opened up after the retreat of much of the bureaucratic mechanisms of the state from social service provision.

This chapter focuses on how the retreat of the "over-burdened" and "cumbersome" state carried civil society organizations (CSOs) in Turkey to the forefront as the new and celebrated stakeholders in the management of the vested fragilities produced by accelerated marketization.[1] On the one hand, it is no doubt futile and pointless to seek a clear breaking point in the way social services were provided in Turkey, and it is difficult to show how the bureaucratic apparatuses have been replaced by civil initiatives in recent decades. On the other hand, this article nonetheless points to a historical reconfiguration of the roles of stakeholders in the Turkish polity. This reconfiguration implies a new political rationality deployed through specific measures in order to maintain the social and political security of the Turkish nation.[2] In other words, the Turkish state does not have a monopoly on securing and governing the socioeconomic security of Turkish citizens against vested fragilities any longer, since it is joined in this by civil and private parties.

I focus on one of the striking implications of this reconfiguration. With the ongoing social restructuring and "liberalization" at hand, the Turkish state started to share not only the *requirement* of social service provision, but also the *duty* to manage and govern the insecurities that were perceived as threatening the Turkish nation. The latter were widely perceived by public opinion as divisive social conflicts centered on religion, ethnicity, and class. They were frequently called "social evils" that allegedly arose out of the insufficiency of the bureaucracy in providing social services, thus alienating segments of society from one another. Social security was reformulated in public discourse as a problematic register that figured as the root cause of all social conflicts in Turkish society. The clunky bureaucratic mechanism had to be transformed toward a shared sense of civic duty to assist the state in securing the integrity, and hence the security, of the nation. Along with what appears as a standard debunking of the cumbersome bureaucratic apparatuses (globally enforced by the World Bank and International Monetary Fund), we also see the emergence of a new political yet "civil" rationality of governing and securing security in the rise of CSOs in Turkey. This political rationality rests on the emergence of a new field or agency of intervention and governance that is mediated through a civic sense of duty to protect the nation against "social evils."

Based on the observation that it is less the substitution of state with civil society and more the emergence of a shared field of collaboration that defines this transformation, I claim that civil society is no less an agent of governance in contemporary Turkey than the debunked bureaucratic apparatuses. In other words, it is not the erosion of the centralized state in favor of civil society as a "liberal force" that defines the neoliberal transformation in Turkey, but rather the emergence of a wide range of civic governmentalities that call public and private parties alike to undertake the task of guaranteeing security against social evils (Foucault 1991, Berry, Osborne and Rose 1996, Dean 1999).[3]

Widely crowned as the novel catalysts of a postbureaucratic transformation toward civic liberties in Turkey in the 1990s, CSOs were engaged in unique governmental relations, programs, and projects within the framework of assisting the state through a series of collaborations. CSOs provided new governmental means for citizens to assist the "paralyzed" and unwieldy state apparatuses in confronting the "risks" and "threats" that were haunting the country. They became "fundamental civil elements"[4] of initiating social transformations in Turkey by providing a new platform of volunteering for and undertaking the task of guaranteeing the security of their nation. What I seek to elucidate in here is, first, the ongoing process that is defined by the particular socioeconomic, political, and subjective vicissitudes and upshots of this "collaboration"; and second, the subjectivity of volunteerism that spans concrete local practices, formative articulations, and disruptions in actually providing services to people. Focusing on these practices, articulations, and disruptions eschews the predominant over-schematic portrayals of global shifts in state-society relations. To that effect, I aim to provide a perspective which replaces the abstract idea of global changes with a focus on emerging political rationalities and performances of local subjectivities in their particularities. The third and most fundamental theme of this article is the emergence of civil society as a governmental plane or register of social action that calls in specific sets of agents to secure the security of the nation by assisting the state. In that regard, it is vital to understand how CSOs and volunteers became the indispensable agents of "acting upon" society and governing the social evils or problems haunting it in the form of "divisive threats" and "risks" (Fisher 1997, Beck 1992, O'Malley 1996, Dean 1999).

I analyze here the governmental projects of one of the most important and powerful CSOs, TEGV (The Educational Volunteers Foundation of Turkey), and the narratives of volunteers working with TEGV in Istanbul with whom I conducted several in-depth interviews.[5] Although TEGV explicitly focuses on education as a specific problem, it was striking to see that TEGV volunteers were consistently reconceptualizing the problem of education as being part of a larger register of risks and threats. Unless so-called responsible Turkish citizens urgently intervened in these problems, uneducated and undercivilized youths were destined to become dangerous subjects, that is, possible perpetrators of all the social evils we know, ranging from petty crimes to ethnic or religious terrorism. In that sense, what defines TEGV volunteers is much less a preoccupation with education than with the civil subjectivity of prudence that "responsible citizens" are being called upon to adopt.

I look at civil society in contemporary Turkey and the political rationalities involved in this novel "civil subjectivity" from an ethnographic vantage point. I focus on how the discourses championed historically by the state (such as modernization and nationalism) could be reasserted and rearticulated by volunteers in everyday practices, along with glorification of civil liberties against the bureaucratic state. The fresh perspective provided by this ethnographic vantage point and the rearticulations it delineates complicate the dynamics of what we wish to call neoliberal transformations. In Turkey, the IMF prescriptions popularly known as structural adjustments do not merely consist of a set of macro policies that restructure the "economy" (if there ever were such a separate space at all). Structural adjustments also comprise a dynamic re-formation of the temporalities and spatialities of everyday lives, leading diverse segments of society to reconceptualize social security and seek their own means to access services like health and education. As a result, the rearticulation of social security as a civil and postbureaucratic political rationality relies as much on the contingencies and subjectivities of local populations affected by the "retreat" of the state, as on macrolevel policies. In that sense, my focus on the shifts in political rationality in Turkey is grounded in an ethnographic perspective on local contingencies and juxtapositions on the level of subjectivity. These contingencies and juxtapositions pose mostly unforeseeable syntheses of diverse ideas, ideologies, or concepts, and they are essential to understanding how neoliberal projects are contested and reinterpreted at different historical moments (Simone 2004). Nothing seems to be neoliberal *as such* before its local articulation and contestation.

Collaborative Subjects

A vital point that should be considered at the onset is that the rhetoric of "assisting the state" (which gradually paved the way for the widespread undertaking of the responsibilities of the state)[6] and the ensuing sociopolitical agency of CSOs in Turkey correlates with the emergence of new subjectivities that glorified "civic responsibilities" of citizens. The state was no longer considered as the paternal supra-agent of providing social services and governing the risks unleashed by social transformations that troubled the sociocultural life sphere of the population. The state apparatus was reimagined and discursively produced as just another initiative among others—it "obviously cannot provide everything for us";[7] we, as citizens, are obliged to intervene in the fate, security, and well-being of our nation through as many civil measures as we can come up with, and assist the state. I intend to elucidate here how this assistance has been ideologically, practically, and discursively articulated in Turkey in the form of a range of subjectivities that promote volunteering in CSOs and assisting the state as civic responsibilities of citizens.

Claiming to embody ideal citizens, the volunteers I met with commonly assumed a superior civil position that transcends the state, whereby "society" can be problematized as an object to be secured and disciplined as a whole (Foucault 1990). This problematization, moreover, seems to be deeply correlated with recent discourses in Turkey on the necessity of incarnating a homogeneous nation, while dexterously managing (or "governing") the socioeconomic conflicts that are either unleashed or aggravated by a restructured and liberalized economy. As will be elaborated below in the section on volunteers, especially after the 1999 Marmara earthquake, narratives on the redundancy of state bureaucracy and red tape gave way to calls for more efficient governance, even among nationalist and Republican circles, substantially legitimizing the retreat of the state from the provision of social services. It was frequently argued that one "cannot expect everything from the state," and citizens were enthusiastically called upon to join civil initiatives in order to assist the "paralyzed state": they had seen that the state was not able to be there when they vitally needed it.[8]

Thus, a range of social conflicts and economic inequalities (which were acutely aggravated by the dramatic failure of the state to provide services after the earthquake to millions of affected people) became the elements of a novel scene of social action directed toward the dangers and risks that preoccupy (or are sometimes posed by) the "disadvantaged others" of Turkish society. Through civil interventions in the "other" (crafted by volunteer subjectivity for disciplining the "other"), the ideal vision of a homogeneous Turkish nation could be reinstantiated in a neoliberal context, in the form of securing society from risks and threats posed by a new epoch (Beck 1992). This especially seems to be the case in Istanbul, where differences among social strata within society become intensely visible and agonistic in urban space, discursively crystallizing in the widespread portrayals of threatening ("disadvantaged") classes versus the threatened ("well-off").

Risks, threats, and dangers that encumber societies in divisive forms and weaken state apparatuses vary across geographies or histories. However, as most of the texts in this volume reveal, there was an increase in local unrest and violence during the decades that followed the 1980s on a global scale. Moreover, although these transcended the existing threshold of local conflicts and divergences (at least in form), we are not always able to reliably identify specific "causes" for them. Nevertheless, one does need to take into account the materially concrete complexity and diversity of these problems haunting societies and the unrest that crystallizes in different yet concrete forms of poverty, inequality, nationalism, exclusion, and so forth. I argue that the particular threats posed by these transformations in varying divisive forms in Turkey correlate with the articulation and dissemination of particular political rationalities of governing everyday lives: volunteerism, empowerment, and prudentialism. These political rationalities catalyze the emergence of new microregimes of "social security" in Turkey by calling the threatened segments of society to *volunteer* and act upon the threatening segments. The latter are *empowered* and responsibilized in order to govern the "threats" they pose to the former. Most fundamentally, the threats in question are supposed to be *prudently* discerned in order to secure the security of the Turkish nation.

Through my research on TEGV, I explored a range of contemporary civil mechanisms that provided the means to govern the "security" and "wellbeing of the population" in Turkey. Widespread among the volunteers of CSOs, these governing practices and strategies depoliticize a whole set of urban questions (like inequality and violence) by reproblematizing them in personal or psychological terms—that is, in terms of self-development and self-responsibilization. Dramatically contradicting the promotion and idealization of civil society as a promising space of freedom and democracy, this chapter points at subjective mechanisms of governance inaugurated by and through civil society, whereby social insecurities are responded to or acted upon by the relatively well-off middle classes and elites in Turkey.[9] Such an analysis will elaborate the concrete socioeconomic neoliberal conjuncture in Turkey through a particular emphasis on the modes of subjectivity that emerge along with it or even that makes it possible.

Turkey in the Post-1990s: Neoliberal Restructuring and CSOs

The 1980s have been considered a significant turning point in Turkish history. The pervasive effect of globalization as a worldwide trend with huge economic and political consequences (economic liberalization being the foremost) has been coupled in Turkey with the postcoup restructuring of the legal and social system under the aegis of the military establishment.[10] In this paradoxical coupling of repressive and liberal transformations in state-society relations, new actors with new demands have begun to make their voices heard. Especially in the late 1990s, Turkey has undergone a rapid political and sociocultural change. As the political landscape has been forcefully and ruthlessly cleared of the intense struggles of left- and right-wing ideological movements of the 1970s, Kurds, Islamists, and feminists have become the new powerful actors of politics, tantalizing the established institutional political order with critiques of the authoritarian experience of modernization. Meanwhile, relations with the European Union set a particular agenda of democratization through which the proliferation of CSOs was further promoted. Due to the combination of several historical factors, the increasing dissemination of CSOs in the 1990s has been celebrated by almost the entire political spectrum in Turkey. It has been widely argued that the crisis of state-centric modernity has given rise to the elevation of civil society to the status of an extremely important actor and arena for the democratization of state-society relations (Keyman and İçduygu 2003). Representing different ideological interests and political demands, civic organizations are considered to be the "expansion of society" against the predominance of the strong nation-state.

Indeed, it would be erroneous to neglect the new spaces of social action that civil society opens. These definitely contribute to a more democratic social and political polity in Turkey, since they provide means of representing different voices that were repressed by Kemalist modernity (Toprak 1996, Keyman and İçduygu 2003). Yet in the new conjuncture that has emerged in the aftermath of the 1999 Marmara earthquake, a particular definition of civil society has begun to be prevalent in the public realm. This definition portrays civil society as a space of intervention in the fateful state of the polity for the sake of assisting and supporting the state, exactly on the points or areas where its legitimacy and effectivity has regressed, rather than as a space of action for the repressed voices to make demands and to pursue political activities.

I suggest that this is an essential point, since almost all the existing analyses and empirical studies focus on the contribution that civil society makes to "democratization" in Turkey (Heper 1991, Toprak 1996), thereby disregarding and even obscuring its emergence as an associational space where subjects *act upon* other subjects in order to assist the state in accomplishing its historic mission of modernization. By volunteering as loyal citizens and taking over the duties of the "weakening state," individuals are increasingly participating in CSOs that are established to empower and responsibilize disadvantaged segments of society concerning "problems" like education and health. This process entails both the emergence of a middle-class elite that assists (rather than make demands on) the state and the ensuing depoliticization of civil society, whereby the CSO is posited as a depoliticizing public actor (Fisher 1997). Furthermore, despite various ideological differences with governments since 1980 and the episodic tensions between major CSOs and the current conservative Justice and Development Party (AKP) government, CSOs were always willing to assist the provision of services, avoiding head-on confrontation.[11] All governments (particularly after 1990s) have welcomed the CSOs working for public service provision, as several projects conducted by TEGV reveal. Similarly, the ideological clash between secularism and Islamism in the 1990s or the tensions between the secularist military establishment and AKP's neoliberal conservatism in the 2000s hardly affected the institutionalization of state-civil society cooperation.

The 1999 Marmara earthquake was a momentous incident in state-society relations in Turkey.[12] The disaster sustained this collaboration between CSOs and the state, and maintained the existing associational definition of civil society as a space of intervention in the fate of the nation. It is primarily after this incident that the state has been questioned in its "conceptual" integrity by almost all social segments that were desperately seeking for other agents in providing social services.[13] CSOs have begun to gain public visibility and legitimacy through widespread and appealing public campaigns organized since the earthquake. The media, academy, and even some state authorities have begun to portray CSOs as indispensable elements. To put it differently, it is only after the earthquake that the discourse of the retreat of the state has been both openly pronounced and acclaimed in the Turkish public. The discourse on the insufficiency of the state in providing social services (like health, education, or pensions) has been ingeniously sutured to various discourses that claimed the indispensability of CSOs. However, critiques of the state were not only celebrations of its death as a cumbersome entity blocking the civil initiative of liberalization but also an acknowledgment of its rebirth as an administrative technician of digital governance, clearing the red tape for the sake of promoting civil society. The "public," as the widespread CSO discourses basically claimed, were pretty convinced that the state was dilapidated in its institutions, and the time had come to get rid of its monopoly on public initiatives. An army of volunteer citizens in CSOs were ready to take over of the obligations that the state could not fulfill anymore.

Thinking through the series of concepts that form what Victor Turner calls social drama ("breach," "crisis," "redress" and "reintegration") (Turner 1974), one can argue that the earthquake apparently opened a *breach* in the political stage. What is remarkable here is the fact that the political trauma exceeded the psychological trauma of well over ten thousand deaths, even transubstantiating it as a motive for promoting political change. This political trauma has become the hallmark of the subsequent phase of *crisis*. The breach that occurred with the earthquake also carried the risk of recurrence. The explicit fear that it was highly probable that such a disaster (or an even worse one) could happen again and that, as "we" have seen, the state will not be able to save "us" was very common among the public.[14] Some even claimed that the state "died under the bricks" and would not recover again. The question that was widely circulated was: what will happen if another disaster emerges? Strikingly, the real specter of danger that haunted "us" was not the probability of a new earthquake, but the desperate vision of a vacuum of responsibility, which once belonged to the state—the responsibility of "prolonging life," as Foucault would have put it. In the first volume of *The History of Sexuality*, Foucault had articulated the shift from the sovereign's power to "take life" toward the modern state's power to "enhance life" (Foucault 1990: 139). The biopolitical production of life has been the ultimate source of state power that dissolved with the event of the earthquake. People lost their sense of security of life (as a provision of the state's being there), thereby diminishing the biopolitical legitimacy of the Turkish state.

The breach that opened up with the earthquake in Turkey was gradually *redressed* through the emphasis on the success of the CSOs and on the necessity of collaborating with the state. Of course, many CSOs continue to exert pressure on the Turkish state and incumbent governments on different issues like human rights, working conditions, women's rights, and so on. Yet one can hardly disregard the fact that the CSOs that pursue the reconstruction of the social realm through the utilization of feelings of responsibility are much more publicly visible and influential in Turkey. In the debates that took place after the earthquake, civil society was conceptually reformulated as being in collaboration with the state. Many human rights defenders or CSOs that are related to the Kurdish problem, poverty, religious freedom, and women's rights have been marginalized and delegitimized for being "ideological." Moreover, the relationship between the CSOs and the state, which is reformulated along the terms of "better governance," requires a rethinking of the distinction between the state and civil society, as has been traditionally emphasized by the liberal understanding of civil society. What is at stake here is not merely the overcoming or sublation of this difference but also the striking culmination of a new sense of citizenship.[15] The new citizen, both loyal to the nation and sensitive to the problems of the population, represents the subjectivity of being a part of civil society not for the sake of freedom and democracy, but to support the state and thereby serve society.

These CSOs assume a place in managing, circulating, and performing what Foucault calls a "conduct of conducts" in neutralizing risks and threats posed by perceived social evils by setting new norms and practices, and thereby acting out a new form of civic governmentality. This process is peculiar to the long and continuing metaprocess of *reintegration*, again in Turner's (1974) terms. In this respect, TEGV is among the most eminent CSOs that emerged as "saviors" after the neoliberal retreat of the state and the ensuing social crisis. However, before shedding some light on the terms of this reintegration through an analysis of TEGV's institutional discourse in comparison to the volunteers' discourse, I would like to elucidate what I understand from the "neoliberal juncture" in concrete theoretical and historical terms.[16] In this way we can construe the historical specificity of the political rationalities that make up neoliberalism in Turkey and relate it to the neoconservative "moral tone" that weaves the social network of social service provision through local-communitarian terms.

Neoliberal Rationalities and Complexities

As Nikolas Rose points out in his early work, although neoliberalism is generally posed as a critique of political government, much of the neoliberal policies around the globe nevertheless retain the presupposition that "the real is programmable" by the authorities: "Neoliberalism does not abandon the 'will to govern'. It maintains the view that failure of government to achieve its objectives is to be overcome by inventing new strategies of government that will succeed" (Rose 1996: 57). Despite the need for caution against deeply problematic portrayals of neoliberalism, imbuing it with an ambiguous form of agency beyond specific localities and temporalities, I underline the relevance of "the new strategies of government" to the local historical constellation of social problematizations in Turkey and elsewhere. These strategies (which are concerned with various issues ranging from health to education) portray actors as subjects of responsibility, autonomy, and choice, while, on the other hand, creating and maintaining a critical distance between formal political institutions and other social actors. The subject imagined by and practiced through neoliberal political rationalities dexterously harmonizes duty and responsibility with free choice and enjoyment. Similarly, Pat O'Malley also emphasizes how the novel technology of "prudentialism" (reducing collectivist risk management to the subject's responsibility of self-management) perforates all spheres of social life (O'Malley 1996: 199–202). He further points out how the emergent language of "working together" signifies a shift of responsibility. Risk management becomes an everyday practice of the self, a moral responsibility, or duty of the self. The individual becomes the main "responsible" agent for managing a series of macrolevel problems ranging from health to crime.

I use the term "neoliberalism" in a similar sense in the Turkish case, denoting an advanced yet loose and dynamic form of political liberalism, which involves the rearticulation of some of the central concepts of liberalism with respect to societal self-responsibilization and risk management that is, a reconstellation of both new and old technologies of subjectivity and political rationality (Foucault 1990, Foucault 1991, Foucault 2001, Burchell, Gordon and Miller 1991, Berry, Osborne and Rose 1996). I consider this rearticulation in Turkey as relying upon the agencies of a diversity of social actors who effectively seek to engineer particular forms of social governance for a variety of purposes, which are mostly irreducible to (or even contradictory with) each other. As many ethnographic studies also demonstrate (Comaroff and Comaroff 1999; Ferguson and Gupta 2002; Rutherford 2004), the analytical concept of "neoliberal governmentality" is heuristically useful in making sense of this and similar instances of rearticulation, since it satisfactorily captures a form of social governance (or a wider political rationality). It pinpoints techniques of discipline that are juxtaposed with technologies of self-government that function as what Foucault calls "conduct of conducts."

One should also note the increasing relevance of the proliferation of new psychological techniques for "marginalized" segments of society (ranging from cheap self-help booklets to engaged NLP seminars) as a basic pillar of the political rationalities that are loosely associated under the banner of neo-liberalism. The striking proliferation of these techniques is acted out not by providing salutary services or benefits, but rather through the active involve-ment and engagement of the marginalized people who are targeted in a whole array of programs that are technically designed to reconstruct them as "active citizens." They entail restoring a sense of self-worth and self-esteem, and engaging people in a continuous process of self-promotion (Cruikshank 1996). Frequently guided by the expertise provided by social, educational, and psychological sciences, these discourses of "acting on the self" redefine a very wide array of problems (ranging from child abuse to educational failure) as being based on the psychological states of people—and especially the urban poor to whom most of the social problems are attributed.

The critique of empowerment projects, however, often points at how these focus on the individual capacities of the poor and consequently minimize the social and political causes of poverty. The poor are encouraged to be entrepre-neurial subjects and to find solutions for their livelihoods through changes in lifestyles that they are supposed to bring about themselves. Hence, the poor are posited as both the problem and the solution to poverty (Kamat 2004, Brin Hyatt 2001). In her study on empowerment programs on Indian women, Aradhana Sharma critically analyzes how the discourse of empowerment is effectively deployed to integrate subaltern women into the middle-class ter-rain of rights and citizenship, turning these marginalized women into law-abiding, self-responsibilized subjects (Sharma 2006: 80).

Moreover, the very portrayal of the advent of these technologies (by works loosely gathered under the banner of "governmentality studies") suffers from a deeply problematic lack of sensitivity to local variations and articulations that make it possible for these technologies to be circulated through a wide range of spaces. However, many ethnographic researches from different parts of the globe reveal a diversity of trajectories in the operation of NGOs and/or CSOs. A number of recent studies on problems of urban poverty and margin-alization in Latin America, for instance, emphasize that a major change is the emergence of the new intermediate sector of nongovernmental organizations, shouldering increasing responsibility for the delivery of social goods (Gonzales de la Rocha et al. 2004). In the Latin American case, researchers usually observe a larger rate of social and political participation by popular classes in social movements that challenge the state on concrete issues and problems, reflecting various forms of collective interests that are rooted in gender, race, and ethnicity. These researches further demonstrate that "the poor" do not blame themselves for "failure" and instead experience a sense of entitlement, recognizing their rights as citizens more than ever (188). Studying AIDS service NGOs in north India, Kavita Misra also notes the increasing acquisition of the language of rights by common people (Misra 2006). Thus, part of the ethnographic data on empowerment programs informs us that empowerment might create an awareness of social inequality and mobilize collective action. Being mobilized by employing the rhetoric of rights and entitlements against forms of social domination, these programs focus more on social change than on improvement of individual capacities. Misra's work in north India competently exposes how the discourse of empowerment is transposed into a discursive strategy that represents a desire to create a transformation from below. When articulated by advocate groups, the discourse of empowerment may open up progressive spaces of political action for disadvantaged groups.

Similarly, the rhetoric of empowerment is redefined by several competing actors with a diversity of political agendas in major urban centers in Turkey. There are CSOs that try to promote human rights, increase political freedom, and demand economic equality, yet there are also other CSOs enacted by nationalist concerns and by desires to ensure security and order in urban space. Obviously, the playing out of this competition does not take place on equal or pluralist terms. Some organizations and projects not only have more salient economic and social resources but also inhabit and speak from a strikingly forceful political and/or ideological terrain, which facilitates an even more perverse and institutionalized hegemony in Gramscian terms. TEGV, for instance, displays a well-established historical alliance between the ideological (modernist/Republican) and economic elites, and vast institutional power. The founders and the executive board of the organization consist of well-established business figures, industrialists, and corporate executives with strong ties to the main economic, social, and educational institutions in Turkey. In my research, I explored the mechanisms through which the well-being and security of the population is "governed" through empowerment projects enacted by CSOs *beyond* the welfare regime of the nation-state. I argue that it is through these mechanisms that the Republican modernist elites of Turkey responded to the haunting social insecurities, which were accelerated and deepened by neoliberal processes of restructuring. It is striking to see that the ideological, discursive, and institutional frameworks associated with the modernist welfare state of the preceding century are not debunked totally, but instead are reutilized in very peculiar juxtapositions of nationalist Republicanism and neoliberal political rationalities and technologies of subjectivity that craft novel governmentalities of civility. Consequently, this analysis elaborates the concrete socioeconomic junctures of neoliberalism in the social realm through a particular emphasis on modes of subjectivity. I elaborate on this through a comparative analysis of TEGV's (institutional) discourse and the volunteer's discourses.

TEGV's Institutional Discourse: Containing Danger and Educating the "Self"

TEGV was founded in 1995 by fifty-five "leading names" from business and academic circles. The foundation provides a comprehensive program of non-formal educational activities aiming to develop personal and social skills in children between the ages of seven and sixteen. Programs are organized in five learning areas, supported by a curriculum and implementation guides, volunteer manuals, and student materials. The books are prepared in collaboration with scientific advisory committees and taught in the foundation's centers, parks, and mobile units throughout Turkey during eight-week terms throughout the year. Since its foundation, TEGV has reached more than one million children with the active support of over 20,000 volunteers at eighty-six locations all over the country. It has considerable public visibility, more than any other CSO in Turkey.

Addressing the Turkish public, TEGV maintains that the state is unable to fulfill its duty in education and asserts that "voluntary institutions, the private sector, and ordinary citizens should share the state's responsibility by supporting the ministry, improving the existing educational system, and creating efficient and applicable educational programs."[17] In this call, the problematization of education becomes central, along with the discourses of "danger" and "lack." The discourse of danger, which is central to the decades-old republican and secularist Kemalist imaginary, is among the fundamental pillars of TEGV's discourse, since it portrays TEGV as a savior akin to the position of the earlier

Kemalists. This is not the least coincidental, since elites and committed supporters of Mustafa Kemal Atatürk's doctrine perceived themselves as guardians of the Republic ever since its first decades. There is a constant yet ambiguously articulated theme of "danger" stemming from some parts or segments of society, against which TEGV appropriates a self-image of protector and savior. Nevertheless, the concrete sources or causes of these dangers, as well as their peculiar nature, are never properly addressed and articulated in unequivocal terms. Interestingly, this ambiguity and representative indeterminacy concerning the specific dangers points at the issues that TEGV refrains from dealing with directly. Naturally, it is futile to expect a civil initiative engaged in nationwide education to address and properly articulate the political traumas of the Turkish polity. However, it is striking that despite the very absence of overt engagement with these "problems" and "social evils" haunting society, the latter are insistently articulated in a wide range of TEGV booklets, brochures, and websites, and equivocally represented as "harm's way" from which the coming generations should be protected.[18] This "harm" interestingly merges the Kemalist perception of threat (frequently attributed to the minorities and Islamists) with the neoliberal problem of risk (unleashed by the increasing socioeconomic inequalities that become visible particularly in urban space).

Looking at the places where TEGV builds its centers, and drawing from the formal and informal interviews that have been conducted, the organization seems to have three broad target concerns. First, the poverty of marginalized segments in the metropolises: this is considered to be creating its own "degenerate" culture, through which it produces "discontent" that is productive of other "dangers." The second concern is immigration from the southeastern provinces and ensuing immigrant activism: this comprises the emerging Kurdish activism among immigrants and different radical-leftist politicizations of social problems in other segments of the population. The third concern is with the rise of Islamism and especially that of "Gülen schools," which provide an alternative means of education as well as other facilities to urban dwellers, yet cause a reactive discontent among the secular elite.[19] These concerns are all interconnected for TEGV. Since the present conservative government no longer wishes to carry on the Kemalist mission of modernizing the nation and cannot struggle against these "dangerous elements" efficiently, TEGV assumes the position of savior.

The education envisaged by TEGV is obviously related to the earlier Turkish modernist mission of creating a homogeneous nation, which entails "generating and sustaining our societal culture," in TEGV's words. TEGV official documents contain abundant claims to its leading, enlightening, and savior role for the entire nation—the typical role assumed by the modernist state in its historiography in Turkey (Zurcher 1993). Yet, beyond the fact that TEGV acts within the framework of modern nationalism and, in a way, sustains or proliferates it, the CSO has a very distinctive discourse that is irreducible to modern nationalist discourse—the discourse of empowerment. For instance, the "abilities" or "talents" prioritized in TEGV centers for development are: first, "personal strategies" such as self-confidence, analytical-critical thinking, self-discipline, and creativity; second, "social strategies" such as communication, empathy, collaboration, problem solving, responsibility, and emotion and stress management; and third, "universal strategies" such as perceiving values, implementing them, and creating a difference. These talents, which connect the personal, the social, and the universal, become the expressions of a new subjectivity. Words that are employed in expressing these talents put a strong emphasis on the "self," on "being active," and on "responsibility." In this sense, the term "individual" is overloaded with qualities, which simultaneously make it self-reliant and self-responsible. Moreover, the task of developing social talents emphasizes the problem-solving ability of individuals, as is strikingly implied in "emotion and stress management." Controlling and directing emotions and stress becomes a social quality that one has to acquire to make life more manageable.

Hence education has been systematically redefined and reproblematized in a particular way throughout the discourse of TEGV. Within this particular problematization, multiple programs are designed in order to create citizens and individuals who are "conscious" of both their own nation and the changing parameters of the globe. Values like "consensus" and "harmony" are emphasized alongside individual responsibility and competition. TEGV overtly emphasizes that its systematic and planned efforts are geared toward achieving specific effects on children. These effects revolve around themes such as autonomy, creativity, responsibility, and cooperation.[20]

The idea that one can shape one's own life is also prevalent in many TEGV's projects. This involves exalting "life strategies" as the fundamental form of knowledge that an individual should acquire. To give an example, the activity dubbed "I can nourish myself" teaches children the "proper" ways of nourishment. This project, an outcome of the cooperation between TEGV and Nestlé on the basis of TEGV's concept of "endowing the children with life strategies," reformulates the problem of nourishment in terms of "consciousness," thereby obscuring the structural inequality that deprives the masses of access to resources of health and nutrition. Through these and similar activities, the problem shifts from lack of access to resources toward lack of knowledge on proper nourishment. There is an explicit concern with the well-being of individuals and their future. However, the chief and sole agent responsible of sustaining this well-being appears to be the individual himself or herself. This project is only one among many collaborative projects enacted through complicated alliances between state institutions, CSOs, and the private sector.

Volunteers as Ideal Citizens: Seeking the Future

Volunteers are the most essential agents through which this discourse (which reproblematizes social problems in specific ways) is articulated, instantiated, and spread. My interviews reveal how complicated forms of power, desire, and fear are embroiled in the volunteer subjectivity. Volunteers are very careful to convey the message of the organization appropriately, and hence quite often seem to identify with its aims. Despite momentary lapses, hesitations, and occasional desperation, they are in a continuous and overt attempt to convince me of the value and importance of volunteering in TEGV. Yet, not surprisingly, their entire narrative also reveals ambiguities and perplexities which confirm that they are not uniform implementers of a similarly conceived homogeneous project. Although they share common social and educational backgrounds and are motivated by similar concerns and desires, they face difficulties in performing their activities with children in marginalized neighborhoods and presenting themselves as "models." Narrating their own performance, they often complain about the "ungovernability" of the children's lives in the face of multiple forces pulling them in different directions. This ungovernability may at some points reinforce their desire to govern, yet at other moments produce unease and self-examination. This elicits practices that are not propounded or even approved by the organization.

Taking for granted the recent retreat of the state from providing welfare provisions in Turkey, volunteers overtly present their aspirations to "support" the state by participating in CSOs. This aspiration makes a continuous and insistent call on the middle class, and demands an efficient governance of society. Middle-class volunteerism reveals how some urban residents can build a particular emotional field in the city, reflecting a desire for cooperation through a micropolitics of alignment (Simone 2004: 12). This fervently expressed demand for an ordered reintegration of the marginalized into urban structures that have been fragmented through neoliberalization reproduces the Kemalist project of top-down modernization through the dual construction of "capable citizens" and "needy *halk* [commoners]."[21] This distinction, which also blames the "educated and capable but insensitive citizens for being irresponsible," presents volunteerism as an ideal space of citizenship and education as the ultimate medium of modernization. Therefore, volunteers commonly believe that many more individuals, or "citizens," should become a part of CSO projects.

By perceiving education as the fundamental cure that will decisively solve all the other problems, and therefore becoming active in relation to the future of the nation, volunteers respond positively to the call of the foundation, which emphasizes "future" and "hope." Therefore they transpose the passivity of "watching" and "worrying" to the necessity of "doing something" and render themselves part of a project that works in professional ways. The discourse on "doing something" also creates a self-responsibilizing effect, leading the volunteers to think that the problems of the country will be solved when all the people become volunteers and do something themselves, and that they can (and indeed should) do something. This pseudocollective way of thinking individualizes the problems, while the representations thereof result in a discourse of "individual responsibility." Within this discourse, problems are technicalized, as a result of which there emerges the expectancy that technical projects will complement where individual efforts fail. This newly emerging space of power summons all the responsible citizens to resolve the problems of their society, while, in the discourse of volunteers, certain families and their children are problematized in such a manner that their life-spheres become spaces of intervention.

According to the volunteers, the children's families cannot provide them with proper means of living. Hence they see themselves as saviors of the poor children of slums. The family is discursively constructed as indifferent, ignorant, lazy, disorganized, and so on. This representation of the family as a bankrupt institution failing to meet the needs of children opens up a legitimate space for TEGV's intervention in "the social" by providing the means for meeting these needs. Moreover, the endless reiteration of the same discourse homogenizes the space to be effectively intervened in. It provides coherence among the subjectivities of different volunteers and renders complicated problems easily governable. The discourse of blaming the family, continuously being put into circulation among the volunteers, productively renders the representations it produces "real," thereby creating a legitimate space of governmentality and its legitimate set of actors. Producing a discursive space of social intervention through educative and moralizing techniques against the "uncontrollable" and "unpredictable" mass of people, TEGV thereby approaches children not only with the courses offered in the education center but also with activities that are envisioned to affect the families and their social environment as a whole.

Parallel to the discourse of blaming the family, unemployment (of the fathers) is portrayed by the volunteers as a problem of lack of will. Fathers are generally portrayed as men who do not work or who invent reasons for not working. Through such representations of lack of will on the part of the poor families, the volunteers' own will and resolution are portrayed as twofold, because they both earn their own money and help others who fail to earn. Moreover, unemployment remains a theme for which the neoliberal feeling of compassion and social responsibility has no place at all (Garber 2004, Berlant 2004). Since this action-oriented approach claims that there always is a job for everybody, the "slothful" are the ones to blame (Woodward 2004: 77). If you do not work, it is your own fault. In the neoliberal economy, where an entrepreneurial culture is becoming more and more widespread, unemployment is turned into a problem of lack of will or talent. In other words, it is reconfigured in terms of what the Comaroffs call an "entrepreneurial subject," who has the task of cultivating and harvesting its will and resolution to empower, perfect, and market itself: You will find a job only if you really want to and are ready to do whatever it takes to get it. Similarly, compassion works only through techniques that are organized to initiate an entrepreneurial sense of self-empowerment in the children and to build the will to transform oneself (Garber 2004). In that sense, in the eyes of the TEGV volunteers, the failed families have either refrained from inculcating this will in their children or were lacking any sense of it. The Comaroffs' work explores the rise of this entrepreneurial subject and, in reference to Foucault's later writings, maintains that this development distinguishes neoliberalism from its historical precursors (Comaroff and Comaroff 2009: 51). In the emphasis on capacity and self-care, our entire existence is expected to serve the market, since the recent neoliberal fantasy demands the mobilization of each and every aspect of one's individuality for the purpose of profit making; the most fundamental capital for an entrepreneur is subjectivity itself. Consequently, we are *all* entrepreneurs who are under a continuous market pressure to find creative means to utilize our most precious capital.

Nevertheless, it is doubtful as to whether all societies or groups around the globe understand the same thing from "entrepreneurialism." Rather than being a coherent systematic project, it is redefined in each specific context in relation to its particular history. What is more interesting is the particular entangling of entrepreneurialism as a current historical impetus with local historicity. Agents with different interests and desires reinterpret it in different ways. The volunteers I spoke to link entrepreneurialism to other projects in their attempts to govern poverty. In other words, they do not want to create an entrepreneurial subject as such, but entrepreneurialism becomes part of a broader heuristic set of complex governance projects to contain urban unrest. Moreover, not only is entrepreneurialism reinterpreted in local contexts but the very interpreters also express their confusion as to its promises.

In their valorization of will as the sole means of bringing success and employment, volunteers seem to feel uneasy at times when they suspect that will might be inadequate for the problems facing society. In fact, most of the volunteers vaguely address the economic destitution of the children and their families throughout the interviews. Nevertheless, when asked whether education is an adequate means of solving these "economic" problems, after a brief hesitation they insist on the primordial importance of education as containing bright potentials and consequences "to come," which will change the children's lives. This insistence on the future consequences of education emphasizes the change of point of view for the future generations. The children are expected to change (unlike their families, who could not), and the future generations are expected to change even more. This narrative of gradual change and development contains an urge to resolve the social problems associated with poverty, migration, and urban segregation, and to lead the children to integrate into the urban life within which they feel alien. The ultimate aim, phrased as "changing their points of view," is to direct and manage the children's subjectivities, especially their dreams and desires, as exemplified in the promotion of their wish to go to the university. When volunteers come to the point of realizing that they cannot promise by any means an immediate resolution of current problems (that is, poverty and many other problematic issues haunting the lives of the children that are not directly mentioned at all), they begin to dream of a distant future in which the children they work with and their families will be in a better condition.

Remedies for a Haunted Nation: Securing Security, Guaranteeing the Future

In the critical literature on educational sciences, it has frequently been argued that "education" has proved to be one of the perfect means of preventing social danger and producing well-regulated forms of liberty by supervising working class children in the nineteenth and twentieth centuries (Hunter 1988, Popkewitz 2000). Similarly, TEGV's relation to the children and to their "integration" takes place not only through having the children participate in "civilized society" by making them become eloquent and self-reflective individuals but also by preventing them from becoming social deviants posing immediate forms of danger. Reaching out to what the volunteers see as a "potential thief," a "usurper," or a "paint thinner addict" is supposed to be helpful in this respect. Through the role model of the volunteer, these potential criminals are to be transformed into obedient citizens who are respectful of the nation and the state. A certain sensibility toward "containing danger" is almost always evident in the discourse of the volunteers. They explain crime through personal traits such as the level of education or material destitution. The pronoun "we" refers to a particular social class that does not commit such crimes, yet will be negatively affected by them. The volunteers abundantly narrate how it has become much more dangerous to live in urban space due to risks that cannot be governed properly by governments and municipalities. If the "danger" that is represented by the "potential thief" is not contained, it will go on harming the class they themselves belong to, rendering the civil initiative of guaranteeing a "secure future" futile. Therefore "we" have to educate these children with patience.

The volunteers' endeavor to take their own precautions against the problem of security by educating and empowering the children (whom they consider potential criminals) to become prudent subjects is itself a perfect instance of prudent subjectivity. Thinking that they can prevent the children from becoming criminals by educating them, volunteers thereby project their own assumed prudential subjectivities to the children. A derivative of entrepreneurial individualism, the prudent individual has to take the initiative concerning security. But the latter term transcends in meaning the usual focus on reduction of crime, and refers more broadly to the biopolitical underpinnings of the political rationalities that make up civil society. It also shows the ultimate connection between volunteerism, empowerment, and prudentialism as the fundamental pillars of civil association in Turkey. This prudential subjectivity fuses the two basic constituents of governmentality: individual and population. The desire for a more moral individual reflects the desire for a more moral and more secure population, which is reflected in anxieties of securing security by articulating a civil sphere/model of conduct of conducts. Every individual who learns the norms of civility renders the ideal of a civilized society more possible. The well-being of the nation, state, and society become exchangeable in this discourse. The "saved child" and the "saved society" are jointly idealized by the volunteers. The fantasy of moralization and betterment spreads from the child to his or her social environment and hence to the whole of society. This line of reasoning feeds even more to the discourse of blaming the family, since it represents the true source of problems as lying in the families, who allegedly fail to initiate the moralization and betterment of their children.

The problematization of the children and their families as constituting a space of intervention, as argued above, excludes many problems like the Kurdish problem, violence, structural unemployment, and so on. To reiterate, although a foundation devoted to education is not expected to address, say, the Kurdish problem, the way in which social problems haunting the security of the nation are associated with education, subjectivity, psychology, and so forth performs the discursive operation of cancelling out specific forms of addressing political problems. As the earlier arguments above hinted, such an exclusion can only be possible through the individualization of social problems. This works on the basis of two discourses: the modernist Kemalist discourse trying to civilize the children and the neoliberal empowerment discourse trying to teach them self-government. In TEGV centers, the volunteers attempt to overcome the basic problem of the "failure to modernize" through daily life practices of Kemalist pedagogy, which can be called codes of civility. Beyond the attempt to develop these codes, volunteers also attempt to induce certain emotions and behaviors in children through novel techniques. These techniques of building self-confidence and creating hopes about the future aim to initiate self-responsibilization among children. In practice, the two intertwine with each other: the children are expected to acquire qualities that will render them "modern" in the Kemalist sense and "self-reliant" in the neoliberal sense. They constitute the fundamentals of a discourse that tries to overcome the insecurity of the neoliberal context by merging the desire for a stable market economy with the desire for a strong Turkey. In this hegemonic discourse, one is expected to be both loyal and responsible, that is, a citizen who is a harmonious part of the homogeneous nation and who is capable of settling one's own problems.

The distinctions and contrasts produced by the volunteers to represent their relations with the local community also reveal how educated and modernized middle classes conceive the migrant residents of poor marginalized neighborhoods. In their contradictory conceptions of the "needy" and "lacking," volunteers reconstruct their own identities by means of their limited encounters with the urban other. It is through the production and reproduction of differences, such as the one between "modern/responsible citizen" and "premodern/needy population," that complex relations of power and intervention can take place. As Timothy Mitchell (2000: 23) argues, the very act of producing differences symbolizes the "performance of the modern," as a result of which the construction of modernity as a project is absolutely related to this incessant production. In their valorization of industriousness, orderliness, and modern art—in their very representation of urban culture and of civilized urbanites—the volunteers portray the poor migrants as "distortions." The existence of the latter poses not only a physical security threat but, perhaps more important, a symbolic threat to the urban culture with which the middle classes identify themselves. Volunteers resort to contrasting representations while interpreting their encounters with the children and the neighborhood, because it is this very contrast that produces the differences between the volunteer and the poor migrant. The volunteer bears a subjectivity that is discursively articulated only in reference to these encounters between the "modern/responsible citizen" and "premodern/needy population." The volunteer in that sense is not a ready-made subject who goes to his or her field (the poor neighborhood) equipped with certain prescriptions to be carried out, but a well-off urbanite with a particular history that attributes an "accomplished" middle class position to the volunteers, and a "lacking" position to the urban poor particularly via these encounters.

Conclusion: Contestations?

Contradictory processes of neoliberalization are at work at different levels, sites, and scales of CSO projects around the globe. As Anna Tsing suggests about the concept of "globalism," one also needs to rethink neoliberalism in relation to the complexity of local modernization and development projects by looking at particular encounters and translations (Tsing 2000). The historically contingent nature of neoliberal governmentality (Gupta and Sharma 2006) confirms that empowerment discourses may produce different consequences at the level of lived experience. This contingency also points at the need for further research on forms of power that are surfacing at the interstices between the state and the CSOs in order to see the dynamics of institutionalized power (Elyachar 2003). David Hecht and Maliqalim Simone (1994: 54) tell us how African societies are headed in many different directions simultaneously since there is no sense of a univocal logic, and how dispersion of social practices are in a constant process of reassembling. In a parallel fashion, they also argue that civil society can manufacture social changes through equivocal ideologies anchored in shifting alliances (102).

The ambiguity in the concrete spaces of "neoliberalism" might better be observed when we look more closely at the dynamics within the poor neighborhoods where TEGV centers are located. Even volunteers themselves mention "resistant" voices from marginalized communities that protest TEGV's presence in the neighborhood. They refer to groups of youngsters who constantly annoy and abuse the volunteers verbally or by painting graffiti. This kind of story signals that there is a space of contestation out there, and not everybody in the marginalized segments welcomes the volunteers. To what extent this narrative of youngster protest can be generalized, or the levels and content of their activities, is worth exploring. The question of how the marginalized are capable of playing with uncertainty needs to be framed in relation to the issues of security technologies and state violence. It is reasonable to believe that "there is always a potentiality for change in cities" (Simone 2004: 213), but the forces restricting this potentiality also need to be addressed seriously. The contestation of urban space and the risks and threats associated with it, albeit variegated among different localities, often involve more dominant and more hegemonic players who seek to enforce order and consensus against chaos.

The enormous investments and huge budgets of large-scale CSOs such as TEGV disclose a desire on the part of economic and social elites to secure order against the increasing ambiguity in urban space. There obviously exist other CSOs, some of which collaborate or compete with TEGV's projects. Yet TEGV not only has more powerful resources to enact its projects but also has the privilege to act in the name of the state and with the support of the state, which further expands its space of legitimacy and intervention. Compared to, say, Hecht and Simone's portrayal of a pluralist space in African cities, the urban space in major cities in Turkey is much less open to contestation, unless backed up by militant ideological movements. Not surprisingly, therefore, rather than supporting resistant and marginal social movements, poor families usually prefer to ally with powerful CSOs, assuming that they would provide more opportunities, especially for their children. Nevertheless, how these relations produce interruptions and subversions in reply to the disciplining projects they are subject to is the topic of another enquiry.

Notes

1   Instead of the widespread term "nongovernmental organizations" (NGOs) I have preferred to use the term "civil society organizations" (CSOs) as a translation of the Turkish term *sivil toplum kuruluşları* (*STKlar*) in order to capture the conceptual reframing of civil society in Turkey in terms of its emphasis on civility as such. What defines CSOs is not a denial of the state apparatus or government involvement, but rather the positing of "another space" of social action that traverses politics, economics, and culture. For a conceptual analysis of the terminological and contextual differences about civil society in the Western, Eastern European, and Middle Eastern contexts, see Akşit, Tabakoğlu, and Serdar 2002.

2   Political rationality or "political reason" is a specific concept introduced by Michel Foucault for understanding the extension of government and the act of governing beyond the formal institutions of the state (Foucault 2001). Similarly, his use of the term "political" implies a novel insight beyond our usual association of politics with the central apparatuses of the state, since governing the population and territory is performed by a wide array of actors, institutions, mechanisms, and rationalities, according to Foucault. In terms of the historical emergence of the nation-state in its European form, he argues that it is not the incarnation of a centralized state or its bureaucratic apparatuses, but the "reasons of the state" (*raison d'état*) that define the modern form of government. In that sense, Foucault argued that the development of the doctrine of raison d'état in seventeenth-century Europe was an example of the emergence of a new rationality of government, or a new "political rationality," which provides the larger framework in which actors, concepts, and mechanisms of government (which include but are not limited to the centralized nation-state) are defined. Similarly, this article conceptually extends its units of analysis by avoiding

an exclusive focus on the state and CSOs as separate actors and moves toward the "political rationality" whereby these actors are thought to be configured and interrelated.

3   Governmentality is a concept that Foucault introduced in his historical analysis of the definitions of government: "Government did not refer only to political structures or to the management of states; rather it designated the way in which the conduct of individuals or of groups might be directed: the government of children, of souls, of communities, of families, of the sick" (Foucault 1982: 221). In that sense, it refers less to a central node that determines conducts, and more to the emergence of a set of techniques and knowledges about how these conducts are to be conducted— that is, it is a conduct of conducts.

4   In Turkish, *toplumsal değişimin temel sivil unsurları*.

5   This chapter builds upon my ethnography of TEGV in Istanbul in 2004–2005, which included institutional ethnography, interviews with TEGV representatives and officials, participant observation on various TEGV centers around Istanbul, discourse analysis of the vast material published by TEGV itself, and semistructured interviews with volunteers.

6   Most of this rhetoric is enriched by novel contributions by the Turkish press, as well as columnists that advocate the "civic necessity" of "intervening" in the fate of society to their middle-class readers.

7   An anonymous sentence that was very frequently expressed in the aftermath of the 1999 earthquake by columnists, news editors, and "fellow" citizens joining live-feeds in a range of TV programs.

8   It is striking that the Turkish state was drastically short of providing most of the vital emergency services that were required to save lives in such a disaster. It was widely argued among the Turkish public at the time that the death toll could have been significantly reduced if there were adequate means and measures to reach the disaster sites with due haste and to rescue the individuals under the debris. Moreover, there were drastic shortcomings in providing tents, medicine, and food to the region, which was frequently expressed in Turkish media through dramatic video footages of individuals who were resentfully asking "Where is the state when we need it?"

9   Here I use the term "middle class" in the way Partha Chatterjee uses it, that is, to describe the national elite in India as a group that tries to be effective in forming the nationalist and modern culture of the country. They are in between the "governors" and the "population," a situation which Chatterjee describes as being the mediator in assuming social authority. The middle-class subject "takes upon him/herself the

responsibility of speaking on behalf of those who were poor and oppressed. To be in the middle now meant to oppose the rulers and to lead the subjects" (Chatterjee 1993: 92). In assuming the responsibility of "saving the nation" and by claiming to represent the people living there, TEGV directors also function as a "middle class" that strives to lead the population.

10 On September 12, 1980, the Turkish armed forces, headed by the chief of the General Staff, General Kenan Evren, took control of the Turkish government. The National Security Council (MGK) declared martial law all over Turkey and dissolved the parliament. The constitution was also suspended. All political parties and trade unions were banned. The generals that carried out the coup frequently referred to threats against the unity of the Turkish nation and against Kemalism and secularism as a pretext, and lumped the various ideological currents of the time under the pejoratively perceived categories of communism, ethnic separatism, and religious extremism. The 1970s had been marked by right-wing/left-wing armed conflicts, which abruptly stopped in the aftermath of the coup. For the next three years the Turkish armed forces ruled the country through the National Security Council, before elections were restored.

11 In this regard, it is difficult to avoid the nationwide protest campaigns in 2007 against AKP and the party's presidential candidate. The protests predominantly mobilized civil society under an overtly political cause against the government. But what is striking is that neither with these protests, nor with other political tensions in which leading CSOs were visible actors, was any aspect of the actual configuration of relationships between CSOs and the state changed. It would thus be safe to say that civil initiatives are relatively impervious to political hassles, however strong the ensuing tensions. Moreover, it is even possible to observe that the discursive integrity of the CSOs has been enlarged via these tensions, joining economic liberalism and liberal conservatism with Republicanism and nationalism.

12 The 1999 earthquake struck northwestern Turkey on August 17. It was centered in İzmit, the eastern neighbor of the city of Istanbul, and had a magnitude of 7.6. According to official figures, the death toll exceeded 17,000 people, while almost half a million people were left homeless. On the other hand, unofficial sources claim that the death toll exceeded 35,000 people.

13 There were many articles in leading newspapers about this issue. Prominent intellectual circles were highly interested in it. The socialist monthly journal *Birikim* and the famous quarterly journal *Cogito* also initiated open forums following the earthquake in their special issues to discuss the agency and responsibilities of the Turkish state.

14   For revealing instances of the expression of this fear in the mainstream Turkish press, see "Turkish Government Fails Quake Test," *Washington Post*, August 29, 1999.

15   It is striking that this novel sense of citizenship transcends the classical separation of the political citizen (*citoyen*) from the private man (*bourgeois*) that finds its essence in "civil society." Despite radical differences in the way political action has been conceived, it is common to portray civil society as a sphere or space that either resists or transcends the political sphere. Conceptually, the way CSOs in Turkey conceive of "citizenship" as a register of agency that could be realized in essence if and only if it is properly disassociated from politics, the state, and ideological convictions, provides a novel and ironical portrayal of civil society as a depoliticized sphere of government and intervention.

16   The data utilized in this chapter are derived from two basic sources: the institutional documents of TEGV, including periodicals, activity booklets, and information provided on their website, and formal and informal interviews I conducted with TEGV volunteers between 2004 and 2006.

17   "Our Reason of Existence," in www.tegv.org.

18   In the text on their reason of existence, featured both in the website and in many of their published materials, TEGV volunteers portray TEGV centers as "magnets for children and parents. Children are drawn to the computers, activities, laughter, and bright colors while parents are comforted knowing their children are in the hands of caring role models learning in a safe, clean environment out of harm's way." There is a constant, yet ambiguously articulated "danger" in their discourse, located in some segments of society, against which TEGV appropriates a self-image of "protector" and "savior."

19   These are the schools of one of the biggest Muslim religious sects in Turkey, the Nurcu movement, headed by Fethullah Gülen.

20   For a worldwide transformation of education, see Popkewitz 2000.

21   Although the word *halk* literally means "people" in Turkish, it is frequently employed by Republican elites to refer to uneducated and traditional masses that are not properly cultivated in Western (or, as is common in the Kemalist discourse, "contemporary and civilized") values. It was a common discursive preference in the press of the pre-1950s Republican period to contrast the cultured "citizen" to the problematic mass of the *halk*, since the presence of *halk* threatens to undo the "cultural and civilizational progress" that was to have emerged after the Republican Revolution.

References

Aksit, B., B. Tabakoglu, and A. Serdar. 2002. "Ulus-Devlet ve Cemaatçi Kültür Arasında Sıkısan/Gelisen Sivil Toplum: Türkiye'de Sivil Toplum Kuruluslarıı Deneyimi." In A. A. Dikmen, ed., *Cumhuriyet Döneminde Siyasal Düsünce ve Modernlesme.* Ankara: Türk Sosyal Bilimler Dernegi ve Imaj Yayınları.

Beck, U. 1992. *Risk Society: Towards a New Modernity.* London: Sage.

Berlant, L. 2004. "Introduction: Compassion and Withholding." In L. Berlant, ed., *Compassion: The Culture and Politics of an Emotion.* New York: Routledge.

Berry, A., T. Osborne, and N. Rose. 1996. *Foucault and Political Reason: Liberalism, Neoliberalism and Rationalities of Government.* Chicago: University of Chicago Press.

Brin Hyatt, S. 2001. "From Citizen to Volunteer." In J. Goode and J. Maskovsky, eds., *The New Poverty Studies: The Ethnography of Power, Politics, and Impoverished People in the United States.* New York: New York University Press.

Burchell, G., C. Gordon and P. Miller. 1991. *The Foucault Effect: Studies in Governmentality.* Hemel Hempstead, England: Harvester Wheatsheaf.

Clarke, J. 1991. *Democratizing Development: The Role of Voluntary Agencies.* London: Earthscan Publications.

———. 2004. *Changing Welfare, Changing States.* London: Sage.

Comaroff, J. L., and J. Comaroff. 1999. *Civil Society and the Political Imagination in Africa.* Chicago: University of Chicago Press.

———. 2009. *Ethnicity, Inc.* Chicago: University of Chicago Press.

Chatterjee, P. 1993. *The Nation and Its Fragments.* Princeton: Princeton University Press.

Cruikshank, B. 1996. "Revolutions within: Self-Government and Self-Esteem." In A. Berry, T. Osborne, and N. Rose, eds., *Foucault and Political Reason: Liberalism, Neoliberalism and Rationalities of Government.* Chicago: University of Chicago Press.

Dean, M. 1999. *Governmentality: Power and Rule in Modern Society.* London: Sage.

Elyachar, J. 2003. "Mappings of Power: The State, NGOs, and International Organizations in the Informal Economy of Cairo." *Comparative Studies in Society and History* 45(3):571–605.

Ferguson, J., and A. Gupta. 2002." Spatializing States: Toward an Ethnography of Neoliberal Governmentality." *American Ethnologist* 29(4):981–1002.

Fisher, W. 1997. "Doing Good? The Politics and Antipolitics of NGO Practices." *Annual Review of Anthropology* 26:439–464.

Foucault, M. 1982. "Subject and Power." In H. Dreyfus and P. Rabinow, eds., *Michel Foucault: Beyond Structuralism and Hermeneutics*. Chicago: University of Chicago Press.

———. 1990. "Right of Death and Power over Life." In *The History of Sexuality*, vol. 1. London: Penguin.

———. 1991. "Governmentality." In G. Burchell, C. Gordon and P. Miller, eds., *The Foucault Effect: Studies in Governmentality*. Hemel Hempstead, England: Harvester Wheatsheaf.

———. 2001. "'Omnes et Singulatim': Toward a Critique of Political Reason." In J. D. Faubion, ed., *Power: Essential Works of Foucault*. London: Allen Lane, Penguin.

Garber, M. 2004. "Compassion." In L. Berlant, ed., *Compassion: The Culture and Politics of an Emotion*. New York: Routledge.

Gonzales de la Rocha, M., J. Perlman, H. Safa, E. Jelin, B. R. Roberts, and P. M. Ward. 2004. "From the Marginality of the 1960s to the 'New Poverty' of Today: A LARR Research Forum." *Latin American Research Review* 39(1):183–203.

Gupta, A., and A. Sharma. 2006. "Globalization and Postcolonial States." *Current Anthropology* 47(2):277–307.

Hecht, D., and A. Simone. 1994. *Invisible Governance: The Art of African Micropolitics*. New York: Autonomedia.

Heper, M. 1991. "Interest Group Politics in Post 1980 Turkey: Lingering Monism." In M. Heper, ed., *Strong State and Economic Interest Groups*. Berlin: Walter de Gruyter.

Hunter, I. 1988. *Culture and Government: The Emergence of Literary Education*. London: Macmillan.

Kamat, S. 2004. "The Privatization of Public Interest: Theorizing NGO Discourse in a Neoliberal Era." *Review of International Political Economy* 11(1):155–176.

Keyman, E. F., and A. İçduygu. 2003. "Globalization, Civil Society and Citizenship in Turkey: Actors, Boundaries and Discourses." *Citizenship Studies* 7(2):219–234.

Misra, K. 2006. "Politico-moral Transactions in Indian Aids Service: Confidentiality, Rights and New Modalities of Governance." *Anthropological Quarterly* 79(1):33–74.

Mitchell, T. 2000. "The Stage of Modernity." In T. Mitchell, ed., *Questions of Modernity*. Minneapolis: University of Minnesota Press.

O'Malley, P. 1996. "Risk and Responsibility." In A. Berry, T. Osborne, and N. Rose, eds., *Foucault and Political Reason: Liberalism, Neoliberalism and Rationalities of Government*. Chicago: University of Chicago Press.

Popkewitz, T. S. 2000. "Rethinking Decentralization and the State/Civil Society Distinctions: The State as a Problematic of Governing." In T. S. Popkewitz, ed., *Educational Knowledge: Changing Relationships between the State, Civil Society, and the Educational Community*. Albany: State University of New York Press.

Rose, N. 1996. "Governing Advanced Liberal Societies." In A. Berry, T. Osborne, and N. Rose, eds., *Foucault and Political Reason: Liberalism, Neoliberalism, and Rationalities of Government*. Chicago: University of Chicago Press.

Rutherford, B. 2004. "Desired Publics, Domestic Government, and Entanglement Fears: On the Anthropology of Civil Society, Farm Workers, and White Farmers in Zimbabwe." *Cultural Anthropology* 19(1):122–153.

Sharma, A. 2006. "Crossbreeding Institutions, Breeding Struggle: Women's Empowerment, Neoliberal Governmentality, and State (Re)formation in India." *Cultural Anthropology* 21(1):60–95.

Simone, A. 2004. *For the City Yet to Come: Changing African Life in Four Cities*. Durham: Duke University Press.

Toprak, B. 1996. "Civil Society in Turkey." In Toprak, *Civil Society in the Middle East*. Leiden: E. J. Brill.

Tsing, A. 2000. "The Global Situation." *Cultural Anthropology* 13(3):327–360.

Turner, V. 1974. *Dramas, Fields, and Metaphors: Symbolic Action in Human Society*. Ithaca: Cornell University Press.

Woodward, K. 2004. "Calculating Compassion." In L. Berlant, ed., *Compassion: The Culture and Politics of an Emotion*. New York: Routledge.

Zurcher, E. 1993. *Turkey: A Modern History*. London: I. B. Tauris.

Other Sources

Birikim 125/126 (Devlet-Toplum Faylarımız Foyalarımız). 1999.Istanbul: Eylül-Ekim.

Cogito 20 (Deprem Özel Sayısı: Depremin Sosyal ve Siyasal Etkileri).1999. Istanbul: Sonbahar, www.tegv.org.

Gündem. 2004. *Eğitim Gönüllüleri*. Istanbul: Aralık.

CHAPTER FIVE

"I'm No Terrorist, I'm a Kurd": Societal Violence, the State, and the Neoliberal Order

Zeynep Gambetti

"'Quien Habla Es Terrorista': The Political Use of Fear in Fujimori's Peru" is the title of one of Jo-Marie Burt's (2006) articles exploring the weakness of civil society in Peru. In the confrontation between the Peruvian regime and the guerilla movement Shining Path, "terrorist" became a strategic label that conveniently associated all oppositional discourses with criminal action in the 1990s. Such is the prevailing tendency in another country, Turkey, whose democratic institutions are paradoxically hailed as a model for the Arab world (Kirisci 2011). After having obtained the international community's accord in listing the PKK (Kurdistan Workers' Party) as a terrorist organization along with Hamas, Shining Path, and the Columbian FARC in 2003,[1] the Justice and Development Party (AKP) government in Turkey has gradually started to use antiterrorist laws to silence protests and civic activism.[2] Since 2009, it has been systematically cracking down on elected Kurdish mayors, rights activists, journalists, and even university students and professors on grounds that they belong to "illegal organizations," mainly the underground urban branch of the PKK.[3]

But although this drift toward authoritarianism under the pretext of legality and democratic proceduralism surely warrants meticulous analysis, the focus of this chapter is slightly different. It looks at the ways in which the ground was prepared from 2005 onward for the public endorsement of increasingly authoritarian measures. I argue that 2005 marks a break in civil society's demeanor vis-à-vis the Kurdish question in Turkey. The chapter intends to show how political and economic factors have converged in transforming civil society into the "willing executioners" of state imperatives.

Put briefly, I claim that the "powerful magi of the Second Coming" of civil society (Comaroff and Comaroff 2000: 331) may well carry the mark of the sovereignty of the market, but this should not be hastily acknowledged to signal the pitting of the nation against the state, market forces against government, the client against the citizen. In the age of governmentality, the sovereign reflexes of the state (Gambetti and Güremen 2005) as exemplified by the post-9/11 strategies of the Bush administration may spell out just the opposite: a locking together of state-economy-society, however they may be defined. It appears likely that the neoliberal privatization of the functions of the state has actually served to reduce the oppositional space between state and society. In theoretical terms, the passage is from Leviathan to Behemoth, an amorphous structure that engulfs state, economy, and society (Neumann 1987). The forms of discursive violence in Turkey provide an interesting vantage point from which to reveal the mechanisms of this tendency.

The Puzzle(s)

The reflections in this chapter are in fact prompted by a series of "puzzles" that seem to elude straightforward explanation. The first puzzle is how to make sense of the 130 or more quasi-spontaneous lynching attempts and numerous other incidents of mob aggression that have taken place since 2005 in a country where outbreaks of collective anger occurred in the past, but rarely at such frequency and intensity.[4] Turkey has a rather grim record of authoritarianism, periodic military interventions, and a strict republican ideology, which, after the 1980 military coup, were combined with a civil war fueling discourses of national security and ultranationalism. This past (and present) could in principle suffice to show that violence is a steady thread that runs throughout the political and social fabric. There is ample scholarly work available on the authoritarian and even totalitarian aspects of Turkish state and society. Still, despite the probability of lynching attempts, one needs to understand why mob anger was vented in *this* specific time period, in *this* manner, and what to make of it.

The second puzzle that complicates the analysis concerns the conspicuous rise of practices and discourses of vigilantism and securitization in the West at about the same time. Although there is no simple correlation between mob violence in Turkey and the flag frenzy in the United States after 9/11 or vigilante practices such as Campus Watch, the similarities are too striking to ignore. Although Turkey cannot easily be compared to Western democracies with respect to its history and institutional setup, the silencing of dissident opinion seems to have followed a logic that is relatively new, here as well as in the West.

A third puzzle is that the Turkish economy shares the plight of many others in being unambiguously thrust into neoliberal globalization. As part of its social effects, neoliberalism "works by multiplying sites for regulation and domination through the creation of autonomous entities of government that are not part of the formal state apparatus and are guided by enterprise logic" (Gupta and Sharma, 2006: 277). It also multiplies the sites of inequality, from the slums that grow around metropolises to the precariousness of income, from the privatization-fueled increase in prices of basic services such as water, electricity, and natural gas, to the competition between multinationals and the underclass (such as in the business of garbage collection).

To be sure, structural reform packages imposed by the International Monetary Fund and the World Bank are effectively rolling back the state in Turkey. But my suspicion is that vigilantism and lynching attempts have actually buttressed the state by aligning civil society and citizens in relation to national objectives. In other words, the neoliberal privatization of the functions of the state may actually have served to reduce the oppositional space between state and society.

The case at hand requires proceeding with utmost caution. The language of violence has been a constant in Turkish official discourse since the 1980 coup. The coup was justified—before, during, and after—as having provided the order and stability that successive elected governments were incapable of securing. This justification effectively conceals the fact that state violence has come to replace the civil strife caused by ideological clashes between social and political fractions in the 1970s. One of the most devastating consequences of military rule was the near-total eradication of the Left, along with its parties and unions, through the imprisonment of its leaders and cadres and the seizure of its property and assets. This has allowed for the top-down imposition of a free market in the place of the previously import-substituting economic model of development. Liberalization of trade, a ban on strikes and union activities, and the implementation of infrastructural measures necessary for the eventual privatization of state economic enterprises—all achieved under the supervision of the military junta—were to lead to the relatively smooth implementation of economic adjustments by civilian governments thereafter.

This process was accompanied by heavy prohibitions on freedom of expression as inscribed into the constitution and the penal code, by the increase in police powers, and the rewriting of school textbooks in the language of duty to the state, national pride, and hostility toward "enemies of the nation." Only a year after the transition to civilian rule, the armed uprising of a part of the Kurdish population under the aegis of the PKK in 1984 served as an excuse for the military to maintain its influence in civilian politics, particularly through the National Security Council. Such expressions as threats to national security, the indivisible unity of the nation, territorial integrity, low-intensity warfare, states of emergency, and extraordinary measures became part of everyday life, especially after 1987. Toward the end of the 1990s, the problem of Islamic fundamentalism supplemented the "Kurdish question," marking the passage to a double-threat perception. A whole generation has thus been molded by various forms of physical, institutional, and symbolic violence.

Despite all this, it must be acknowledged that the lynching attempts that this chapter will focus on began only after the war with the PKK had momentarily ebbed.[5] Party leaders and journalists ascribed the mob incidents to the "growing impatience of the people" with Kurdish demands for recognition and with the failure of the government to uphold national pride in negotiations with the European Union. Without doubt, the growing nationalist sentiment owed as much to the various "injuries" dealt by the EU to haughty representations of Turkishness as to the ineffectiveness of the government to solve the Kurdish question through peaceful means.[6] In Turkey, nationalism has indeed become an ideology that cuts across the political spectrum—from what remains of the Left to the ultra-right and Islamist parties—from 1980 onward. It has taken hold of the language and horizon of politics. But by representing the lynching attempts as outbreaks of nationalism and by driving in the message that the nation was a moral and unified bloc, both the media and state officials tended to overlook the fact that citizens were now taking onto themselves the responsibility of policing dissenters and would-be enemies. Civil society, armed with patriotic values, was rushing to fill in the gap presumably left open by the state.

Another very significant void in public debates on societal-level outbursts of anger was any mention of what political science literature calls "post-peace accord violence." Mob violence figures among the various forms of aggression and criminality that often mark the period of passage to peace after prolonged civil wars. The internalization of violence as a norm in dealing with personal or social problems has given rise to a "culture of violence" in settings as different as Northern Ireland, Sri Lanka, South Africa, and Guatemala, for instance (Steenkamp 2005; Jarman 2004; Godoy 2002, 2004). Violence is normalized and legitimized by the very practice of war, and also by the discourses of the state that represent war as sacrifice, as patriotic duty, and as service done to an ultimate noble cause. Violence, in other words, becomes a prized value.

In Turkey, the failure of mainstream public opinion to come to terms with the two violent sequences in the country's recent history—the 1980 military coup and the war with the Kurds in the Southeast—accounts for why nationalist discourse continues to monopolize public discourses. The failure to move beyond the boundaries set by official ideology forecloses the possibility of a public consideration of the social effects of the lived experience of war. Even the term "war" is absent from mainstream discourse: the coup as well as the armed conflict in the Southeast are represented as police operations, as restoration of order and stability or as purification of the national body of "harmful elements."

Briefly put, the state is the ultimate arbiter of truth, morality, and subjectivity in this political set-up. This is probably why the target of mob violence in Turkey was neither the state nor society at large, as was the case in Guatemala (Godoy 2002, 2004). The agents of violence were not part of the population that experienced the war; on the contrary, the majority of the lynching attempts occurred in regions far removed from the Kurdish-populated Southeast. Violence did not manifest itself in the form of generalized criminal practices (theft, mugging, drug dealership, and so on), which are present, of course, but either remain petty or are "cleanly" operated by big mafia networks. In other words, vigilantism in Turkey does not compare to that in South Africa, where crime control initiatives constitute the main vigilante groups (Buur and Jensen 2004). Rather, social violence broke out along the ideological fault lines dictated by the state, coming closer to what Rosenbaum and Sederberg (1974) call "establishment violence."

It is the paradox of the devolution to civil society of the state's duty of maintaining order and the simultaneous *étatisation* of society that prompts further reflection. Outrageous as it may seem, lynching attempts can be considered as a form of civil initiative or voluntary enterprise, and thus point to the emergence of a peculiar subjectivity, that of the "officer-citizen."

The Violence

The first lynching attempt reported in the press was on April 6, 2005. Five members of TAYAD, a Leftist group, were attacked while distributing tracts in Trabzon, a major metropolis in the Northeast.[7] A crowd of around 2,000 people reportedly gathered upon rumors that the Turkish flag was being burned, and began beating the five activists, who were actually protesting prison conditions in the country. The police intervened, but the crowd insisted that the activists be handed over to them, shouting: "We will burn those who dare burn the Turkish flag," "This is Trabzon, there is no way out of here," and "This is not Mersin."[8] What these would-be lynchers were alluding to was the infamous Mersin incident, where a Turkish flag was reported to have been trampled and burned by Kurdish youngsters participating in the *newroz* (Kurdish New Year) celebrations on March 21, 2005.

The particular feature of the Mersin incident was not the incident itself but a statement made by the chief of staff the day after. It triggered what the BBC called a "flag frenzy" that gripped the whole country.[9] "Innocent festivities organized to celebrate the coming of spring," he said,

> have been pushed so far as to provoke the insolence of attacking the glorious Turkish flag, a symbol of the great Turkish nation and inch by inch bedecked with the blood of martyrs, by a group that has not received its share of values. The Turkish nation has seen good and bad days in its long history; besides its innumerable victories, it has also experienced treasons. But never did it have to face such ignominy in its own fatherland by its own *so-called citizens* . . . This is treacherous behavior. Being the citizen of a country, breathing its air, drinking its water, filling one's stomach, and then daring to raise one's hand against the flag, a country's most sacred common value, can be nothing other than heedlessness, depravity, and perfidy. Friend or foe, everyone should understand that neither the country's indivisible integrity nor the glorious Turkish flag, a symbol of this unity and integrity, has been abandoned. First the great Turkish nation, and then the Turkish Armed Forces that emerged from its bosom, are ready and have sworn to protect and look after the country and the flag, exactly as their

ancestors did, and, if necessary, to shed the last drop of their blood for this. We advise those who misinterpret our dignity and solemnity, our patience, those who are after mistaken deals, who attempt to put the Turkish Armed Forces' love of country and flag to test, to look into the pages of history.[10]

One of the severest declarations made in recent years, this speech was spectacularly performative in the existential sense of "world-creating."[11] It reordered the discursive field in such a way as to reset priorities and targets, identify the characteristics of the "nation" as an entity and agent, and reconstruct its past, present, and future. It assigned the armed forces an organic place within the nation, reminding the latter of its duties and values. It pitted this "nation" against the "so-called citizen," which was reconstructed as a rather suspicious element. It assigned an outside to the nation, an outside that is paradoxically located within.

The distinction between enemy and stranger is relevant here. Although the figure of an enemy provides for political identification with the state as the guarantor of the principle of determinacy, strangers "articulate ambivalence and therefore challenge the (modern) ordering activity which relies on reducing ambiguity and uncertainty by categorizing elements" (Huysmans 1998: 241). As Mesut Yeğen (2006) notes, the chief of staff's speech revealed a shift of paradigm in the official representation of Kurds from "would-be Turks" to "so-called citizens," signaling a loss of faith in their capacity to assimilate. One should also add that it served to diffuse the enemy (the PKK) into the whole fabric of society. The ambivalence of the figure of the Kurd as a "so-called citizen"—one of us and yet not one of us, for he hasn't had his share of the authoritative distribution of values—generalized the threat perception. Danger was no longer attached to an identity; it could come from anywhere, everywhere.

And although it was not yet clear whether the flag had been trampled or burned, the chief of staff's speech had taken immediate effect. First came declarations by almost all of the political leaders in Ankara, reiterating more or less the same words, irrespective of their position within the ideological spectrum. The "Turkish people" were getting impatient; the national sensitivity of the "people" was being offended; the Mersin event was an incident of "provocation." The flag frenzy began the next day. As if they were a file of soldiers, official institutions, business associations, people from all professions, the media, civil society organizations, and "simple" citizens distributed flags to passers-by, hoisted them outside buildings, and organized rallies that competed with each other to tote the largest possible flag, fabricated expressly for the purpose.[12] And, finally, mob violence began.

The first series of thirty lynching attempts reported by the press between 2005 and 2007 occurred immediately after the Mersin incident. Most of them targeted either Kurdish individuals or radical Leftist groups, as was the case with TAYAD activists in Trabzon.[13] Several attacks took place in the conservative Black Sea coastal region. But mob violence also spread to other parts of the country, particularly to those provinces with a heavy population of Kurdish migrants from the Southeast. Except in three incidents, most of the Kurds who were attacked were seasonal or resident migrant workers.[14] In Seferihisar on the Aegean coast, for instance, two fights broke out between Kurdish migrants and locals, wherein five Kurds were almost killed and nine Kurdish families had to be evacuated from the district under the supervision of the gendarmerie upon threats that they would be lynched.[15] Their abandoned houses were broken into, the furniture left inside was destroyed, and huge Turkish flags were hung from the windows.

What was surprising, though, was that public anger was vented overwhelmingly against groups or individuals who were mistaken for supporters of the Kurdish cause. TAYAD activists were attacked for a total of eight times in different provinces, six of these happening in the Black Sea region. Turkish Communist Party militants distributing the party's newspaper, members of the Socialist ESP making a press statement, and Federation for Fundamental Rights activists handing out tracts were all subject to mob violence on grounds that they were "terrorists." In one incident, two students putting up a poster of Mahir Çayan, one of the legendary Marxist-Leninist revolutionaries of the 1970s, were severely beaten by a mob that later went on to attack the local branch of the pro-Kurdish party, BDP.[16] In each incident, an association was being made between dissident activism and the PKK.

On another register, intellectual gatherings also received their share of mob frenzy. To cite a few instances, an academic conference on Ottoman Armenians was postponed because of violence and, when it finally took place, was ambushed by angry crowds;[17] the presentation of an academic report on the forced migration of the Kurds was broken into and had to be postponed;[18] a photography exhibit commemorating mob violence that occurred in Istanbul in 1955—during which non-Muslims had been attacked and their shops and houses vandalized—was itself vandalized (*Radikal*, September 7, 2005).[19]

There was a short lull in the political and ethnic lynching attempts between September 2006 and June 2007, but mob violence resumed after another chief of staff Internet communiqué, coming at a time when the PKK had stepped up its armed operations in Turkey:

> These terrorist operations have clearly revealed the real intentions of the separatist and racist [PKK]. The time has come, for those individuals or organizations that use the highest values of humanity such as peace at home and abroad, freedom and democracy as shields to protect the terrorist organization, to see the real countenance of these events. The Turkish Republic is confronted with an approach that regards its national and unitary structure as passé. . . . It is beyond doubt that the terrorist operations, which have [recently] surfaced and are growing in number, are a result of this type of twisted thinking and of those who directly and indirectly advocate them. . . . The Turkish Armed Forces expects the grand Turkish nation to demonstrate a massive counter reflex against this type of terrorist event.[20]

Once again, the chief of staff was reordering the discursive field, but this time with a clear attempt to asscociate peace activists and democrats with the PKK. The very definition of "terrorism" was being extended to include not only all Kurds but also those Turks who were critical of a military response to the Kurdish problem, who pushed for more democracy, transparency, and plurality in the country, or who questioned the centralized and unitary set-up of the republic. Immediately afterward, as was the case with the first chief of staff speech in 2005, several civil society organizations wasted no time in calling for "silent rallies" against terrorism. The late Türkan Saylan, head of the Kemalist association ÇYDD, was quoted as denouncing all countries that provided money and arms to the PKK and as defending the "people's right" to react: "Terrorism can be combated when the state, government, army, administrators, and the nation join hands," she said.[21]

The second series of lynching attempts, although also occasionally targeting leftist groups, was predominantly directed against Kurds. The most destructive among them took place after various PKK raids on military and police personnel. When twelve soldiers were killed in Dağlıca on October 21, 2007, for instance, week-long outbursts of violence ensued wherein whole Kurdish neighborhoods were besieged, Kurdish businesses vandalized, coffee houses broken into, BDP branches stoned, and several people beaten up by angry crowds all over Turkey.[22] Likewise, Adana's Dörtyol district became the scene of frenzied attacks on people and buildings after four policemen were ambushed by the PKK in July 2010. The electric atmosphere in the district was amplified when Kurdish politicians wanted to pay a visit to the victims of mob attacks. Angry crowds patrolled the streets for four days. The aftermath of the PKK's attack on Silvan in July 2011 was again marked by sporadic lynching attempts throughout the country. A host of other clashes between Turks and Kurds took place without any PKK-related news to spur them.[23]

Among the mob frenzies that were totally out of place in this context was a gigantic attack on a gypsy community in Manisa, after which the community had to be moved elsewhere. In Istanbul, the opening of an art exhibit was mobbed by residents in the neighborhood who were displeased by the snobbish manners at the cocktail party. It became more and more frequent to see crowds outside of courthouses or police stations, wanting to get their hands on criminals or suspects. Unverified rumors were enough to mobilize crowds in most occasions.

It is important to note that few people actually died in all this frenzy.[24]These were *attempts* at lynching, but imagining what would have happened if the crowds had actually managed to keep the targeted persons in their grip is next to impossible. The police or gendarmerie intervened sooner or (mostly) later to stop murder from being committed. Public hanging, burning, or stoning are not among the usual habits of the Turkish mob since 1980, although one fatal (but fortunately exceptional) incident happened in 1993.[25]

In a kind of "mimicry of war" (Anna Tsing), the lynching attempts that followed the chief of staff's declarations provide clues as to the "national sensitivity" of this curious entity that had been construed as dormant since the 1980 coup: "the people." The slogans emitted by the angry crowds in all of the attacks ("Down with the PKK," "We don't want any PKK in this town," "Love it or leave it"[26]) indicate that they mistook leftist groups for PKK sympathizers. University students protesting the detention of their friends were harassed on two occasions in Edirne on grounds that they were "terrorists."[27] On one occasion, a small group protesting Ankara's decision to send troops to Lebanon was mistaken for the PKK. How the hostility was framed—lumping all opposition groups under the category of the PKK—was relatively new, but the underlying logic was already established during the long years of war. The flattening out of differences, particularly between PKK militants and all of the Kurds, was now being extended to include every type of protestor. The gist of the matter is that the PKK was being turned into something like an empty signifier under which to articulate all antistate opinion and activity.

How elected politicians reacted after the lynching attempts reveals that new boundaries were being drawn concerning legitimate violence. Weber's classical formulation of the state as the entity that retains a monopoly over the legitimate use of violence was undergoing an alteration. Whereas during the war, legitimate (and extralegal) violence was indeed under the control of the state, the right over life and death was now being passed on to "society"—or rather, to bodies within it that had *not* been marked as "expendable" by official discourses. Those citizens who were directly associated with "the people" and to whom indirect acknowledgment was granted through impunity, were actually taking onto themselves the full responsibility for the letter of the law.

After the first incident on April 6, 2005, Prime Minister Tayyip Erdoğan made a statement declaring that the sensitivity of the people was of utmost importance: "May no one take advantage of this sensitivity," he added.[28] Another good example of the government attitude toward lynching was a declaration by Erdoğan that patience had its limits.[29] Most politicians and journalists portrayed the lynchings as "justified outbursts of anger." This discursive strategy pointed beyond the probability that the "people's sensitivity" was shared by opinion leaders. It redrew the boundaries of legitimate violence. Exculpating the would-be lynchers and normalizing their sensitivity was a crucial step in the process that consisted of blurring the distinctions between state and society.

Another step was to incriminate the victims of lynching, but not the members of the mob. In almost all of the cases, the victims were taken under custody and even arrested for provocation and causing public unrest. One of the accusations is illustrative of the procedure usually applied. The Edirne police told university students who demanded protection upon seeing angry crowds gathering around them that the crowds were using their "democratic rights," just as the students were. In the police records, the crowds were called "citizens" while the students were "individuals who continued to provoke the crowds and the police officers despite warnings."[30] Five of the victims were arrested, while neither the would-be lynchers nor the police officers accused of nonassistance were indicted.[31]

The Turkish state, under the auspices of the army, had already officially begun this process of fusing state and society by arming villagers in the Kurdish southeastern region and according them a salary as "village guards" (*korucu*) in the 1980s. This tactic was also used in Guatemala (*patrullas de autodefensa civil*) and Peru (*rondas campesinas*), serving to divide and rule (Godoy 2002; Burt 2006). Civil war, in principle, means that the state has already lost its monopoly right on the use of violence, since another entity in society has devolved this right onto itself. Incapable of penetrating fully into society, the state uses civilians as an ersatz security force. That is to say that the state itself transfers this monopoly to citizens. Civil wars or low-intensity wars are particularly effective in blurring the distinction between soldiers and civilians. The system of arming civilians (mainly villagers) not only spreads a politics of fear but also seriously damages feelings of belonging, solidarity, and trust within local communities.[32] But whereas lynching and mob violence soared in communities having directly experienced the war in Guatemala, and "popular justice" (*justicia a mano propia*) came to be practiced in these same communities for lack of trust in the official judiciary system (Godoy 2002: 644), a paradoxical situation seems to have emerged in Turkey. The "people" aligned themselves along the ideological lines constituted by the state, while at the same time posing themselves as more étatist than the state, as a sort of "excess" of the state, an excessive state. This authoritative coming into being of an army of citizens around the patriotic mission of protecting the unity and integrity of the nation-state is more reminiscent of Germany in the early 1930s than of Guatemala in the 2000s.

What does all this point to, theoretically speaking? Based on a Hobbesian (and Hegelian and Weberian) representation of the state, sovereignty has been conceptualized, in studies on Turkey and elsewhere, as the form-giving and boundary-making power of law. Hobbes's Leviathan is the not-so-metaphorical figure of the state as order imposed on a natural state of disorder, of structure molded out of shapeless chaos—in short, of identity grafted on to indistinction. While forcefully distinguishing the public from the private, state from society, and the universality of law from the particularity of social existence, Hobbes's representation is caught up in its own dilemma of having to specify the exact boundaries between these. State and society come into being simultaneously: the one cannot exist without the other. The state has been erected by the transfer of the power and natural rights of individual bodies onto a third entity whose sole condition of existence is this transfer. But the language of rights is an abstraction that in no way exhausts the real (lived, concrete, material) activity of the field now designated as "society," the field where the individual bodies that made the initial transfer are engaged in everyday life practices. The question of the actual relation between state and society cannot be fully absorbed into the juridical model of sovereignty, for this is where the boundaries become fluid, unidentifiable. and open to negotiation. Within this context, Foucault's reconceptualizing of the state beyond the paradigm of sovereignty, as one locus of power among a multiplicity of relations that shape and construct norms, boundaries and subjectivities, populations and disciplined bodies, provides a way out of the dilemma.[33] Studies on governmentality effectively account for the simultaneous individualization and homogenization that mark the constitution of "order" in modern societies. Abstract and legal definitions of legitimacy (or normality) are shown to be porous, owing to the power strategies employed by a multiplicity of agents within the grey zones of everyday activity. These "zones of contestation" (Buur and Jensen 2004: 145) or indistinction point to the limits of state sovereignty, but at the same time indicate how the latter is constituted and reconstituted in its relation to "society."

As such, the state tradition in Turkey does not exhaust itself in the representations it offers of itself through laws and official discourses, but must be explored in the concrete practices that constitute its power. The lynching attempts emerge in the zone that Das and Poole (2004) call the "margins of the state." They attest to the point where state jurisdiction fades, but is also continually refounded through the state's appropriation of "private justice." Like the local strongmen, the brokers, and the paramilitary, the lynch mob is situated between law and its outside, but with a difference: the mob is not the (un)officially acknowledged representative of the state. In ethnographies conducted at these margins, the "question of the origins of law emerges, not as the myth of the state, but rather in the form of men whose abilities to represent the state or to enforce its laws are themselves premised on the men's recognized ability to move with impunity between appeals to formal law and forms of extrajudicial practice that are clearly construed as lying outside, or prior to, the state" (Das and Poole 2004: 14). The lynch mob is the other side of the coin: by reappropriating the power initially transferred to the state, the lynch mob functions as a reminder of the ultimate dependence of the state on compliance by society. It demands that the agents of law and order take up the challenge of confronting the substantial (as opposed to the procedural) ground of their ability to represent the state. The lynch mob thus destabilizes the legal definition of legitimacy and puts it up for negotiation, thrusting it into the grey zone where the "officer-citizen" is located. The latter is in fact the point of intersection between the state's official ideology and its practical being.

Legal Vigilantism

One can confidently say that trust in the judiciary as an independent third power delivering the justice inscribed in rational and universal laws has always been very low in Turkey. On the contrary, the opinion that the judiciary simply executes what power dictates is quite common. Irrespective of the form that the state can take, or of the particular ideology that happens to order its practices and norms in a given historical period, it seems to be the sole purveyor of legitimacy (Kadıoğlu 1998: 13). Thus, instead of accounting for the emergence of what can be called "legal vigilantism"—the now widespread phenomenon of protesting crowds outside of courthouses—by citing the decrease in trust in procedural justice as the main reason, another explanation must be found.

The most puzzling development in the 2005–2007 period was that, although terrorism and separatist activity were on the decline in Turkey, the country's legal structure was readjusted to align with Patriot Acts and antiterror laws being promulgated in the West. A week after the first chief of staff speech, for instance, the promulgation of a new (reformed) penal code was postponed for two months. The new code was expected to remove restrictions on freedom of speech and opinion. It was eventually revised to do just the opposite: restrictions and penalties became heavier. A year later, a draconian antiterror law was passed. How is one to make sense of this?

The fact is that after the PKK leader Abdullah Öcalan was caught and imprisoned in 1999, civil society, the media and academia had become polyphonic. The mainstream political agenda mainly consisted of debates over increasing civil society activism, cultural rights, and legal and structural reforms in view of European Union membership. Such relatively "bold" propositions as redefining citizenship to remove its ethnic underpinnings, launching TV and radio programs in Kurdish, demanding Kurdish-language education, restructuring the National Security Council, probing into the motifs and consequences of the 1980 coup, and even initiating academic debate over the question of the Armenian genocide were being made, one after the other.

This effervescence was brought to a halt between 2005 and 2007. Instead, new actors began to appear: Kemal Kerinçsiz, a lawyer who was unheard of until then, became the chief protagonist in a series of law suits filed against such prominent intellectuals as Nobel prizewinner Orhan Pamuk and writer Elif Şafak for "insult to Turkishness." Numerous trials took place in this vein. The journalist Perihan Mağden was tried for having defended conscientious objection and was insulted for being "the PKK's concubine."[34] The worst case was that of the Armenian journalist Hrant Dink, who was accused of insulting Turkishness and interfering with legal procedure. Dink paid with his life for the "negative publicity" he received during his trial: he was assassinated in January 2007. The circumstances of the assassination and of the trial remain controversial, even as this chapter is being written.

The trials against intellectuals became pretexts for making rallying calls to citizens willing to fulfill their "national duty": "The time has come to say no on legitimate grounds to enemies of the Turks," wrote Kerinçsiz, for instance.[35] The legitimate grounds in question was the courthouse, and the means of "saying no" was the lawsuit. Courthouse patios became spaces in which demonstrators hassled with each other, throwing eggs and bottles and engaging in fistfights.

The Orhan Pamuk trial was the most sensational among these lawsuits. Not only law but also the courthouse was reconstituted into a battleground. Pamuk had declared in an interview to a Swiss magazine that 30,000 Kurds and a million Armenians were killed in Turkey. Following a campaign in right-wing newspapers against him, a district governor in Isparta ordered that Pamuk's books in local libraries be removed and destroyed. Incidentally, this written order came a few days after the 2005 *newroz* celebrations that sparked the first lynching event. Pamuk was branded a "minority racist."[36] A witch hunt for his books was instigated in the district, only to be countered by the provincial governor's move to annul the order and open an investigation about the district governor. An Islamist-nationalist party (BBP) declared its support for the book ban and called Pamuk an "ungrateful, so-called writer." The BBP press release was revealing: "An official of the state should take the side of the state; if one of them is being punished for doing this, then traitors are being given leeway."[37] The support Pamuk was getting from writers abroad and from European parliamentarians who were present at the trial caused a nationalist uproar such that groups gathered outside the courthouse shouted: "Are we under foreign occupation here?"[38] The prominent mainstream newspaper *Hürriyet* began its report of the trial with these words: "The Orhan Pamuk trial is closely watched by the EU and the European Parliament, which have turned Turkey into a target in their debates on freedom of opinion."[39] When the trial was postponed owing to a procedural issue, demonstrators outside attacked the van carrying Pamuk, hitting it so hard with their fists that the front window cracked. Among the slogans chanted was this one: "Sold-out traitors, the fatherland expects nothing of you!" A few days later, Pamuk's accusation was thrown out of court for procedural reasons.

The trials of intellectuals thus turned into spaces in which reactionary forces within civil society settled accounts with progressive circles. This was simultaneously the sign of the breakdown of the state and its relocation or reconstitution in civil society, akin to an enactment of justice by civilians—a "mimicry of the state," just as lynching attempts are "mimicry of war." What is peculiar in these instances is that the "people" act as if they *are* the state: they appropriate and resignify the state function of dispensing justice. The age-old liberal ideal that makes of the state an embodiment of the will of the people seems finally to have come true.

This development signals a new dialectic whereby the state is being continually refounded, not only "through its (not so mythic) appropriation of private justice and violence" (Das and Poole 2004: 14) but also through society's (not so mythic) appropriation of public justice and violence. The ethnic, political, and economic bias inherent in the latter comes into the open through the intervention of civil society. Whereas official discourse had always to be cloaked under the legitimating catchwords of democracy, universality, impartiality, and the public good, civil society is not under the same constraint. The "people" give voice to the will that covertly grounds the reason inherent in Law. As Godoy (2002: 659) provocatively argues, the devolution of the state's monopoly of violence to society not only "democratizes" terror but also invalidates the representation of civil society as virtuous and respectful of human rights, and standing against the state.

The Neoliberal Context: Politics of Fear or Fear of Politics?

The economic bias underlying the state's own practices deserves special attention for the ideologically unexpressed division that it adds to binaries already defining state power (legal/illegal, legitimate/illegitimate, public/private). In Turkey, economic problems that manifest themselves in migration, seasonal labor, purchasing prices, or the lack of control over economic processes are hardly expressed in these terms, but become entangled in discourses of security. The discursive and effective falling out of grace of class struggle in the age of neoliberalism is evident not only in the individualized language of performance and flexibility but also in the replacement of previous threat perceptions such as unemployment or stagnation with the political economy of terrorism.

I will refer to two events in Turkey to demonstrate the profitability of violence. The first event occurred in the summer of 2006. The fall in hazelnut purchasing prices spurred a major protest rally, reportedly gathering 100,000 people in the town of Ordu in July 2006. Despite the use of tear gas and the arrival of gendarmerie units to assist the local police, the road blockade lasted eight hours.

What was of interest was the use of the language of terrorism by both the protestors and state officials. One of the banners at the July protest read: "Terrorism is separatism, but isn't having people go hungry also separatism?"[40] Another one said: "Are you obliging us to take to the mountains?"[41] This was a direct allusion to the PKK, whose militants use the expression "taking to the mountains" to mean that they have joined the armed organization. Prime Minister Erdoğan himself likened the Ordu protests to terrorism and reportedly went as far as to claim that the roadblock had been organized by illegal organizations.[42] Another public declaration in the same vein came from a ruling party deputy: "Terrorist organizations that could not establish a foothold in the Black Sea region are now using hazelnut as an excuse. These incidents prepare the ground for terrorist organizations."[43] As a matter of fact, the protestors in the Ordu rally were questioned by the antiterror division of the Police Department.[44]

Meanwhile, seasonal Kurdish workers were beginning to arrive in the region for hazelnut harvest. Sakarya's local authorities decided, without prior contacts with representatives there, to refuse the right to work to seasonal workers.[45] Several workers were forcefully sent back upon arrival. They were probably intercepted at train and bus stations and asked to name their contractors. In September, one of the districts of Sakarya became the scene of a lynching attempt against Kurdish seasonal workers.[46] This incident did get some coverage, but mostly as an "ethnic row" in newspapers. The relationship between social class and ethnic division seemed to escape the attention of media commentators. Indeed, the relationship between interracial violence and economic conditions, although quite well established in scholarly work, continues to elude popular representations. But lynching is not unrelated to economic strife or perceptions of it. In the United States, for instance, Olzak (1990) finds that during periods marked by populist challenges to white political and economic supremacy, fluctuations in the price of cotton and increasing competition in the labor market were the main triggers for an increase in lynching practices between 1882 and 1914. Beck and Tolnay (1990) similarly show that mob violence against blacks in the Deep South corresponded to adverse economic conditions, especially those affecting the financial fortunes of marginal white farmers.

The economic factor behind the government's attitude toward hazelnut producers cannot be grasped without a few words on the sector itself. Turkey's Black Sea region ranks first in world hazelnut production, accounting for 75 percent of global production and 95 percent of global trade in hazelnuts. As much as eight million people, a significant proportion of whom are seasonal workers from the Kurdish-populated southeastern Turkey, live off hazelnut production. Whereas the purchasing price for hazelnuts was around 6.5 liras per kilogram in 2005, the 2006 price was 2.5 liras, the lowest in decades. The purchasing price was also below the 3.5 liras per kilogram cost of production. Instead of doing anything about this, the government was putting the blame on Fiskobirlik, the union of hazelnut producers' cooperatives. The farmers in Ordu were actually protesting how foreign buyers were being favored over the domestic producer, how the government and Fiskobirlik were indifferent to the plight of farmers, and how one of the prime minister's advisors, Cüneyt Zapsu, a merchant trading hazelnuts in international markets, was abusing his political power to keep prices low. Zapsu was actually shortselling, as most merchants tend to do in this sector, that is, selling the crop before it is produced and without actually owning it. Shortsellers profit from this transaction by buying the crop once the harvest is over at a lower price. This puts a downward pressure on prices, even under such conditions of quasi monopoly as Turkish hazelnut production.

One of the organizers of the Ordu hazelnut protest expressed the (real) problem thus: "A million people were torn out of the countryside. This was the largest migration in twenty-five years. These people didn't go to work in industry, they went to the urban slums. What we call the problem of public security in big cities has to do exactly with that."[47]

What the organizers and various banners (such as "Should we stop being farmers and become purse-snatchers?" "Do not make the peasants join the army of unemployed!") were saying was that the alternatives to complying by the rules of the market were to be unemployed, to become a thief or, as a third option, a terrorist. But by articulating an economic claim to terrorism, state officials were resignifying class struggle. Their rhetoric suggested not only that national security was to take first place in the hierarchy of social problems and threats but also that all problems were to be reformulated as problems of "security." While dissidence in all of its political forms was being equated with terrorism (that is, with the PKK), so also were class claims.

The second major incident revealing the newly discovered *dispositif* of incriminating social demands occurred in Hopa on May 31, 2011. The main opposition party, CHP, and various socialist groups used Prime Minister Erdoğan's electoral visit to the district as an occasion to protest the sell-out of rivers and streams to the private sector as part of a government scheme to privatize electricity production. Riot police immediately intervened, pouring so much tear gas on the protestors that one retired schoolteacher died of a heart attack. In the hassle with the police that lasted for some time, Erdoğan's convoy was stoned and one of his bodyguards fell off the top of a bus. Erdoğan made the following comment after the incident: "Bandits have seemingly descended upon Hopa."[48] Those who were opposing the privatization of water and electricity were affiliated with the main opposition party, which, in turn, was affiliated with a socialist formation (Halk Evleri) renowned for its clashes with the police during rallies, which then (finally) was associated with the pro-Kurdish party BDP, which, on numerous occasions was directly or indirectly accused of having organic ties with the PKK by the prime minister. The chain of equivalences that Erdoğan constructed thus ended up affiliating a social protest with terrorism.

The follow-up to the event revealed how the equivalence was translated into legal practice. Protestors were first charged with causing public disorder, but then the accusation was changed to "membership in illegal organizations."[49] The heads of local party branches were taken under custody and their houses searched. Several people who demonstrated in solidarity in other parts of the country were also detained. Charges against a deputy from the BDP were illustrative of the arbitrariness of the accusations: he was accused of being a terrorist because he had participated in an illegal revolutionary organization in the 1970s.[50] Riot police remained in the town for weeks. The event even became a pretext to consider setting up a permanent riot police headquarters in the district.[51]

The economic background of this apparently excessive establishment reaction to protests in Hopa is that the eastern Black Sea region is very rich in high-altitude water resources. In fact, of around 2,000 hydroelectric power plants that the government plans to construct all over Turkey, the majority are to be situated in this region. While the Erdoğan government claims that there is a need to open the electricity sector to market competition to reduce production costs, growing awareness of the social costs of allowing usage rights to the private sector has roused significant opposition from civil society. Numerous groups have mobilized together with local farmers to take judiciary action against the construction of dams in natural reserves, to publicize the cause in newspapers and other media, and to organize local resistance teams. These groups were reviled on various occasions by the prime minister, on grounds that they were "misleading public opinion" and even "downright lying."[52]

According to the president of the Human Rights Association, Öztürk Türkdoğan, oppositional leftist forces are eyed suspiciously by the establishment because they have power among the marginalized, are defending the right to decent housing, have acquired environmental consciousness, are siding with students, and are voicing general discontent: "Ultimately the government doesn't like this kind of insubordination and wants to eliminate it by using the pretext of [membership to] illegal organizations."[53] A group of six NGOs that visited Hopa after the eventful visit of the prime minister have indeed reported that the locals feared the police would also knock on their doors: "Although they are still in solidarity with each other, they were under the shock of the crackdown . . . and whereas they had resolved to struggle for their rivers against the hydroelectric plants and were demonstrating peacefully, they were astounded at being attacked by the police."[54]

These and other considerations, which are beyond the scope of this study to spell out, lend support to the idea that the discourses of security (in this case in the form of the fight against terrorism) and the criminalization of dissent serve important functions in neoliberal market economy. Some, of course, would not agree. Niklas Rose claims, for instance, that in devolving onto themselves the will of the exiting welfare state, neoliberal subjects "reconceptualize themselves in terms of their own will to be healthy, to enjoy a maximized normality" (1996: 52). He therefore claims that the coherence that Marxist theory attributes to mechanisms of rule in capitalist societies no longer holds in the age of neoliberalism. Authority relations are to have become reversible: "what starts off as a norm to be implanted into citizens can be repossessed as a demand which citizens can make of authorities" (59). Thus, the neoliberal market mechanism with its array of expertise, and multiple social technologies and subjectivities, is construed as a potentially "liberating" field.

But when the rhetorics and practices of security are grafted onto the neoliberal "will to govern" (Rose 1996: 53), subjects come to equate happiness with security, thus adjusting their activities in accordance with officially designated national security goals. The optimism concerning the pluralization of sites of regulation not only covers up what Žižek (1997) calls the "cultural logic of multinational capitalism"—false freedom of choice between objects of consumption, identities, lifestyles, even forms of resistance— it also hides from view the continued centrality of the state as a logic of rule and an immense locus of power, incomparable to any of the multiple powers diffused in society. As pathbreaking as they can be, sociological and anthropological studies have often fallen into the trap of equating the state with public administration, just as political scientists have done before them. Social institutions and civic activity not categorized as "public" by law are taken to be "private," thus nonstate. The proliferation of such nonstate spaces of decision and action then appear as a new dynamic that challenges state authority and opens up the possibility of creative strategies of resistance. But if the state did not consist of government programs, bureaucracies, and checkpoints—if it were seen as the division of the social and political field into the haves and the have-nots of power; if it were understood as a hegemonic structure of meaning that organizes life activity through this division— then it would become possible to understand why the rhetoric of security had to accompany the neoliberal comeback of civil society. Huysmans (1998: 232), for instance, distinguishes between security as a "thick signifier" and security as a definition or concept. The former is a logic, the latter implies specific content, such as "environmental security," "world security," "societal security," and so on. Any potentially democratic (in the ancient sense of *demos-cratos*) and, by this virtue uncontrollable, transformation of the available field of action will have to be countered by a reordering that brings back the prospect of control by any possible means. Government at a distance is *government* only when control is effectively exercised over souls and bodies. Civil society is a rewarding place to begin with, since when subjects themselves espouse and implement strategies of control favorable to the renewal or maintenance of order, the unequal distribution of power that underlies it will cease to be apparent.

I am arguing that what La Boétie and Tocqueville, each in his own manner, conceptualized as a voluntary submission to power merits more attention today. Whereas security discourses toughen and spread the logic of rule both horizontally (across the globe) and vertically (down to civil society), neoliberal discourses naturalize and spread (again both horizontally and vertically) the logic of capitalist inequality. The concurrence of the two results in the belief that there is no alternative either to the market or to compliance. For neither the state nor capitalism can bear alternatives: their functioning depends on their success in being the "only game in town" because both are distributive mechanisms that cannot exist without the unequal distribution of power and wealth.

Conclusion

The dispensation of justice by citizens themselves may appear to be symptomatic of the collapse of the state under the pressure of neoliberal ideology and practice. But the idea that neoliberal economy would push back the state with its centralized mechanisms of rule and replace them with more participatory forms of governance has proven to be extremely ambivalent. As the Turkish case shows, citizens may indeed become "more participative" in policing dissent, handing out guilty verdicts, and keeping class conflict under bay. While global capital amplifies existing inequalities through new exclusionary practices, it also seems to call on the willful engagement of civil society. The language of the "failure" of the state to deal with increasing crime, new sources of societal risks, poverty, and exclusion fails itself to take into account how the state can reclaim the lost domain by authoritatively ushering its citizens back in line through the rhetorics and practices of security. The ongoing patterns of violence result in the criminalization of dissenting identities and the simultaneous absolution of citizens who take on the role of the state of removing threats to national interests. Not only do dissenters thereby become bodies that can be eliminated, but society itself becomes a branch of the state.

Such must have been the horror felt by eighteen-year-old Evrim Demir who set herself on fire in her own backyard. In the letter she left behind she wrote: "I'm not a terrorist, I'm a Kurd." Is this not lynching par excellence?[55]

Notes

1   Council Decision 2011/70/CFSP of January 31, 2011, updating the list of persons, groups, and entities subject to Articles 2, 3, and 4 of Common Position 2001/931/ CFSP on the application of specific measures to combat terrorism, *Official Journal* L 028, February 2, 2011, P. 0057–0059, http://eur-lex.europa.eu/LexUriServ/Lex-UriServ.do?uri=OJ:L:2011:028:0057:01:EN:HTML.

2   Human Rights Watch 2010.

3   See Scholars at Risk press release, November 9, 2011, http://scholarsatrisk.nyu. edu/Events-News/Article-Detail.php?art_uid=3197; and International PEN news bulletin, November 1, 2011, http://www.internationalpen.org.uk/go/news/ turkey-ragip-zarakolu-moved-to-high-security-prison.

4   More than two-thirds of the lynching attempts had political or ethnic motives.

5   After the capture of its leader Abdullah Öcalan in 1999, the PKK declared a unilateral ceasefire that lasted for five years. It ended the ceasefire in June 2004 and resumed armed operations, but these were more sporadic than systematic during the entire period between June 2004 and April 2005, when the lynching attempts began. In 2006, serious fighting broke out and the war was resumed once again, so much that the Turkish Armed Forces crossed the border into Iraq to hit PKK camps in June 2007.

6   The EU's hesitations and the ambivalent language used concerning Turkey's full membership are considered as insulting by a growing portion of public opinion.

7   TAYAD is the Association of Solidarity with the Families of Convicts and Detainees.

8   *Milliyet*, April 7, 2005.

9   Jonny Diamond, "Flag-waving frenzy grips Turkey," BBC News, March 24, 2005, 15:35:41 GMT, http://news.bbc.co.uk/go/pr/fr/-/2/hi/europe/4379675.stm.

10 *Milliyet* and *Radikal*, March 23, 2005; emphasis added. Note that "heedlessness, depravity, and perfidy" (*gaflet, dalalet ve hıyanet*) are words that come from one of Mustafa Kemal Atatürk's speeches.

11 Despite the poststructuralist use of the term, I refer here to the original sense, as used by John Austin and developed by Barbara Cassin and Michael Warner.

12 The Higher Council for Radio and Television called on all channels to put a Turkish flag on the screen; public prosecutors, governors, police chiefs, and university rectors organized "flag rallies"; several employers as well as workers' unions and local chambers of commerce called for flag campaigns. Flag sales soared. *Milliyet*, March 25, 2005.

13 Threats of lynching also stopped a gay-and-transsexual rally from taking place in the city of Bursa.

14 One of the most violent events in the first series of lynching attempts occurred in Bozüyük in western Turkey. Ultranationalists were informed of the arrival of over two coaches carrying Kurdish activists to a rally in support of the imprisoned leader of the PKK. Around 3,000 people gathered in the town center, armed with Molotov cocktails, sticks, and stones, and set fire to one of the buses. Over fifty-five people were injured; *Ülkede Özgür Gündem*, September 9, 2006. In another incident in Istanbul, a group of Kurdish protestors were tear-gassed and chased by the police into a gypsy-populated neighborhood. There, neighborhood residents took to the streets with long knives, axes, sticks, and shovels to help the police round up the protestors. Ironically, the press reported the events as "Roma citizens reacting to the group [of protestors] intervened" in the situation (Haber7.com, April 2, 2006). Whereas gypsies are rarely called "Roma" either in the press or in popular language and are rarely considered citizens, they had suddenly been promoted to that status and had acquired a distinct culture for joining in the now socialized and democratized activity of policing dissidents. They were to become victims of a massive lynching attempt later on in Manisa, in 2010. In the third incident, a local branch of the pro-Kurdish BDP was stoned in Sakarya.

15 *Milliyet*, August 23, 2005; *Hürriyet*, May 22, 2006; *Ülkede Özgür Gündem*, May 23, 2006. Another such incident occured in Konya's Bozkır district (central Anatolia), where a dispute resulted in over thousand people attacking the local Kurdish coffeehouse. Over twenty Kurds had to leave the district; *Ülkede Özgür Gündem*, August 31, 2006.

16 Peace and Democracy Party (BDP) is the latest name of the pro-Kurdish legal political party, which has not ceased to reestablish itself under new names after being banned through successive constitutional court decisions. At the time of the particular lynching attempt mentioned here, the party was called DTP, but to avoid confusion, the acronym BDP will be used throughout this text.

17 *Radikal*, September 26, 2005.

18 *Hürriyet*, July 6, 2006.

19 *Radikal*, September 7, 2005.

20 *Milliyet*, June 7, 2007.

21 *Milliyet*, June 8, 2007.

22 *Radikal*, October 22–28, 2007; *Bianet*, October 25, 2007.

23 In Bursa's İnegöl, fighting started out between Turkish and Kurdish minibus drivers the day before the Dörtyol attack, turning the district into a war zone in no

time. In 2007 through 2009, several incidents, one of them fatal, took place wherein mobs, counting at times in the thousands, attacked BDP festivities (Sakarya) and convoys (İzmir), harassed people for speaking Kurdish in public places, tried to beat up women going to work in the fields (Mersin), set houses on fire, and turned inter-city buses and hospitals into scenes of lynching.

24   Although the figures are not reliable, one person was killed in an intersect fight in a mosque, one Kurdish worker died of wounds incurred by the lynching mob in Sakarya, and two people died of heart attacks when confronted with would-be lynchers or the riot police in Sakarya and Hopa, respectively.

25   Mass riots of a more organized sort, basically instigated by ultra-right and Islamist parties and encouraged by various government officials, had produced such atro-cious events as the Malatya (1975, 1978), Kahramanmaraş (1978), and Çorum (1980) massacres before the military coup. The visible fault line in all of these was the Alevi-Sunni divide, which grafted itself onto the Left-Right divide (Alevi-Left vs. Sunni-Right). But the single most serious incidence of mob violence experienced after 1980 was the 1993 Sivas Madımak event. Sunni Islamist groups set fire to a hotel harboring intellectuals that participated in Alevi celebrations in the city of Sivas, killing thirty-five people. All other cases of summary executions and mas-sacres in the post-1980 era were (un)officially conducted by state forces.

26   *Ya sev, ya terket* is the Turkish version of "Love it or leave it," adopted from the United States in the years of the Vietnam War. The slogan, in use in Turkey since the 1970s, has resurfaced in the 1990s and has been circulating persistently ever since.

27   This incident shows how arbitrary detentions can get in Turkey. The students under arrest had been taken in for protesting university registration fees. Their friends were nearly lynched when they organized a demonstration of solidarity with them, but were then accused of "terrorist propaganda" (*Radikal*, January 5, 2010).

28   *Milliyet*, April 8, 2005.

29   This comment was made after a shopkeeper started shooting at Kurdish demon-strators in Istanbul. Erdoğan continued by saying that since the demonstrators were provoking material damage, "the citizen" (meaning the shopkeeper) would natu-rally take up his arm to defend himself (*Milliyet*, November 4, 2008).

30   *Radikal*, March 31, 2010.

31   *Radikal*, October 10, 2010. In stark contrast, sixteen members of the mob were immediately detained after they attempted to lynch a police officer in the Kurdish-populated Yüksekova (*Radikal*, March 2, 2011).

32   Little or no research has been done (or can be done) on the effects of the *korucu* sys-tem, extensively used in southeastern Turkey. Although reliable figures are hard to

come by, an estimated 58,500 village guards were on the state's payroll in 2003, and an additional 12,500 were "voluntarily" acting as guards in twenty-two provinces, all of them in the east and southeast.

33 Cf. Introduction in this volume.

34 *Radikal*, June 8, 2006.

35 *Radikal*, September 9, 2006.

36 *Milliyet*, March 31, 2005.

37 *Milliyet*, April 1, 2005.

38 *Radikal*, December 17, 2005.

39 *Hürriyet*, December 17, 2005.

40 Yalçın Bayer, "Açlık ve Öfke," *Hürriyet*, August 1, 2006.

41 *Radikal*, July 31, 2006.

42 *Bianet*, August 1, 2006, http://www.bianet.org/2006/08/01/83125.htm.

43 *Radikal*, September 20, 2006.

44 *Hürriyet*, July 31, 2006.

45 *Radikal*, August 5, 2006.

46 *Hürriyet*, September 8, 2006.

47 *Radikal*, August 1, 2006.

48 *Hürriyet*, June 1, 2011.

49 *Bianet*, June 16, 2011.

50 *Milliyet*, October 17, 2011.

51 *Radikal*, August 8, 2011.

52 *Milliyet*, August 11, 2010.

53 *Bianet*, June 16, 2011.

54 *Bianet*, June 7, 2011.

55 I owe the information and the comment to Pınar Öğünç, "Az Sonra: Dev Ekranda Linç Keyfi," *Radikal*, July 20, 2011.

References

Beck, E. M., and Stewart E. Tolnay. 1990. "The Killing Fields of the Deep South: The Market for Cotton and the Lynching of Blacks, 1882–1930." *American Sociological Review* 55:526–539.

Burt, Jo-Marie. 2006. "'Quien Habla Es Terrorista': The Political Use of Fear in Fujimori's Peru." *Latin American Research Review* 41:32–62.

Buur, Lars, and Steffen Jensen. 2004. "Introduction: Vigilantism and the Policing of Everyday Life in South Africa." *African Studies* 63:139–152.

Comaroff, Jean, and John Comaroff. 2000. "Millennial Capitalism: First Thoughts on a Second Coming." *Public Culture* 12: 291–343.

Das, Veena, and Deborah Poole. 2004. "State and Its Margins: Comparative Ethnograpies." In V. Das and D. Poole, eds., *Anthropology in the Margins of the State.* New Mexico: School of American Research Press; Oxford: James Currey.

Gambetti, Zeynep, and Refik Güremen. 2005. "Did Somebody Say Liberal Totalitarianism? Yes, and Despite the 5½ (Mis)uses of the Notion." *Rethinking Marxism* 17:638–645.

Godoy, Angelina Snodgrass. 2002. "Lychings and the Democratization of Terror in Postwar Guatemala: Implications for Human Rights." *Human Rights Quarterly* 24: 640–661.

———. 2004. "When 'Justice' Is Criminal: Lynchings in Contemporary Latin America." *Theory and Society* 33:621–651.

Gupta, Akhil, and Aradhana Sharma. 2006. "Globalization and Postcolonial States." *Current Anthropology* 47:277–307.

Human Rights Watch. 2010. *Protesting as a Terrorist Offense: The Arbitrary Use of Terrorism Laws to Prosecute and Incarcerate Demonstrators in Turkey.* New York: Human Rights Watch.

Huysmans, Jeff. 1998. "Security! What Do You Mean? From Concept to Thick Signifier." *European Journal of International Relations* 4:226–255.

Jarman, Neil. 2004. "From War to Peace? Changing Patterns of Violence in Northern Ireland, 1990–2003." *Terrorism and Political Violence* 16:420–438.

Kadıoğlu, Ayşe. 1998. *Cumhuriyet İradesi, Demokrasi Muhakemesi.* Istanbul: Metis.

Kirisci, Kemal. 2011. "Turkey's 'Demonstrative Effect' and the Transformation of the Middle East." *Insight Turkey* 13:33–55.

Neumann, Franz. 1987. *Béhémoth: Structure et pratique du national-socialisme 1933–1944.* Paris: Payot.

Olzak, Suzan. 1990. "The Political Context of Competition: Lynching and Urban Racial Violence, 1882–1914." *Social Forces* 69:395–421.

Rose, Niklas. 1996. "Governing 'Advanced' Liberal Democracies." In A. Barry, T. Osborne, and N. Rose, eds. *Foucault and Political Reason.* Chicago: University of Chicago Press.

Rosenbaum, H. Jon, and Peter C. Sederberg. 1974. "Vigilantism: An Analysis of Establishment Violence." *Comparative Politics* 6:541–570.

Steenkamp, Chrissie. 2005. "The Legacy of War: Conceptualizing a 'Culture of Violence' to Explain Violence after Peace Accords." *Round Table* 94:253–267.

Yeğen, Mesut. 2006. *Müstakbel Türk'ten Sözde Vatandaşa*. Istanbul: Metis.

Žižek, Slavoj. 1997. "Multiculturalism, or, the Cultural Logic of Multinational Capitalism." *New Left Review* 225:29–51.

CHAPTER SIX

Public-Private Partnerships in the Industry of Insecurity

Nandini Sundar

A weakened state structure is like a flagging army; the commandos—i.e. the private armed organizations enter the field and they have two tasks: to make use of illegal means, while the State appears to remain within legality, and thus to reorganize the State itself.
—Gramsci 1971

This chapter discusses the phenomena of "public-private partnerships" in the discourses and practices of the contemporary Indian state. These partnerships involve the use of individuals or private groups to enact the violence of the state against vulnerable sections of the citizenry (such as Muslims, dalits or former 'untouchables,' and adivasis or indigenous people) whom it cannot legitimately kill while maintaining its universalist discourse, or to engage in forms of battle that it cannot lawfully engage in itself (such as death squads and private militias).

The use of proxies and partners is scarcely new or peculiarly Indian. However, as Sen and Pratten point out, while reflective of globalization and neoliberalism at a macro level, "the effects of community policing reforms, of privatised security industries, and of state sponsorship of vigilante groups are each mediated by localised cultural and historical repertoires" (Sen and Pratten 2007: 19). As this essay shows, over years of counterinsurgency and what Brass refers to as an "institutionalised riot system" (Brass 2004), the Indian state has developed an extensive inventory of practices in which impunity is guaranteed to both state and nonstate actors. These practices have acquired a new ideological resonance under neoliberalism, where the state's self-justifying monopoly over violence gives way to an openly declared "partnership and participation" with a range of groups to whom violence is outsourced. "Degrees of agreement, or apparent agreement, within such normative frameworks establish lines of inclusion and exclusion" (Duffield 2005: 34; see also Gupta and Sharma 2006).

The agreement the Indian state brokers, however, is not even necessarily to a shared ideology, but to a share in the spoils from those defeated, a mercenary arrangement of immediate advantage. In the case of renegade militants, the people with whom it makes these arrangements are often those whom it sought first to destroy, inviting political movements to feed upon themselves. In the process, citizens at large lose their voice, becoming faceless ciphers clutching their insecurities to their naked selves, for they no longer have a state to turn to—that thin cloak of legality that liberal democracy afforded. And "civil society," too, from which the state draws its agents, loses its liberal innocence of being a bulwark against the excesses of the state.

Public-private partnerships (PPPs), as traditionally defined, can take a number of forms, but basically involve contractual partnerships between the public and private sector for carrying out operations that have traditionally been regarded as falling in the public domain. The stated aim is to bring private resources into public projects rather than vice versa, and such partnerships are normally justified on the grounds of efficiency and cost effectiveness. Where the operations are devolved into the hands of the local community, PPPs are also claimed to result in greater legitimacy, social inclusion, and responsiveness (Osborne 2000; Savas 2000). On the other hand, PPPs face the classic principal-agent problem, with problems of accountability, differing agendas, and organizational difficulties. The exponential growth of private military firms illustrates the complexities of the PPP strategy—even as they bring "efficiency" and post-Fordist flexibility into the military business, they build upon military capacity developed at public interest, benefit from public resources like mining contracts handed over by insolvent regimes, or gain from tax payer–funded wars (that is, they transfer public resources into private hands). Above all, they face serious problems of accountability, as illustrated by Dynacorp's behavior in Iraq and Afghanistan (see Singer 2008; Duffield 2005). Singer notes that the privatization of military activity goes back to an earlier tradition, where the state did not have a monopoly over violence.

In the Indian context, however, even as the state supports or, more accurately, calls into existence private violence and vigilantism, it simultaneously asserts its monopoly on legitimate violence and thus its claims to stateness (Weber 1970) by asking insurgent groups like the Maoists or the Kashmiri and Naga militants to hand over their arms, asserting that it will not negotiate with them unless they "give up violence." We see, then, in the government's support for vigilantism not an abdication of the claim to being a legitimate liberal democratic state, or a lack of state capacity, but rather an expansion of options or greater market choice in the use of violence. In the Indian case, the private armed organizations coexist alongside a million-strong army, several well-equipped paramilitary forces, and a regular police force to deal with any violations or militancy by the victims. They act together, the state and the nonstate, the police and their agents—with the latter visibly degenerate but the police often no less so—with a repertoire ranging from extrajudicial killings and torture to routine rent seeking.

Bruce Campbell argues that death squads exist precisely because ideas of citizenship, state accountability, adherence to the rule of law, and state monopoly over violence are now established in international discourse (Campbell 2000: 14–15). Death squads have the major advantage of enabling deniability (12). In India, it is true that there is a constitutional guarantee of citizenship whose promise has held the country together, and the threat of judicial oversight is present enough to make (officially deniable) death squads an attractive proposition. On the ground and for the communities involved, however, connections between the police and these squads or individual renegade killers are barely concealed and, on the contrary, are often advertised, precisely because their function is to instill terror.[1] These do not always, of course, have the desired effect. Because the associations between police and renegades are so public, these so-called private killings are often followed by large public demonstrations against the state.[2]

Moreover, and perhaps unusually for a state that claims to be a democracy, the two main parties in power in India, the Congress and the Bharatiya Janata Party (BJP), have consistently organized mobs. These range from small "squads" to attack cultural, educational, or artistic expression, and even women drinking in pubs, claiming that they "hurt community sentiments,"[3] to large frenzied gatherings that openly orchestrate violence against minorities. The best-known examples of this are the massacre of Sikhs in Delhi in 1984 and the genocide of Muslims in Gujarat in 2002. In both cases, the attacks were organized by members of the ruling party, who also ensured police inactivity and complicity. Here "deniability" was sought by calling it mob anger.[4]

For the BJP in particular, but also for cadre-based parties on both the right and left—like the Shiv Sena and the Communist Party of India

(Marxist), which have ruled the states of Maharashtra and West Bengal, respectively—vigilantism is not a response to an exceptional situation but rather a permanent condition of the way that the relation between party and state is organized, with the cadre and the ruling party dividing up the space of civil society and the state between themselves.[5]

In the following sections, I give some examples of how public-private partnerships in organized violence have played out in practice in India, before concluding with a discussion of its implications for security and citizenship. The first relates to the demolition of a fifteenth-century mosque, the Babri Masjid, that was allegedly built over the birthplace of the Hindu God Ram. The Ramjanmabhoomi movement resulted in a wave of riots across India, and large numbers of deaths. Here, the blame was displaced onto popular faith. However, the involvement of the government or party is necessarily an open secret, since, as a judicial commission (the Justice Liberhan report) on the demolition of the Babri Masjid makes clear, the real aim of the movement was to get the BJP to power, precisely on the basis of their ability to uphold the faith of Hindus even when it meant going against the law. What was important for BJP supporters was the calculated ability to break the law while claiming to be a law-enforcing party. It is also not coincidental, as Rajagopal (2001) points out, that the Ramjanmabhoomi movement and the rise of the BJP were associated with liberalization of the economy and a rejection of Nehruvian secular socialism.

The second example relates to state-sponsored attacks on over six hundred villages said to be supporting Maoist guerillas, using a combination of state security forces and vigilantes, in forest- and mineral-rich central India. State violence was successfully portrayed in the media as popular resentment against the Maoists, in an effort to deflect direct state responsibility and claim the legitimacy of civil society. But simultaneously, the state repeatedly and publicly justified the use of local vigilantes as the only way to counter Maoist guerrillas, citing its own lack of reach into interior forest villages. The key factor here was the state's faith that a middle-class public would accept violations of law and human rights when it came to questions of national security, backed by the strength of a development discourse that portrayed mining and industrialization as the only way forward, thereby justifying state repression to access "national resources."

The third example relates to the use of death squads by the police to target human rights activists, as well as the promotion of fake insurgent groups to fight against real insurgent groups. Keeping the conflict going provides a convenient rationale for sections of the state like the security forces, who benefit from increased expenditure on national security to extend their own reach.

What these cases point to is not an overarching plan by the Indian state to perpetuate disorder, but a set of family resemblances, a repertoire of practices, competencies, and relations between sections of the state and sections of civil society that can be crafted or summoned into being as and when needed. In each case, the advantages accrue to particular groups in both society and state, while disorganizing society and state at large. What is also important is that while a democratic constitution and the rule of law sometimes come in the way, requiring deniability, most of the time the usefulness of these partnerships lies precisely in the muscular assertion of mutual benefit.

The "Joint Common Enterprise": The RSS at Work

(5) PRIVATE ARMIES
16–11–1947
The All India Congress Committee has noted with regret that there is a growing desire on the part of some organizations to build up private armies. Any such development is dangerous for the safety of the State and for the growth of corporate life in the nation. The State alone should have its defence forces or police or home guards or recognized armed volunteer force. The activities of the Muslim National Guards, the Rashtriya Swayamsevak Sangh and the Akali Volunteers and such other organizations, in so far as they represent an endeavour to bring into being private armies, must be regarded as a menace to the hard-won freedom of the country. The A. I. C. C. therefore appeals to all these organizations to discontinue such activities and the Central and Provincial Governments to take necessary steps in this behalf.[6]

Despite the Congress's exhortations, the Rashtriya Swayamsevak Sangh (RSS), never gave up its attempt to create a private army. Ostensibly a "cultural" organization set up in 1925 to promote a "Hindu nation" in which members of minority religions would occupy a subordinate role, one of the basic aspects of RSS membership has been physical and military training.[7] The RSS was banned in 1948 after one of its (allegedly former) members killed Mahatma Gandhi for ostensibly being pro-Muslim, and again during the Emergency (1975–1977), when people were arrested across the political spectrum.

The RSS operates through several fronts, of which the political wing, the BJP, is the best known. It also has fighting wings like the Vishwa Hindu Parishad and the Bajrang Dal, as well as a range of "soft" educational and service wings like the Vidya Bharati, which runs schools; the Vanvasi Kalyan Ashram and Seva Bharati, which run hostels for deprived children; and so on. Although these organizations claim to survive on contributions from individuals, rather than government support, in fact their expansion has coincided with periods when the BJP has been in government, whether at the central (1998–2004) or state level (see Sundar 2006). But in contrast to its shadowy and secretive past, the RSS is now a mainstream organization, mainly thanks to the Ramjanmabhoomi movement, following which the BJP's political fortunes improved spectacularly, so that it was able to become the main opposition party and, in 1998, take over power at the center.

In the run up to the demolition of the mosque, the RSS and its fronts mobilized across the country, collecting bricks from every corner of India in order to build the temple at Ayodhya. BJP leader L. K. Advani's *rath yatras* (chariot processions) through the country gave him public and bloody visibility, as communal violence followed in the wake of his processions. The VHP also created a cadre of workers, known as *kar sevaks*, for the purpose of building the temple. Having succeeded in demolishing the mosque, BJP leaders then tried to address those dismayed by such naked disregard for the law, so as to cover all fronts. Advani called December 6 "the saddest day of his life," while other BJP leaders described the demolition as the work of "agent provocateurs," an act by "anti social elements who had infiltrated the kar sevaks," and the kar sevaks' work as "the surfacing of pent up suppressed feeling" (Noorani 2000: 75).

A commission set up to enquire into the demolition, headed by a former Judge, Justice Liberhan, took seventeen years to submit its report (Liberhan 2009), getting forty-eight extensions. It was tabled in Parliament only at the end of November 2009, six months after it was submitted, and that too, only after a newspaper leaked its contents, indicating that the ruling Congress also had little interest in challenging its political adversary. In the meantime, far from facing criminal charges, the people involved, like Atal Bihari Vajpayee and L. K. Advani, had gone on to become the prime minister and home minister of the country, respectively, between 1998 and 2004.

Although the Liberhan report reveals little that was not already known at the time, its interest lies in the detail that it provides regarding what it calls "the joint common enterprise," showing the complicity of the state government (which was ruled by the BJP at the time), the senior civil servants posted in charge of the local administration (some of whom later went on to fight elections under the BJP banner), and the local constabulary (which did nothing to prevent the demolition), among others:

> The joint common enterprise of planning by the political, religious and the operational leadership had the unstinted support of the government in power as well as that of the BJP, RSS, VHP and the other members of the Sangh Parivar. It may not be abject in fact, to hold that the government had been subsumed in the Ayodhya campaign and had become a de facto appendage of the Sangh Parivar. (Liberhan 2009 para 132.8)

> The main object of the Joint Common Enterprise on the 6th December 1992 was to construct the temple or any other substantive act to show the Karsevaks that construction of the temple was started by the government and that it had taken all steps to achieve their electoral promises in this regard. This was essential for use in elections in the future, as subsequent elections successfully showed. (Liberhan 2009 para 132.12)

The Liberhan report shows how, far from being unexpected or accidental, the demolition was carried out by a skilful combination of groups. "It was declared that a guerrilla strategy would be adopted for Karseva on sixth of December 1992" (133.4). But this "guerilla strategy," including the movement of weapons, took place with the full support of the state government of Uttar Pradesh, and the actual demolition was equally well planned. Liberhan notes that there were four sets of people involved—the first was a group of kar sevaks who performed for the television cameras by climbing the domes, hoisting flags, and so on; another consisted of skilled workers who actually performed the demolition; a third group of kar sevaks "kept the police and administration at bay, by throwing bricks and other missiles for public consumption or providing the defence to be invoked later at the appropriate time"; and a fourth group consisted of religious preachers and political leaders who incited and cheered on the kar sevaks from a public platform (131.4–131.7).

In this case, the "joint common enterprise" also extended to the judiciary. In 2010, the High Court decided the long-standing title suit to the "disputed site" largely in favor of the "Hindus," giving them two-thirds of the area, and treating the demolition of the mosque as a fait accompli. The case is now pending in the Supreme Court.

The intertwining of the state and sections of the citizenry in a mutually strengthening spiral of prejudice that the Liberhan report illustrates brings strength to particular political parties who may be in power at any moment in time, but it has serious consequences for the long-term legitimacy and thus security of the state and citizens. While one section of citizens (here Muslims, or those who believe in a secular state) are distanced from the security that comes with the basic certitudes of citizenship and the rule of law, other sections who have become complicit with the state are also more insecure. Not only does the delegitimation of the state that comes from its partisan action engender resentment among excluded groups, leading to some support for terrorist actions, but the guilt of complicity further polarizes the perpetrators in a cycle of remorseless self-righteousness.

The Organized Poor as Security Threat: The Case of Salwa Judum in Chhattisgarh

Polarization as an instrument of state policy is also seen at work in the government's handling of left-wing challenges to the state. But unlike the Hindu-Muslim divisions that existed even prior to the Ramjanmabhoomi movement, here the aim was to split hitherto united communities and villages.

In April 2006, the prime minister of India declared that the Naxalites, as Maoist guerilla fighters in India are popularly called, represented the biggest security threat to the Indian state. Thus far, state discussions of terrorism or security issues had routinely coalesced around the neighboring state of Pakistan and the Indian Muslims as the enemy within. The Naxalite movement, on the other hand, was located largely in a "socioeconomic" context, as not "merely" a law-and-order problem, but one born out of a development deficit. In the last few years, however, in what Huysmans calls the performative function of security labeling, noting that "the signifier 'security' does not describe social relations but changes them into security relations" (Huysmans 1998:232), the Indian government has converted the Naxalite "problem" almost exclusively into a security issue. In October 2009, for example, a series of half-page advertisements in national and local newspapers, with gruesome photos of people killed by Naxalites, was carried under the heading "Naxalites are nothing but cold blooded murderers."

In Home Ministry statements on the Naxalite problem, although "development" does figure, it is only invoked to counter the Naxalites and not because the citizens of India have a right to land reform or security of tenure and employment. Instead, the emphasis is on an effective "police response." The police, too, couch this in terms that require huge expenditure, for instance, on mine-protected vehicles, helicopters, the fortification of police stations, and so on, rather than simply greater professionalism and courteous treatment of the public. This, despite the fact that police behavior and contempt for villagers is a major cause of support for Naxalism.

It is not coincidental that this securitization has accompanied a renewed round of "accumulation by dispossession," David Harvey's (2003) phrase to describe the continuity of what Marx called primitive accumulation: "those moments when great masses of men are suddenly and forcibly torn from their means of subsistence, and hurled as free and 'unattached' proletarians on the labour-market," a time when "conquest, enslavement, robbery, murder, briefly force, play the great part in accumulation" (Marx [1887] 1983: 669). The government and industry see mining, steel plants, and Special Economic Zones—which take over huge tracts of agricultural land, offer significant tax concessions to corporate houses, and deny regular labor laws—as the new vehicles of India's economic growth. On the other hand, people's movements see them as the prime symbol of dispossession, as the culmination of the growing neoliberal trend away from the earlier ideals of socialist economic development across society premised on land to the tiller, unionization, and large-scale employment. For the government, the livelihood insecurity of those who will be displaced is less important than the "security threat" their protest against displacement poses to the state.

Clearly sensing that Maoist strength lay not in their arms but in the reach of their ideology and the support they enjoyed within the villages, the Government of India consciously promoted a policy of promoting "local resistance groups." As the Ministry of Home Affairs annual report of 2003–2004 stated:

> The States have been requested to explore the feasibility of appointing Special Police Officers (SPOs), Nagrik Suraksha Samitis (NSSs) and Village Defence Committees (VDCs) in the villages affected by Naxalism. These

local groups are required to. . . expose other misdeeds of the naxal outfits and their leaders. This will help reduce the over ground support to the naxalites. (Ministry of Home Affairs Annual Report, 2003–2004, para 3.145)

Under a "Security Related Expenditure" scheme, states are compensated by the federal government for any anti-Naxalite expenses, including those for "local resistance groups," opening the way for many cash-strapped states to project a greater threat from Naxalites than they actually pose.[8]

In June 2005, the state of Chhattisgarh duly set up its "local resistance movement" in one district, Dantewada, christening it Salwa Judum,[9] and claiming that it was a "spontaneous, self-initiated people's movement" led by villagers who were fed up with years of Naxalite oppression in the form of grain levies and frequent calls for strikes. The core of this movement consisted of local youth who were recruited as special police officers and security forces, but initially the movement also mobilized large numbers of villagers, who were threatened with fines or beatings, to accompany them. The Salwa Judum burned and looted several thousand homes (644 villages were affected according to government records), killed several hundred people, and raped many women. Over fifty thousand villagers were forcibly moved to government-run camps, while another hundred thousand or so fled to neighboring states to avoid the violence.

Both in the Supreme Court, where Salwa Judum excesses were challenged,[10] and in public, the BJP-ruled government of Chhattisgarh has continued to justify the Salwa Judum as a voluntary movement, variously describing it as a "Gandhian movement," and the "fragrance of the forest." Even more than in the demolition of the Babri Masjid, where the Congress has been reluctant to act against the BJP, the two parties have acted in concert against the Maoists. Indeed, the Congress leader of the opposition in Chhattisgarh was the visible face of the Salwa Judum on the ground, while the Home Ministry at the Congress-ruled center also defended the Salwa Judum as an example of "local resistance" to be replicated in other states.

However, a plan drawn up by the head of the district in 2005 clearly lays out the modalities of a "people's counterinsurgency" plan, including identifying "friendly" and "enemy" villages, creating village defense committees, and appointing special police officers to assist the regular police as informers:

If we want to destroy the Naxalites totally, we will have to adopt their strategies, or else we will not be successful. However many police forces we get, we will find they are inadequate. . . . For this we too will have to form village defence squads like the Naxalites. For this SPOs and trustworthy people from the village defence committees will have to be given licenses and guns. (District Collector, Dantewada 2005, Chapter 4, para 18)

Some of the special police officers (SPOs) appointed in accordance with this plan were surrendered Naxalites or their village-level workers known as Sangham members, while others, especially minors, signed up thinking they were getting a government job. The SPOs have been critical to identifying the Naxalites, sometimes pretending to be visiting Maoist squads themselves, and thus catching supporters out. Many of them have relatives on the "other" side, and their aggression is fueled by fear as they accompany security forces to villages.

In 2011, the Supreme Court declared the use of local youth as special police officers unconstitutional, citing their youth and lack of training as harmful to both themselves and others. The judges also castigated the government for its rapacious exploitation of the area for mining and other purposes. Not only were its economic policies neoliberal, the court argued, but even when faced with the inevitable consequences of these disastrous policies in the form of increased social unrest, the state's response was neoliberal—relying on cheap young cannon fodder to fight the insurgency rather than well-trained forces:

> To pursue socio-economic policies that cause vast disaffection amongst the poor, creating conditions of violent politics is a proscribed feature of our Constitution. To arrive at such a situation, in actuality on account of such policies, and then claim that there are not enough resources to tackle the resulting socio-political unrest, and violence, within the framework of constitutional values amounts to an abdication of constitutional responsibilities. To claim that resource crunch prevents the State from developing appropriate capacity in ensuring security for its citizens through well trained formal police and security forces that are capable of working within the constitutional framework would be an abandonment of a primordial function of the State.[11]

Despite this rejection of its policies, the state government, with full central support, has circumvented the court's orders by forming the SPOs into an "auxiliary armed police force." They are no longer, they argue, arming civilians because these civilians are now part of a legal force. Indeed, the progression from the 1861 colonial police act—which first envisaged SPOs as being drawn from warring sections of the public at times of emergency for limited periods in order to restore peace—to the Chhattisgarh auxiliary force ordinance of 2011, which envisages long-term use of SPOs in counterinsurgency operations, marks an interesting shift in policing. Polarization rather than peace becomes the raison d'être of appointing SPOs.

In the meantime, the state has also increased the strength of its regular paramilitary forces, sending some 70,000 men into battle against the Naxalites. "Operation Green Hunt" began in September 2009, and it is likely that eventually the army will be used. The methods that the paramilitary security forces use are the same as those used in the first phase by the Salwa Judum—combing operations, arson, and extrajudicial killings, even if the attacks on villages are more sporadic than at the peak of the Salwa Judum, when three or four villages were burned every day. So is the combination of what are called "special police officers" (home guards) and regular police and paramilitary. Only the label is different.

While the government talks of the Maoist security threat, it has nothing to say about the insecurity of ordinary villagers faced with combing operations, the constant drone of helicopters, and the arbitrariness of arrests. Villagers have stopped going out of their homes in the evening, or tending their fields at night, leaving their crops to be eaten by wild animals. Several have started moving their household possessions to safer sites.

Until recently, Maoists or the issues they represented—impoverishment and exploitation—were within the political framework of the Indian state. Increasingly, however, they are being externalized and rendered unintelligible. As Huysmans argues, the issue is not just the capacity of the state to meet daily threats to security—which in the Naxalite case it could perhaps have done through efficient policing—but its power to provide "ontological security" by ordering society: "This requires that those 'elements' which cannot be classified, which are ambivalent, and thus have a capacity to render problematic this ontological function of the state system, have to be eliminated, possibly through enemy construction" (Huysmans 1998: 242).

Renegade Militants, Government-Sponsored Counterinsurgents, and Other Civilian Impersonators

To personate is to act or represent himself or another.
—Hobbes [1651] 1958

In *Leviathan*, Hobbes makes a distinction between the actor, the one who represents, and the author, who owns the words and actions of the actor. When the authority is evident, says Hobbes, "the covenant obliges the author, not the actor." The author acts as surety (Hobbes [1651] 1958: 133–136). The Indian Penal Code prescribes punishment for those impersonating government officials, or wearing clothes and carrying tokens used by public servants (Sec 170, 171). It does not, however, prescribe any punishment for public servants acting through civilians to kill other civilians. The public "authorship" of private acts, so routinely practiced by law enforcers, is not recognized by the law. If criminal violence, according to the Comaroffs, "does not so much repudiate the rule of law or the licit operations of the market as appropriate their forms" (2006: 5), what accounts for a rule of law that mimics criminal violence?

The use of renegade militants to fight insurgent groups or the financing of new insurgent groups to counter existing ones is a well-tested tactic of the Indian government, as of governments across the world. In Punjab, during the late 1980s and early 1990s, a legislator noted that "the government agencies had been creating many armed vigilante groups out of anti-social riff raff, so as to infiltrate and neutralize genuine militant outfits. The outrages they committed were routinely blamed on the separatist groups" (Kumar and Singh 2003: 105). Sometimes, the same activities were carried out by police in plain clothes, or police informers called Cats dressed as militants, as this testimony shows:

> That on the intervening night of 8–10–1991 and 9–10–1991 at about 1 am a Police party in civil clothes came to the Complainant's house and woke up the Complainant and her husband namely Bachan Singh who were sleeping in the Verandah of the house. They took away Bachan Singh into the courtyard and shot him dead in front of the Complainant. They also raised slogans of "Bole So Nihal" in order to impress upon the Complainant that the alleged killers were not Policemen but they were rather militants. (VFF/0259, VFF/0260, VFF/0261, reproduced in Voices for Freedom 2007: 286)

In Andhra Pradesh, where many of the Naxalite leaders originate, and where there is a strong human rights movement that has meticulously recorded extrajudicial killings over the years, the government has deliberately encouraged private killer gangs not just to target the Naxalites but also to suppress any questioning of their illegalities by human rights groups. A letter by the Human Rights Forum in Andhra Pradesh to the home minister of the state (September 1, 2005) brings out the degree of state complicity:

> For the last one decade the State has been hearing of and seeing killer gangs describing themselves by various names such as Green Tigers, Tirumala Tigers, Kranti Sena, etc. Now we are hearing of Narsa Cobras and Kakatiya Cobras. Threats are publicly being issued by these outfits, mainly to persons working in civil rights organisations or various mass organisations alleged by these outfits to be close to the Naxalites. That these are not idle pranksters is attested to by the fact that a number of murders have been owned up by these outfits saying that they have committed the murders.
>
> Green Tigers claimed to have killed Sri T. Purushotham of Andhra Pradesh Civil Liberties Committee (APCLC) in the year 2000 and Azam Ali in the year 2001. Someone calling himself Singamalai of Tirumala Tigers claimed to have kidnapped and tortured Dr. G. Laxman of APCLC in 2004. The Kranti Sena claimed to have killed a number of rural supporters of the Peoples War in the 1990s.
>
> Though this has been going on for more than a decade now, the government's response has been a deafening silence. Who are these faceless gangs? How can the government of any civilized country turn a blind eye to the presence of self-proclaimed killer groups in the midst of society? How is it that the government has not a word to say about them? In the case of the Naxalites, the police do a thorough investigation and have in their possession all the personal details of the leaders and the cadre of the Naxalite groups. A hunt goes on for them day and night. Many are arrested and some are killed. But how is it that by contrast there is no whisper from the government or the police about these gangs? It is as if they do not read the papers and have never seen the claims these outfits make to the authorship of crimes of violence, and the threats they hold out to activists.
>
> Would it be unfair to conclude from this that the government is not unhappy to have these vigilante gangs around? Perhaps because what the government cannot directly do, these anonymous killer gangs can, and the

government, if challenged, can pretend to be busily investigating the matter. In all the crimes of violence listed above, some investigation has been done, some individuals have been charged, and tried and acquitted by the courts. But there is not a word about the gangs themselves.

Elsewhere, the Human Rights Forum writes that these killer gangs were composed of former Naxalites who, encouraged by the state, had taken to crime. The police also contacted people within the party and paid them to kill their comrades. In addition to killing Naxalites and civil rights defenders, they were allowed to act as mafia, settling private disputes over land, and giving the police a cut of the money. While the police claimed that the people in gangs were victims of Naxalite violence, a possibility that the Human Rights Forum did not rule out, given the high levels of Naxalite violence on people they consider informers, they add:

> Often, the abusive phone calls made by the Cobras has revealed awareness of facts that only the police know. Secondly, threats in the name of Cobras or from anonymous persons from the areas where these gangs operate have been issued pursuant to injury or insult caused to the police or to old favourites of the police. Thirdly, the police are gleefully inactive in the face of the increasingly blatant violence in the name of the Cobras. (Letter from Human Rights Forum to other human rights groups in the country, 2005, personal collection)

In the northeast of the country, as well as in Kashmir, both of which have a proliferation of insurgency outfits, the line between who is supported by the state and who opposes it and why continues to be thin. By one estimate, there are 109 armed rebel groups in the northeast, of which 40 operate out of one state, Manipur, alone. The organizations are distinguished by ethnic composition, by whether they are "active" or "inactive," whether they are banned or not (South Asia Terrorism Portal, cited in Baruah 2007: 9). As Baruah writes, "Not all armed groups are rebels. For instance, many locals believe that some of them have come into being at the behest of security and intelligence agencies combating insurgency. Although it is hard to confirm such charges, warfare between rival militias—especially following ceasefire agreements signed by a militia faction and the security forces—sometimes neatly serves official counterinsurgency ends of the moment" (Baruah 2007: 9). The existence of such multiple groups also helps the government to keep in place the Armed Forces Special Powers Act of 1958, under which the army has sweeping powers to shoot and kill civilians on mere suspicion, with almost complete immunity from prosecution. As several civil liberties groups have pointed out, the act has been singularly ineffective in terms of its stated objectives of ensuring peace, since under its regime, the number of insurgent groups has gone up hugely. However, this explosion of groups is seen by the government as one reason why the act can never be repealed, since there is no one major group it can negotiate with. The proliferation of these groups also keeps public insecurity at a constant pitch—not only are they vulnerable to arbitrary arrests, killings, and frisking by the police but also face "taxation" by the insurgent groups and restrictions on their movements.

Conclusion

If one allows that liberal legality always involves a tension between legal and discretionary forms of violence (Huysmans 2004: 328; see also Derrida 1992), governments have to justify this discretion as being in the name of the political community as a whole. In other words, they have to argue that democracy is being violated for its own sake (see Singh 2007 on how extraordinary emergency laws are justified).

Unlike counterinsurgency under military rule, in the Indian context counterinsurgency efforts underpinned by vigilantism are positively celebrated as a defense of democracy, a flowering of plural (progovernment) sentiments, or "local resistance groups" against the tyrannies of the Maoists. A similar logic also applies to the BJP justification of the Babri Masjid demolition—as an act of resistance to the alleged fifteenth-century Mughal demolition of the Ram temple and the subsequent support of the postcolonial state for the status quo. "Democracy" thus comes to take on a specific character, requiring the creation of a new political community, if necessary by suppressing the political choices that people have actually made. In "states of exception," this tendency is enhanced, as when the top police chief of Chhattisgarh says that the only problem in the government's war against the Maoists is that the people support the Maoists. Differences with the state are externalized onto civil society, through "people's movements" like the Salwa Judum, "nonstate" associations that mesh seamlessly with the state, and which oppose genuine people's movements. As Huysmans says: "rather than a technique of mediating the gap between an existing people and political elite, representation becomes a technique through which the leaders call into being a people" (Huysmans

2004: 333). Samaddar argues that this tendency is especially visible in post-colonial societies like India, with their legacy of authoritarian laws meant to control the natives: "colonial constitutionalism" oscillates between "a Rousseauistic consent-governed theme" where the state represents the will of the people, and the spirit of "constitutional engineering" (which meant constructing elaborate rules for domesticating disobedience of an unruly society and putting a hazardous polity in order) (Samaddar 2007: 25).

Even as the state claims universalism, its everyday practice is meshed with opportunist support for vigilantism. Mob violence by fronts of the BJP and Congress are routinized as "joint common enterprises," and spokespersons for both parties routinely appear on TV accusing each other of genocide (in 1984 and 2002), with no legal action whatsoever being taken or expected. In the case of Salwa Judum, there is no pretence even at enacting the charade of parliamentary democracy, where the ruling party and the opposition are meant to act as checks on each other. Both are united against the people.

In the public-private partnerships that create insecurity in India, the logic of private vigilantism acting together with state support plays itself out to create a particular kind of state of exception: one, as Agamben noted, that was marked by the force of law, a situation where law is *deliberately* suspended (as against its everyday suspension in application) but simultaneously enforced (Agamben 2005: 59). Private vigilantism represents a particular kind of enforcement, and coupled with the use of security laws directed only at certain sections of the population (Muslims but not Hindus, even when the latter have been found to be involved in terrorist acts; Maoists but not politicians who incite mobs to kill), and a partisan media, can effectively distance certain sections of the population from everyday citizenship. Even as some individuals are drawn into the orbit of the state, others are silenced, because the enemies are now from within their own communities, their neighbors, or people they used to know. Dividing publics is particularly effective, since it reduces the possibility of framing alternatives to such states of exception, and restoring the rule of law. Just as in the invocation of the "ancient hatreds" that divide Shias and Sunnis to deflect questions regarding the American occupation of Iraq, the state's creation of counterinsurgent groups in the northeast of India is used to justify its draconian laws and security operations, and create the image of an amorphous hydra where no negotiated settlement is possible because there is no singular other to talk to.

These "partnerships" between the state and certain sections of society in acts of vigilantism mirror the logic of neoliberal "public-private partnerships" in specific ways. As with privatization, and sweetheart deals, which may benefit some corporates and politicians, but disadvantages low-level workers who are thrown out of a job, the state here, rather than "rolling back," rolls sideways into civil society, reorganizing itself in terms not just of its administrative boundaries but also of the social background of the forces it represents. Saying that both sides benefit through PPPs is not enough—we need to specify the actors who benefit through such arrangements. Under private vigilantism of the Salwa Judum kind, criminal leaders often work directly with the more powerful elements of the state and industry to acquire land, in the process marginalizing more lowly employees of the government, who are entrusted with the everyday task of documentation, and whose jobs may be on the line should the state ever decide to assert legality. The proliferation of (nonideological) insurgent groups at the behest of the state may help the counterinsurgency apparatus to expand its power, but reduces the room that ordinary people, even legislators, have to engage in ideology-based politics. Some informers use state patronage to eliminate private rivals, thus harnessing public ends to private means (see also Kalyvas 2006).

On a long-term and structural level, rather than bringing the strengths of both parties to a partnership, PPPs in state-mob violence reduce the strength of each party to the arrangement, and the outcome is widespread public insecurity and lack of accountability. Not only does the state lose long-term legitimacy, but the bonds of solidarity often identified as part of civil society are weakened, with mutual mistrust spiralling between citizens and suspected informers. From Hobbes to Agamben, the social contract is suspended when the state is no longer able to provide security. "The obligation of subjects to the sovereign is understood to last as long and no longer than the power lasts by which he is able to protect them. For the right men have by nature to protect themselves when none else can protect them can by no covenant be relinquished" (Hobbes [1651] 1958: 179). The alternative, for Agamben, to the force of law, is "civil war and revolutionary violence" (Agamben 2005: 59).

But revolutionary violence itself—through its renegades and doubles—turns inward and begins to feed on itself in the face of state divisiveness. The state's relentless molding of individuals into its own image as power flows along networks of patronage and spoils creates rent-seeking corrupted individuals to match a rent-seeking corrupted state. Who then will prosecute the revolutionary civil war and in whose name?

Notes

1   The renegades go by the names of Cats in Punjab, Tigers and Cobras in Andhra Pradesh, as well as Ikhwan (tr. "brothers") in Kashmir and SULFA (Surrendered United Liberation Front of Assam) in Assam. For some reason, animal imagery appears to be popular with the police.

2   See Gossman 2000; Kumar and Singh 2003 on Punjab; Voices for Freedom 2007; Nanda Talukdar Foundation and Human Rights Law Network 2009.

3   For example, front groups of the Hindu Right have attacked art exhibitions by India's best-known artist, M. F. Hussain, for depicting Hindu goddesses in the nude, and a Congress-supported gang attacked the Bhandarkar Research Institute in Pune for assisting scholar James Laine in his revisionist reading of the Marathi political icon Sivaji.

4   In 1984 the massacres were portrayed as a popular reaction to the killing of Prime Minister Indira Gandhi by her guards. Her son (and future prime minister) Rajiv Gandhi famously said, "When a big tree falls, the ground will shake." In 2002, Narendra Modi, Gujarat's chief minister, justified the genocide of Muslims as a response to the burning of a train coach in which fifty-eight Hindu *kar sevaks* (Hindu activists) died, quoting Newton as saying "every action breeds a reaction."

5   In 2007 the CPI (M) government in West Bengal justified its cadres attacking villagers who were resisting land acquisition on the grounds that they were upholding state sovereignty.

6   Congress resolution reproduced in the *Collected Works* of Mahatma Gandhi (*CWMG*), 97: 480. I am grateful to Dilip Simeon for bringing this to my attention.

7   The RSS has no formal membership but works through *shakhas*, or places where boys and men meet for an hour a day to do physical exercise and military style drill, which includes training in martial arts and learning to wield a stick or a knife, ostensibly for self-defense. They also receive ideological training.

8   Estimates of the People's Liberation Guerrilla Army, which was formed in 2000, suggest that they have about 7,300 weapons for 10,500 armed cadre nationwide, a 25,000-strong people's militia, and 50,000 members in village-level units. Showing how figures of Maoist arms and incidents of attack belie the threat they constitute in the security imagination is not to say, however, that the Maoists do not see themselves as a serious armed challenge. The Maoist fetishisation of militarism is

connected to their goal of capturing state power through armed struggle. The combination of Maoist self-projections as a significant military force and government projections of them as the greatest security threat make it difficult for independent observers to point out the limited nature of the Maoist military threat.

9   The government translates this Gondi word as peace campaign; other Gondi speakers, however, insist that it really means a "purification hunt." The imagery of vermin and extermination is more in keeping with the language used by the government and unthinking journalists to describe areas of Naxalite influence: "Naxalite infested areas."

10   Nandini Sundar, Ramachandra Guha and EAS Sarma vs. State of Chhattisgarh, WP (Civil) 250/2007; Kartam Joga, Manish Kunjam and Dudhi Joga vs. State of Chhattisgarh and Union of India, WP (Cr.) 119/2007.

11   Nandini Sundar and Ors, Judgment by Justice Sudershan Reddy and Justice S. S. Nijjar, July 5, 2011.

References

Agamben, G. 2005. *State of Exception.* Translated by Kevin Attell. Chicago: University of Chicago Press.

Baruah, Sanjib. 2007. *Postfrontier Blues: Toward a New Policy Framework for Northeast India.* Washington, D.C.: East West Center.

Brass, Paul. 2004. "Development of an Institutionalised Riot System in Meerut City, 1961 to 1982." *Economic and Political Weekly*, October 30, 2004, 4,839–4,848.

Campbell, Bruce. 2000. "Death Squads: Definitions, Problems and Historical Context." In Bruce B. Campbell and Arthur D. Brenner, eds., *Death Squads in Global Perspective: Murder with Deniability*, 1–26. New York: Palgrave Macmillan.

Comaroff, J., and Comaroff, J. 2006. "Law and Disorder in the Postcolony: An Introduction." In J. Comaroff and J. Comaroff, eds., *Law and Disorder in the Postcolony*, 1–56. Chicago: University of Chicago Press.

Derrida, Jacques. 1992. "Force of Law: 'The Mystical Foundation of Authority.'" In Drucilla Cornell, Michel Rosenfeld, and David Gray Carlson, eds. *Deconstruction and the Possibility of Justice*, 3–67. New York: Routledge.

District Collector, Dantewada. 2005. "Work Proposal for the Jan Jagran Abhiyan." Typed manuscript. Dantewada District Collectorate, Chhattisgarh.

Duffield, M. 2005. *Global Governance and the New Wars: The Merging of Development and Security*. London: Zed.

Gandhi, M. K. *Collected Works of Mahatma Gandhi (CWMG)*, Vol. 97. 2001. New Delhi: Government of India Publication Division.

Gramsci, A. 1971. "State and Civil Society." In Quintin Hoare and Geoffrey Nowell Smith, eds., *Selections from the Prison Notebooks*. 206–276. New York: International Publishers.

Gupta, A., and Sharma, A. 2006 "Globalisation and Postcolonial States." *Current Anthropology* 47(2): 277–304.

Gossman, Patricia. 2000. "India's Secret Armies." In Bruce B. Campbell and Arthur D. Brenner, eds., *Death Squads in Global Perspective: Murder with Deniability*, 261–286. New York: Palgrave Macmillan.

Harvey, David. 2003. *The New Imperialism*. New York: Oxford University Press.

Hobbes, Thomas. [1651] 1958, 1961. *Leviathan,* Parts I and II. Edited by Herbert W. Schneider. Peterborough, Ont.: Broadview.

Huysmans, J. 1998. "Security! What Do You Mean? From Concept to Thick Signifier." *European Journal of International Relations* 4(2):226–255.

———. 2004. "Minding Exceptions: The Politics of Insecurity and Liberal Democracy." *Contemporary Political Theory* 3:321–341.

Kalyvas, Stathis. 2006. *The Logic of Violence in Civil War.* Cambridge: Cambridge University Press.

Kumar, Ram Narayan, and Amrik Singh. 2003. *Reduced to Ashes: The Insurgency and Human Rights in Punjab*. Kathmandu: South Asia Forum for Human Rights.

Liberhan, Manmohan Singh. 2009. *Report of the Liberhan Ayodhya Commission of Enquiry*. New Delhi: Government of India, Ministry of Home Affairs, http://mha.gov.in/uniquepage.asp?Id_Pk=571.

Marx, Karl. [1887] 1983. *Capital: A Critique of Political Economy, Vol. I.* London: Lawrence and Wishhart.

Ministry of Home Affairs, Government of India. 2003–2004. *Annual Report*. New Delhi.

Nanda Talukdar Foundation and Human Rights Law Network. 2009. *Secret Killings of Assam*. Guwahati and New Delhi: Nanda Talukdar Foundation and Human Rights Law Network.

Noorani, A. G. 2000. *The RSS and the BJP: A Division of Labour*. New Delhi: Leftword Books.

Osborne, Stephen P. 2000. *Public-Private Partnerships: Theory and Practice in International Perspective*. London: Routledge.

Rajagopal, Arvind. 2001. *Politics after Television: Hindu Nationalism and the Reshaping of the Public in India*. Cambridge: Cambridge University Press.

Samaddar, Ranabir. 2007. *Technologies of Rule*. London: Anthem Press.

Savas, E. S. 2000. *Privatization and Public Private Partnerships*. New York: Seven Bridges Press.

Sen, Atreyee, and David Pratten. 2007. "Global Vigilantes: Perspectives on Justice and Violence." In David Pratten and Atreyee Sen, eds., *Global Vigilantes*, 1–24. London: Hurst.

Singer, P. W. 2008. *Corporate Warriors: The Rise of the Privatized Military Industry*. Ithaca: Cornell University Press.

Singh, U. 2007. *The State, Democracy and Anti-Terror Laws in India*. New Delhi: Sage.

Sundar, Nandini. 2006. "Adivasi vs. Vanvasi: The Politics of Cconversion and Re-conversion in Central India." In Satish Saberwal and Mushirul Hasan, eds., *Assertive Religious Identities*, 357–390. New Delhi: Manohar.

Voices for Freedom. 2007. *Smoldering Embers*. Charleston, S.C.: Booksurge.

Weber, M. 1970. *From Max Weber: Essays in Sociology*. Edited by H. H. Gerth and C. Wright Mills. London: Routledge and Kegan Paul.

CHAPTER SEVEN

Does Globalization Breed Ethnic Violence?

Georgi M. Derluguian

The discussions of globalization's darker side assume a direct causal link between the central process of global integration and the peripheral reactions presumably manifest in ethnic violence, organized crime, and religiously motivated terrorism. The prevalent interpretations in scholarly and especially in the public political discourse typically evoke the long-running tropes of cultural difference and social psychology. Depending on political perspective, the unsettling effects are then blamed either on Western imperial arrogance and capitalist greed or, conversely, the maladjustment of Third World societies to market discipline and liberal cosmopolitan modernity.

This polemic suggests that, after a hiatus of nearly a quarter century, the problems of world underdevelopment and its discontents once again emerge centrally on the agenda. And once again we are confronted with essentially the old question: does modernization breed revolutions and the dangers of totalitarianism? Today it is rather phrased like this: does globalization breed violent anti-Enlightenment reactions? Can democracy take a root in non-Western societies? Remarkably, it is the same Samuel Huntington, whose darkly prophetic *Clash of Civilizations* (1995) established the conservative stance on the jeopardies of globalization, that, at the peak of Vietnam war, posed this question regarding modernization in his influential monograph *Political Order in Changing Societies* (1968).

Back in the early seventies, Charles Tilly vigorously responded to Huntington's challenge and demonstrated that revolutions tended to arise from far more complex historical causality than merely modernization. The same now applies to globalization. This hegemonic locution is too broad, fuzzy, and slippery—just as modernization before it—to provide us with a useful frame for analysis. Taking inspiration in Tilly's classic "Does Modernization Breed Revolution?" (1973), I want to extend the arguments in two directions. One is Immanuel Wallerstein's world-systems perspective. Here we can obtain a meaningful explanation to the question of why the collapse of developmentalist state projects produced such a massive recoil to peripheral patterns. Furthermore, I use the concepts of habitus and social capital developed by Pierre Bourdieu to bring back into the focus of analysis the class dimension of global social organization.

The goal is not to join the debates on globalization or terrorism in their present form. Instead, the goal is to reframe the arguments, suggest a synthetically theorized alternative explanation, and above all to invite further discussion among the social scientists concerned with the ongoing world transformation. Admittedly, these are no small claims. Therefore I outline up front the alternative perspective, followed by the brief demonstration of how it might work in explaining the patterns of Soviet disintegration. We might then be able to discuss how common these patterns are elsewhere in the world.

Alternative Explanation

Globalization serves the all-encompassing locution of the contemporary hegemonic discourse. It directly refers to the revived teleology of market-driven economic progress that presumably should produce a cascading self-propellant dynamic across all other social arenas. In particular, the rhetoric of globalization optimistically misrepresents as a new beginning the catastrophic end of the erstwhile industrializing states of socialist as well as national liberation variety. In these locales, the waning of developmentalist hopes, the erosion of central governance, and the introduction of competitive elections and privatization unleashed principally two kinds of adaptive strategies. Their combinations, embedded in historical contexts, largely account for the outcomes registered across the reemerging peripheries. The first strategy, pursued by the bureaucratic elites and the ascendant political interlopers, is corrupt patronage that relies on privatizing the state offices, or what the Weberian scholars call neopatrimonialism (Eisenstadt 1973; Jowitt 1992). It is conducive to comprador oligarchies, weakened states, and the decay and criminalization of civil societies. The second reactive strategy seeks to mobilize ethnic and religious solidarities (rather than merely identities). Objectively, it is directed against what Polanyi (1944), referring to the nineteenth-century wave of globalization, called the market destruction of the substance of local societies. But subjectively, the evocation of traditional communities tends to scapegoat other ethnic communities, weak corrupt governments, and, increasingly, the global American "plutocracy."

The violent ethnic politics of recent years did not arise in a direct reaction to globalization. Rather, these were desperate and particularist attempts to cope with the worldwide wave of dismantling the developmental regimes (see Evans 1995, ch.10) which in extreme examples amounted to the collapse of states (Bunce 1998; Reno 1998). These states became impossible to sustain, and thus they were abandoned by their ruling elites because they could no longer deliver on the main legitimating promise of progress and national development, that is, the fairly rapid equalization of socioeconomic conditions in their countries with those of core capitalist states.

To put it differently, the peoples of former Yugoslavia, the Chechens and Abkhazes in the Caucasus, the warlord factions in the Congo, and the Islamist radicals in Algeria went into fighting not over the ancient animosities or in defense of their cultural identities challenged by the new big "McWorld" (see Barber 1996; and its critique by Beck, Greer, and Ragin 2000). They all fought, fight, and will fight, in different ways, over what to do about their suddenly delegitimated states and the drastically devalued modern economies that these states once nurtured and sheltered. Moreover, the conflicts are fought over the gravely serious issues of who will profit, who will bear the costs, and who will support whom in the new system of capitalist property rights.

Yet ethnic violence is neither an automatic reaction rooted in the historically consecrated collective identities nor, in fact, is it the first choice of the people who might get involved in such violence. Their likelier first choice would be democratization, albeit not the "shallow" democratization limited to the electoral procedure and competition among the elite actors. It is rather the "deep"—a hard-nosed realist would say utopian—social democratization that seeks to open a broadly equitable access to the flows of power and goods, give voice to and ensure the self-management rights of the work, residential, and cultural communities. Historically, this has been a predominantly proletarian agenda of democratization in modern Western states (Rueschemeyer et al. 1992). In the past, it could coalesce in some political form in the situations where wage laborers, from manual workers to the educated wage-earning specialists, found themselves in a position to effectively lay claims on modern states. This became structurally possible in the late nineteenth century, and especially after the depression of the 1930s and the world wars of 1914–1945, when proletarians came to prevail among the core states' military recruits, employees, and voting citizens.

Even more than in the core capitalist states, analogous structural conditions for proletarian democratization were created in the Soviet Union and later in many other revolutionary industrializing states. Arguably, for the time of their duration these states remained the evolving postrevolutionary dictatorships that practiced the propagandistic dissimulation of people's democracy. Nevertheless, the shortage economy of rapidly industrializing states also created a constant need for worker enthusiasm and microgroup autonomy to overcome anarchy in production (or, for that matter, in fighting serious wars), while the party-state apparatus at the point of production rendered transparent the actual exercise of power and class inequalities (Burawoy and Lukács 1992).

It has been a long-standing Trotskyist expectation that socialist proletarians will eventually rebel against the state bureaucracy (Deutscher 1953). This prediction, though not entirely wrong, willfully overlooked two other possibilities. First, that the less ideologically committed fractions of technocratic managers could dump the defunct ideology, turn the state assets that they administered into privately or corporately owned capital, and seek profitable alliances with the global capitalist partners (see Eyal, Szelényi, and Townsley 1998; Solnick 1998; Woodruff 1999; and King 2001). The second possibility is that the industrializing state can simply collapse, which removes the main object of proletarian claim making and the key condition of democratization. State breakdown makes it likely there will be lateral struggles among shifting coalitions of locally embedded contenders. These are commonly viewed as ethnic conflicts because enterprising patrons, emerging from all ranks of society, advertise their intention to protect a particular community. This is what the Serbian communist apparatchik Milosevic did at the famous 1987 rally in Kosovo, the rogue Soviet General Dudayev did in 1991 in Chechnya, and various ragtag warlords did in Africa. It is a central message in al-Qaeda's propaganda of global jihad.

Still, why are these conflicts ethnic? Few alternatives remain after the agenda of state-bound democratization became pointless, because of the evident erosion of state institutions; because the state-created industrial assets and bureaucracies, which embedded the existence of proletarian groups, turned into liability in the face of global markets; and because structural unemployment now verges on permanent lumpenization. The Serbs, Chechens, Algerians or, for that matter, the presumably quiescent Chinese, do not have much in common except that they all live in world locales that are incompletely industrialized and only partially and recently urbanized, and thus where the modern formal institutions are often superficial or downright superfluous (Woodruff 2000). In such locales they know from daily practice how much one's life chances depend on the access to various patrons and informal networks. And when these people become convinced that they face the prospect of marginalization in the new, competitive-restrictive set of arrangements, they sometimes fight back—if they can find a mobilizing platform.

Collective Actors

If the preceding arguments seem provocative, here is the central claim: class matters crucially in explaining today's ethnic conflicts. The enshrined triad of race-gender-class in reality treats social classes as an afterthought, the residual category inherited from the not-too-distant past when Karl Marx was regarded a canonical pioneer of social analysis. Powerful criticisms have since been leveled against the Marxist scheme which was, granted, at the same time quite rigid, economistic, and faithfully deterministic. But what heuristic utility survives from the notion of class? Instead of plunging into the abstract debates regarding social categorization or the comparative merits of Marxist versus the Weberian approaches to stratification, let me try to demonstrate how class might be still salient. In doing this, I will be borrowing conceptual tools from Pierre Bourdieu who, himself being a trenchant critic of Marxist orthodoxy, in fact has shown perhaps the most promising ways of extending the critical analysis of society. In his lifetime Bourdieu was predominantly concerned with France. I am going to sketch here the social structure of my own native society, which was once engendered and contained within the mighty jurisdiction called the Soviet Union. By showing how Bourdieu's variety of class analysis might apply to the realities of Eastern Europe before and after the collapse of communist rule, I also hope to demonstrate the utility of this approach to the contemporary world.

The Ruling Bureaucracy

The fundamental condition of our world is that over the last century it came to be ruled by bureaucrats. States immediately come to mind—but let us not forget the economic corporations which are, in essence, bureaucratic organizations designed to organize and control market niches. In the Soviet experience, economic corporations were fused with the command structures of state and single party. Moreover, their key rationale was not profit expressed in monetary terms but rather the creation of economic assets that could be deployed for the purposes of defense, enhancing the state's international prestige, and managing its population, who doubled as state employees and army recruits. Emerging from a brutal civil war and designed for the geopolitical climate of world wars, the Soviet developmentalism was of a distinctly military-industrial variety. In this, it was remarkably successful, as attested by the victory in 1945 against the formidable machinery of Nazi Germany followed by the sustained Cold War competition against the vastly richer America.

But was the USSR capitalist? In retrospect, this once burning question seems redundant. The USSR, like all other developmental states from Japan and fascist Italy to Turkey, and all sorts of import-substituting or export-oriented dictatorships across the Third World, functioned as the collective vehicle of power that the ruling elites of various peripheral countries constructed in the course of the twentieth century. The original kind of profit was expressed in the collective good that, to use a Weberian term, might be called power-prestige. This collective asset engendered various privileges for those in the commanding heights of the developmental state. The privileges carried the temptation of making them private, legally guaranteed, portable, and inheritable. In theory, bureaucrats are employees like anybody else in the social organization of modern mass production, except that they work from behind their special desks. But since these desks are special in possessing the power of decision making, various opportunities emerge that are commonly called corruption. And corruption is a dangerous strategy because it is, at least in principle, punishable by superiors and because it provokes the ire of those located lower in the same hierarchy. Thus the elite feels impelled to promote privatization and democratic elections—albeit always bounded and conditional in order to secure the safe transition from public service to private elite status. These strategies might be meaningfully conceptualized in Bourdieu's terms as conversions of capital: the administrative social capital of positions, connections, and insider knowledge of power converted into the political capital of decision making and into business opportunities through privatization. In the actual political history of recent decades, things did not always look as straightforward. Transitions from one form of power to another are bound to be messy and fraught with many dangers because elite actors viciously compete among themselves on the way to exit; because grievous mistakes of overestimation and delusion happen when pursuing ideological utopias; and, moreover, because other members of society might also see their utopian opportunities and dangers in the moments of transition.

Proletariat

Ironically, this designation fell in ideological disrepute precisely when the proletarianization was at its historical height across the world. Who wants to be called a proletarian? Yet, I suspect, the majority of us are proletarian in a crucial measure: our livelihoods depend on regular wages, because incomes from commerce, farming, rents or, for that matter, corruption are not available. The vast centralization of the Soviet industrial state created the historical situation in which a majority of the population became proletarianized, especially in big towns. This condition extended from the "classical" shop-floor workers to the service employees such as clerks or hairdressers, and to the highly educated specialists like engineers, medical doctors, and educators—all in the formal employment of the state. Everywhere in the world, regardless the ideological formulations of power, proletarization has been growing apace with the extension of the bureaucratic organization of state, economy, and social reproduction.

The crucial feature of contemporary proletariats is that they are typically controlled not by individual capitalist owners but rather by the impersonal bureaucratic hierarchies. Hence the political vector against hierarchical regimentation of work and life that first became apparent in the student revolts of 1968—if you wish, the first revolution that owed more to Max Weber than to Karl Marx. In Eastern Europe, the youthful activism of the 1960s played an especially explicit role in undermining the erstwhile structures of bureaucratic control—even if by their symbolic delegitimation rather than immediate destruction. These events become understandable if we move from the ideological rhetoric of civil society to the analysis of social capital held by the rising generation of young specialists.

In 1968, the first surge of political activity to update the institutions of bureaucratic control took the form predominantly of a democratic movement, mainly because the all-encompassing hold of the Communist Party over production and social life was preventing the new intelligentsia from deploying its technical capabilities effectively and from gaining status and power commensurate with its growing significance. The bureaucratic power of ruling communist parties, however, proved stronger and more resilient. This is why the unfinished business of 1968 had to be vigorously resumed in 1989 and conducted with a "wind of madness" that has been perceptible in the revolutionaries' adherence to the least plausible of ideologies—namely, the monetarist ideology of ruthless "economizing" as the road to the wealth and power of the West (Arrighi, Hopkins, and Wallerstein, 2001). Here I would observe that the deployment of neoliberalism by East European revolutionaries against what to them was their old régime should not seem such a paradox, given that these Soviet-made and alienated intelligentsia nurtured a deep distrust of any bureaucracy; in the dichotomous vision of Cold War they regarded the West as their ideal and sought to convert the existing ideological paradigm of state socialism to its complete opposite.

What the forces of change did not realize in 1989 was that the road of neoliberal reform or what was then called economic shock therapy was leading them—or at least most of them—not to the promised land of North America but to the harsher realities of South America or worse. Instead of harnessing industrial conflict to the democratization of political institutions and the restructuring of economy toward a more stable social-democratic regime like in Spain after the death of Franco, the majority of East Europeans faced a severe decline if not a destruction of state powers and thereby the state's contradictory founding counterpart, civil society. The popular reactions to this new harsh situation ranged from frustration and cynicism to promises of building alternative moral communities as the loci of primary loyalty and protection that could be offered, at least in the short run, by a nationalist movement's replication of stateness and a fundamentalist movement's negation of stateness. In between, however, came various intermediate alternatives that integrate people "outside the law" (and thereby outside civil society) and become centers for all manner of illegal relational activities, whose spheres of circulation reach throughout the larger society and often abroad, as well. These are societies mostly closed to outsiders and known today by such names as "the mafia," "shanty towns," "inner cities," "drug-lord domains," "warlord fiefs," and so on.

Subproletarians, the Awkward "Non-class"

A crucial marker of peripheral social structure is the prevalence of subproletarians. Referring to his early Algerian experience, Bourdieu (1973; 1994: 21–24) admitted to the particular elusiveness, yet crucial importance, of the subproletariat category. Bourdieu emphasized the short time horizon of the subproletarian habitus and the underlying violence, which he related to the generalized unpredictability of subproletarian existence. This observation meshes well with Stinchcombe's (1997) argument that institutionalization extends the range of the predictable future.

This awkward "residual" class differs from proletarians in the crucial measure of wages that do *not* provide the basis of subproletarian household income, even though wages are occasionally earned. Other incomes are derived from multiple sources: subsistence production, various "informal" (untaxed) market profits, gains from criminal activity, gifts, and charities (Portes and Böröcz 1988). Since the subproletarians are historically and geographically a very motley category, let me describe some localized examples.

The subproletarians are not necessarily paupers from shantytowns, though certainly many are very poor, and they normally live in haphazardly built family homes with garden patches and chickens roaming in the backyard. The disorganized lives of subproletarians episodically offer various opportunities, though the associated hazards might seem excessive to people with more stable social positions. Today on the outskirts of any big city in Eastern Europe, one sees new ostentatious houses with Mercedes-Benzes in the driveways that serve as the flashy manifestations of violent entrepreneurs rising from the Soviet-era shadow economy (many of these cars were stolen in Germany and resold through a chain of intermediaries). Such opportunities for subproletarians were, and remain, principally of two kinds: semilegal labor migrations to zones offering higher wages (Siberian oilfields, the metropolitan economy of Moscow, and now the West) and various forms of smuggling, from early fruits produced in households to that most profitable of all agricultural produce, illicit drugs. Such skills and connections constitute the typical social capital of subproletarians.

Several differences between the proletarians and subproletarians are readily apparent. Subproletarians seem more "ethnic" than do the workers who have experienced the leveling effect of an urban industrial lifestyle. Subproletarians tend to have large patriarchal families. In the Caucasus and Central

Asia, the large size of families is usually considered a Muslim tradition, but it also serves as a demographic strategy to maximize household labor and social capital (acknowledged in several interviews). Among fighters in the recent ethnic wars, a strikingly large number came from subproletarian families with several sons.

A crucial difference between proletarians and subproletarians is how they relate to the state. For the post-Soviet proletarians, the state remains the key provider of social structure and benefits. Subproletarians, by contrast, regard the state as a nuisance if not a threat, represented by greedy police and street-level officials, the "jackals." Avoidance of the state is their daily sneaky strategy. But in the times of state breakdown, the subproletarian masses could raise their "street" or "crowd" voice.

Exiting the Developmental State

Let me now put this scheme into historical perspective and sketch how as the USSR collapsed, a range of nationalist strategies were produced in its wake. The outcomes could be explained in the main as the complex, historically structured, yet still often contingent *pas-de-trois* of bureaucrats, highly educated proletarians, and the usually "invisible" subproletarians.

First of all, why did the supposedly totalitarian regime agree to give up its control over society? Perhaps because totalitarianism is just an ideological construct that posits an immovable tyranny where none could exist. Historians (for an update and very wise summary, see Lewin 2005) have demonstrated how unstable communist rule was at any moment in its history. Three sorts of pressures continuously destabilized all developmental states, whether Leninist or not. The first was interstate competition against the much stronger Western powers that kept Soviet rulers perennially feeling inferior and defensive. The second was the typical tendency of bureaucrats to entrench their positions and limit the scope of intervention by their superiors. Finally, the complex effects of social dynamics unleashed by the industrial transformation exerted pressure—and how could it be otherwise in a country that began the twentieth century with a predominantly agrarian and illiterate population and ended with one of the highest rates of urbanization and education in the world?

In the 1950s, under Khrushchev's bold if rambunctious leadership, the Soviet bureaucracy undertook their self-emancipation from the dread of Stalinist terror and the inhuman workloads imposed during industrialization and war. The effect, however, was to unleash escalating expectations in the society at large, especially among the educated specialists concentrated in big towns. Two kinds of towns existed in the USSR: the industrial centers where ethnic mixing was occurring on the basis of Russian language and modern culture, and the capitals of Soviet ethnic republics, which were subject to the Leninist variety of affirmative action. Correspondingly, we obtain two kinds of educated specialists with different composition of social capital and politics vectors. While in big industrial towns the new intelligentsia pursued essentially social-democratic project of collective bargaining for benefits and making their managers accountable, in the capitals of national republics it was rather the new national intelligentsias who sought greater cultural and artistic autonomy from central government and the right to lead their national communities. The combination of three vectors—technocratic reformism, the social-democratization of generic "scientists and engineers," and the cultural demands of national artistic intelligentsia—produced the effervescence of Eastern Europe in 1968, in the USSR as well as in Czechoslovakia, Poland, and Yugoslavia.

The dramatic events of 1989 were so transformative and sweeping precisely because they had their dress rehearsal in 1968. The intervening conservative reign of Brezhnev's generation could not last forever (even if it appeared so at the time) because it could not solve any of the structural challenges that had brought the experimentation of the 1960s in the first place: keeping up with America, dismantling the political structure inherited from Stalinism, or making the midlevel bureaucrats more accountable and dynamic. Hence Andropov's reforms from above soon followed by Gorbachev's perestroika.

What does this have to do with explaining ethnic conflicts of the nineties? A lot, in fact. One cannot understand why these conflicts arose without first explaining why nationalism was *not* a major issue before 1989. State repression of presumably ancient passions is demonstrably not what happened. Nationalism emerged as central only after several years of liberalization. It was Gorbachev's policy that provided hugely optimistic expectations of a reformed socialism and peaceful integration of Soviet bloc with the prosperous West. Nationalism in this atmosphere was a fringe phenomenon.

Separatism moves to center stage in 1989 when it became apparent that Gorbachev could not deliver on his optimistic, if fuzzy, promises. The bureaucrats governing the republics and industrial sectors, watching their positions threatened by democratization, rather desperately began transforming their administrative capital into political capital invested in sovereign national states, or else the economic capital of private firms. This explains why the erstwhile communist apparatchiks so readily defected to the causes of nationalism and neoliberal reform. In the process, these escaping bureaucrats sought selective alliances with the previously oppositional members of intelligentsia and specialists who could help them formulate the new legitimating discourses of power, whether nationalist or neoliberal, and also help to diffuse the pressures from the opposition.

This strategy of converting administrative prerogative into economic capital and the politics of national independence worked more or less smoothly in the parts of Soviet bloc that enjoyed immediate proximity to the erstwhile Cold War divide. In the geographical band winding from Estonia across Poland and Hungary down to Slovenia, the stakes of European integration seemed credible, which exercised a mighty stabilizing effect. Consider the simple fact that the capital of Lithuania, Vilnius, before 1939 belonged to Poland, or how numerous ethnic Hungarian populations are in Slovakia, Romania, and Serbia. And yet there was peace.

Ethnic violence was confined to the southern tier of the USSR, extending from Moldavia across the Caucasus and Central Asia. Why, despite vast differences in cultures, histories, and religions, did this geographic band register so much ethnic violence? In short, the answer is: too many subproletarians in this less well-developed region, and the prevalence of corrupt bureaucratic patronage that proved very vulnerable to violent disruptions. The acute rivalries among the networks of bureaucratic patronage cracked open the window of opportunity into which the national intelligentsias burst with their demands for greater political influence. The subproletarians remained a silent "dark mass" until the unwinding political and economic destabilization directly threatened their livelihoods and/or promised fabulous opportunities in the newly criminalized politics and markets. In the majority of instances, the bureaucratic elites still managed to reconsolidate their position, if only at the price of ever more fabulous corruption and the extension of ethnically formulated patronage. Let us now see in a couple of empirical examples how this happened.

Nomenklatura Oligarchic Restoration
Once the USSR was disbanded in December 1991 and the Russian Federation gained its unexpected independence, Yeltsin's weak new regime had to

balance conflicting pressures at three levels: the West expected increased openness to global capitalist flows in exchange for the International Monetary Fund's loans; Moscow's neoliberal technocrats and financiers aspired to become a "comprador intelligentsia" (Eyal, Szelényi, and Townsley 1998) mediating between global capitalism and Russian industries; and the former communist governors were still in control of the provinces. Industrial proletarians and managers, who once dominated the Soviet economy, utterly failed to constitute the class-based political forces. The managers, still guided by their Soviet-era connections and habitus, lobbied Moscow to have the flow of resources continue, but the revenues available to the Russian government dropped by a factor of almost three (Popov 2000). The prospect of massive bankruptcies undermined the bargaining and redistributive powers of managerial corps and weakened the resolve of proletarians. It was exactly what the neoliberal economic reformers were hoping for: bankruptcies and top-down restructuring would attract outside investors; but there was little actual money flowing from Wall Street and very few Russian goods, other than mineral resources, that could be exported on the world market.

The provincial governors faced the immediate sociopolitical consequences of neoliberal reform. Without having to read Karl Polanyi's 1944 classic regarding "double movement," the governors fell back on their old political habitus and the inherited networks of bureaucratic patronage that were now deployed against the market threats to the substance of their provincial societies. Learning in the process and emulating each other, the governors devised two key arrangements. The first was nominal self-privatization of enterprises under the existing management, in order to gain full control of resources. Second, the governors led the industrial managers in building circuits of barter exchange that assured the survival of bankrupt enterprises despite their frozen bank accounts (Woodruff 1999). It also bound industrial managers and workers powerfully to their governors and cut down the amount of local resources flowing to Moscow.

The data gathered during field research in the North Caucasus region shows that a great many (perhaps three-quarters) of the new rich were either themselves former nomenklatura or close relatives (mostly sons) and clients. Besides, a few locally prominent businessmen obtained their current positions through contentious politics. They included a number of nationalist oppositionists who during perestroika came to the threshold of nomenklatura and tried to leap ahead by supporting the revolutionary cause in 1991–1992.

Subsequently they defected, accepting flattering offers from the official establishment. The remainder of new capitalists rose from the criminalized smuggling economy with the connivance of venal officials.

What held these provincial networks together might be called the minimal trust of despair. Barter schemes were conducive to continuous conflicts, rampant corruption, and asset stripping. In the absence of effective legal enforcement, private protection and adjudication proliferated widely. At first, organized crime rushed in to claim the lucrative protection market but, in the latter 1990s, as the local political machines acquired more cohesion, the mobsters' rule was rolled back. This did not mean, however, that the rule of law prevailed. Rather, police and the quasi-official protection agencies won a larger share of economic flows (Volkov 2002).

These shadowy and ruthless intraelite politics left the majority of the population mystified, cynical, and feeling powerless—alas, not without reason. In the 1990s, the circle of political contenders was sharply reduced to the factions of neo-nomenklatura officials and oligarchic entrepreneurs. The intellectuals and proletarians no longer mattered as producers of material or symbolic goods. Profits and power were now generated not in production but in finance and trade exchange linked to global flows.

The proletarians of near-defunct industries, however, continued to be dependent on their workplaces. This dependency took many material forms, from whatever wages were being paid, to the hot water flowing to their apartments from the industrial boilers of nearby plants. Yet it went far beyond material benefits. The professional capital of proletarians is collective-dependent and embedded in their workplace: an operator of a blast furnace must stay close to his furnace and among his coworkers. Moreover, from the time of Stalinist industrialization, these enterprises provided the nuclei of communities, the sites of daily interactions, and the very tangible materialization of Soviet modern civilization in action. With the drastic devaluation of their industry-embedded social capital, the former Soviet proletarians lost their collective voice and soon their very identity.

The Vodka Rebellion

All big mobilizing programs were now discredited: socialist developmentalism, proletarian social democratization, the quest for national independence, the neoliberal promise of markets. Yet not all was quiet, for there still remained the subproletarians, who were mostly excluded from the officially sponsored patronage. Instead, these subproletarians relied on their own networks, which could be mobilized for political purposes and in forms homologous to the local subproletarian culture. This could be clearly seen in the recent bootleg wars in the North Caucasus, which produced the largest political mobilizations since the collapse of the USSR.

The end of the Soviet alcohol monopoly produced a fabulously lucrative, fragmented, and violent market. The majority of vodka capitalists were socialist-era black marketeers and street toughs who, keeping to their class, continued to live in the same subproletarian quarters. When they built their ostentatious walled mansions, these nouveaux riches could not fail to pave the whole street, or to provide natural gas lines for the neighborhood, or build a new mosque and sponsor respected elders on pilgrimages to Mecca.

For a while, Moscow turned a blind eye to the booming trade of bootleg vodka in the North Caucasus, probably afraid to unsettle the political balance in the volatile region bordering on Chechnya. In 1998, though, Russian border guards suddenly began to enforce customs duties on the raw alcohol smuggled from Western Europe across the porous frontiers of independent Georgia. This started a year-long standoff, during which border guards were regularly fired upon from the mountaintops, hundreds of hostages were seized by gangs, notorious bootleggers were assassinated, and bombs exploded in town markets. The bootleggers, quickly learning a new defensive strategy, ran for elected office across the region. For the ruling bureaucratic cliques of the North Caucasus, the political activism of the rich and popularly admired bootleggers posed an unexpectedly dangerous challenge. It was defused by begging Moscow for help. Federal prosecutors readily brought criminal charges against the politicized smugglers.

In the Republic of Daghestan, this provoked the two Hachilayev brothers (both former boxers and celebrity smugglers) to launch an abortive rebellion that was proclaimed as the beginning of an Islamic revolution. The Hachilayevs' rebellion was crushed by the Daghestani police, with the help of "angry citizens," who were, in reality, private ethnic militias of various state officials (Derluguian 1999). The mysterious conflict eventually calmed down. The vodka industry, though shaken, continues to provide the region with its main source of cash, redistributed through the networks of bureaucratic patronage and private charities. Yet after 2000, Putin's centralizing regime has apparently improved tax collection by scaring the smugglers and accentuating the dependency of regional elites on Moscow.

Future Prospects

These days the veteran fighters in the ethnic wars of the early 1990s remain mostly unemployed, a few went on drugs, and the luckier ones became private guards or bootleggers. Still others traveled to Islamic schools abroad and brought back stories of their encounters with Osama bin Laden, who was described in the interviews with great awe as the ascetic saintly man who had quit the life of privilege and corruption for the caves of Afghanistan. But, contrary to the alarmist predictions that cited ethnic traditions and the historical precedent of jihad against the Russian imperial conquest in the nineteenth century, the native North Caucasus communities were not swept by religious fanaticism. Though mute and profoundly tired of mobilizing, the urban educated populations remain prevalent in the social structure which, at least so far, perpetuates the modern secular dispositions. The rest was accomplished by police repression in the wake of September 1999 apartment bloc bombings across Russia, which Moscow officials blamed on the North Caucasus Islamists, and especially after Putin allied himself with America's "war on terror."

Nevertheless, the prospect of future rebellions is not at all implausible. The ruling elites, like those virtually anywhere else in the emerging post-communist periphery, is precariously suspended in the web of personal deals that periodically get too tangled. One of the most robust generalizations formulated by the comparative sociologists of revolutions finds the neopatrimonial regimes, especially those of "sultanistic" variety, particularly susceptible to being overthrown. The disruptive events like the bouts of market volatility, the succession of big patrons from within, and interventions by the stronger political actors from without (like Moscow's crackdown on bootleggers or the "war on terror") always threaten to aggravate the feuds among the peripheral élites. Such crises in the future will be creating opportunities for radical contenders who up to that point remain latent. But will they be revolutionary forces or rather rebels with a different cause?

There is now plenty of empirical evidence suggesting the likelihood of the latter possibility. Consider the last decade's experiences of Afghanistan or Algeria, Nepal, and Sri Lanka; Peru, Colombia, and even Chiapas if we control for the Internet imagery of subcomandante Marcos. Or consider the frightening dynamics of more than a dozen collapsing states in sub-Saharan Africa; the former Yugoslavia's Kosovo and Macedonia; the formerly Soviet

Uzbekistan and Tadjikistan, and moreover, Chechnya. These examples indicate that the likeliest contenders would be ethnic separatists, various kinds of fundamentalists, or the smuggler warlords who emerge from the peripheries within peripheries: the subproletarian slums and also the immigrant ghettoes of core capitalism.

World-systems theory (Wallerstein 2004) suggests that the likelihood of nonrevolutionary destructive contention derives from generalized systemic conditions: the absence in the contemporary geoculture of a legitimate ideological alternative, and the end of Cold War geopolitical competition. These conditions deny the potentially revolutionary contenders in the peripheries the resources of political recognition and international solidarity that were amply enjoyed by the national-liberation guerrillas of the 1950s–1970s. What remains as the bases of contention are various networks of predominantly local character and the traditional solidarities embedded in ethnic and religious communities (which can be carried far across state borders by modern communication). A related condition is the relative weakness of dependent peripheral states, whose legitimacy and coercive powers are eroded by the same foreign dependency and corrupt practices that sustain the ruling regimes (see Reno 1998). At this point globalization, namely, the global forces structuring these forms of neodependency, indeed become a major potential cause of future ethnic conflicts.

The overall conclusion should now be clear. Globalization was not the direct cause of ethnic violence in the newly emergent post-Soviet peripheries. The common cause of post-Soviet ethnic conflicts was the breakdown of central governance occurring in a state that had historically institutionalized nationality in its affirmative action practices and used to operate through the layers of ethnically formulated networks of bureaucratic patronage. But if market globalization was not the cause, further down the road it does become the major structural condition for the perpetuation of contention in ethnic and fundamentalist forms.

The immediately obvious effect of globalization is to shift the wrath of the masses from their increasingly irrelevant national or local governments to the world's dominant group construed as "American plutocrats." The latter, due to the enormous social and physical distance, assume mythical proportions in popular imagination. Such distance makes the usual forms of contention impossible. Nonetheless, a strongly negative emotional background remains and is expressed in the recent spread of anti-Americanism and, by implication, anti-Semitism. These generally remain at the level of impotent feelings, but on September 11, 2001, a daring group of conspirators showed how ideological fantasies could materialize.

The second effect of global market restructuring on the character of peripheral contention is perhaps more consequential. The connection, however, seems less evident because of its deeply structural nature. Additionally, it is buried under the weight of ideological clichés. I mean the social and political effects of deindustrialization in the former developmental states. Postcommunist transitions were widely assumed to result in democratization by liberating the latent civil societies and creating new property-owning middle classes. This is one of the central tenets of neoliberalism (see Eyal, Szelényi, and Townsley 1998, ch. 3). Indeed, in past epochs the middle classes—artisans, petty bourgeoisie, entrepreneurial farmers, or autonomous professionals—were often found in the forefront of democratization in Western countries. In the capitalist core, historical conditions favored the existence of large middle classes in the first place. Yet even there, as Tilly (1997: 210–211) can attest with the authority of detailed expertise, the success of democratization alliances often depended on the active support of proletarians.

In post-Soviet countries the new middle classes turned out to be not as big and autonomous as in the capitalist core. Not surprisingly, they feel very ambiguous about democratization in locales where wealth is linked to political patronage and foreign connections, where income disparities are large, and where the presence of underemployed workers and subproletarian masses perennially threatens them with social problems and political unpredictability. The persistent fantasy of postcommunist middle classes has been Pinochet rather than Jefferson. So far, the hegemonic vision of neoliberalism imposes political conformity on the peripheral states. The result, however, is only a shallow emulation of electoral procedures and capitalist transaction technologies. David Woodruff (2000) provides an illuminating discussion of disjuncture between the veneer of conformity to the hegemonic project of globalization and the profoundly different bases of social power in the realms of peripheral neopatrimonialism.

This poses the question: what has been actually achieved by the latest worldwide wave of democratization in the 1980s and the 1990s? We need to know what the relationship was (negative, positive, or nonexistent?) between the actual structures of domestic politics in various countries and the new geoculture of human rights, internationally monitored elections, and their effects on the credit ratings of governments. Does the globally induced form of democratization continue or subvert the older-running structural trends that have been engendered by developmentalist proletarianization? Can the global democratization eventually grow deeper local roots, and if so, by what social mechanisms? Or will the veneer peel off when the global climate changes again? We might ask as well whether deindustrialization and the resulting social marginalization of the populations in so many countries makes likelier a global confrontation among the neonativist political forces, drawing their support from angry masses and acting in opposition to the global capitalist forces and the peripheral compradors. In other words, through what processes could the *Clash of Civilizations* become a self-fulfilling prophecy?

References

Arrighi, Giovanni, Terence K. Hopkins, and Immanuel Wallerstein. 2001. "1989: The Continuation of 1968." In George Katsiaficas, ed., *After the Fall: 1989 and the Future of Freedom*, 5–51. New York: Routledge.

Barber, Benjamin. 1996. *Jihad vs. McWorld*. New York: Ballantine Books.

Beck, Bernard, Scott L. Greer, and Charles Ragin. 2000. "Radicalism, Resistance, and Cultural Lags: A Commentary on Benjamin Barber's *Jihad vs. McWorld*." In Georgi Derluguian and Scott L. Greer, eds., *Questioning Geopolitics: Political Projects in a Changing World-System*, 101–110. Westport, Conn.: Praeger.

Bourdieu, Pierre. 1973. "The Algerian Subproletariat." In I. W. Zartman, ed., *Man, State, and Society in the Contemporary Maghreb*, 83–89. London: Pall Mall.

Bourdieu, Pierre. 1994. *Nachala*. The Russian translations by Natalia Shmatko. Moscow: SocioLogos.

Bunce, Valerie. 1998. *Subversive Institutions*. New York: Cambridge University Press.

Burawoy, Michael, and János Lukács. 1992. *The Radiant Past: Ideology and Reality in Hungary's Road to Capitalism*. Chicago: University of Chicago Press.

Derluguian, Georgi. 1999. "Che Guevaras in Turbans." *New Left Review* 237 (September–October):3–27.

Deutscher, Isaac. 1953. *Russia: What Next?* Oxford: Oxford University Press.

Eisenstadt, S. N. 1973. *Traditional Patrimonialism and Modern Neopatrimonialism*. London: Sage.

Evans, Peter. 1995. *Embedded Autonomy: States and Industrial Transformation.* Princeton: Princeton University Press.

Eyal, Gil, Iván Szelényi, and Eleanor Townsley. 1998. *Making Capitalism without Capitalists: Class Formation and Elite Struggles in Postcommunist Central Europe.* London: Verso.

Huntington, Samuel. 1968. *Political Order in Changing Societies.* New Haven: Yale University Press.

———. 1995. *The Clash of Civilizations.* New York: Norton.

Jowitt, Ken. 1992. *New World Disorder: The Leninist Extinction.* Berkeley: University of California Press.

King, Lawrence P. 2001. "Making Markets: A Comparative Study of Postcommunist Managerial Strategies in Central Europe." *Theory and Society* 30:493–538.

Lewin, Moshe. 2005. *The Soviet Century.* London: Verso.

Polanyi, Karl. 1944. *The Great Transformation.* New York: Farrar and Rinehart.

Popov, Vladimir. 2000. "Shock Therapy versus Gradualism: The End of the Debate." *Comparative Economic Studies* 42(1):1–57.

Portes, Alejandro, and József Böröcz. 1988. "The Informal Sector under Capitalism and State Socialism: A Preliminary Comparison." *Social Justice* 15(3–4).

Reno, William. 1998. *Warlord Politics and African States.* Boulder, Colo.: Lynne Rienner.

Rueschemeyer, Dietrich, Evelyn Huber Stephens, and John D. Stephens. 1992. *Capitalist Development and Democracy.* Chicago: University of Chicago Press.

Solnick, Steven L. 1998. *Stealing the State: Control and Collapse in Soviet Institutions.* Cambridge: Harvard University Press.

Stinchcombe, Arthur. 1997. "Tilly on the Past as a Sequence of Futures." Review essay in *Roads from Past to Future* by Charles Tilly, 387–409. Lanham, Md: Rowman & Littlefield.

Stinchcombe, Arthur. 2003. "The Preconditions of World Capitalism: Weber Updated." *Journal of Political Philosophy* 3(4) (December):411–436.

Tilly, Charles. 1973. "Does Modernization Breed Revolution?" *Comparative Politics* 5:425–447.

———. 1997."Democracy Is a Lake." In Tilly, *Roads from Past to Future*, 193–216. Lanham, Md.: Rowman & Littlefield.

Volkov, Vadim. 2002. *Violent Entrepreneurs: The Use of Force in the Making of Russian Capitalism*. Ithaca: Cornell University Press.

Wallerstein, Immanuel. 1995. "'Declining States, Declining Rights?' Response to Charles Tilly (1995)." *International Labor and Working-Class History* 47 (Spring):24–27.

Wallerstein, Immanuel. 2004. *The World-Systems Analysis: An Introduction*. Durham: Duke University Press.

Woodruff, David. 1999. *Money Unmade: Barter and the Fate of Russian Capitalism*. Ithaca: Cornell University Press.

————. 2000. „Rules for Followers: Institutional Theory and the New Politics of Economic Backwardness in Russia." *Politics & Society* 28(4) (December):437–482.

CHAPTER EIGHT

Guarded (In)visibility: *Violencias* and the Labors of Paralegality in the Era of Collapse

Rossana Reguillo Cruz

Passions resurge, but as intensified extremes—explosive, paroxysmal—as a radical, infernal violence. They always precipitate the arrival of death; they are fascinated by the live scene of death. Between the two extremes, violence takes on two symmetrical figures: one is that violence which is invisible, interior, projected over itself, in the secret of the body, which brutalizes and confuses. The other is exterior, hypervisible. It is that violence that further extends the surrealist image of enlightenment, of total war, of the immediate and witnessed death of the victim.
—Oliver Mongin

The *dispositif* is not there to execute man, but rather, man is precisely there because of the *dispositif,* to provide a body upon which it may write its aesthetic work, its bloody lettered inscription with its florilegia and adornments. The Officer himself is no more than a servant of the Machine.
—Michel Löwy

It is the abysmal quality of *violencias* that endows them with their mystified and exterior quality, a quality with which a good part of the social sciences identify through an act of pure seduction.[1] In order to be "understood"—elevated to the rank of explanation both as common sense and as reason of a second order—they require a double movement. The first isolates their codes from the broader set of social codes, thus enabling the observer-analyst to situate him/herself in a position to qualify and attribute; and the second is that other movement which is constituted by the translation of the code into a language that is capable of endowing it with intelligibility, or to circumscribe it to a framework that is able to neutralize the anomaly that *violencias* perform, and make that anomaly patently visible by grounding it in a semantic universe that seeks to safeguard "normality."

Tension and paradox. Thinking that thinks *violencias* must anchor analysis in a *place* that enables the construction of a "point of view" that can at the same time constitute itself as a strategy of displacement through which the binary oppositions commonly utilized to understand *violencias*—anomaly-normality, exterior-interior, good-bad, violent-nonviolent—may be de-essentialized. It does little good, in my opinion, to think in terms of "good *violencias*" and "bad *violencias*," or in terms "legitimate *violencias*" or "illegitimate" ones. This is particularly the case at a time when contemporary societies are facing the hollowing of institutions and of the hegemonic (and legitimate) meanings they have been assigned. The state itself, moreover, is not spared this crisis despite its claim to the "monopoly of legitimate violence." Accelerated transformations have overwhelmed the categories and concepts with which we understand the world.

From this perspective, my objective here is to approach *violencias* from a "place," that of legality, and from a constant "displacement," rhetorics of security. What interests me here is both the analysis of and situated reflection about the effects of *violencias* upon institutionality and sociability, as well as the political uses of security as spaces and practices through which these may be contained. This strategy leads me to the central hypothesis of the chapter: Contemporary *violencias* have inaugurated a border zone, an order open to constant definition, a space of dispute between asymmetrical and incommensurable forces that powerfully exceed the legal-illegal binary. I would also like to argue that *violencias* constitute a space of transit, a "vestibule" between an order that has collapsed and other that has not yet come to be, but which is in the processes of becoming—thus their enormous foundational power and their simultaneous celerity.

Legality Defied and the Emergence of Paralegality

One summer morning in 2005, the city of Piedras Negras in the Mexican state of Coahuila awoke to total devastation. Torrential rains, floods, and mudslides had cut the city off completely and had reduced most of the area to ruins. On that morning, the priest in charge of the main Catholic parish in the city answered a loud knock on his door. What he found was the driver of a gigantic trailer truck who greeted him and handed him a note that read

"With warm regards, from Osiel Cárdenas." The trailer contained blankets, water, medication, food, and toys for the children affected by the tragedy. Cárdenas, the great don of the Gulf Cartel and undoubtedly one of the most powerful drug kingpins in Mexican history, had arrived on the scene well before the Mexican state, which found itself increasingly unable to respond to the numerous emergencies of that catastrophic summer.

Scenes like this one are repeated on a daily basis across Latin America. Yet beyond the anecdotal, these performances of power that ratify the growing empowerment of drug traffickers in diverse arenas of social life reveal, along with the debilitation and corruption of state institutions, something much more profound: the compensation of a lack, of an absence, of a crisis in meaning. Through these regular performances, the *narco* makes visible the deterioration of the reigning symbols of order and at the same time generates its own. And while these may be linked to a specific political contingency, they are in fact performances that appropriate themselves as their own referents, such that each time the *narco* appears in the public sphere there is an explicit negation of any other "exterior" instance.

On September 6, 2006, in the middle of the political crisis that followed the July 6 presidential elections and amid a climate of high social polarization, a commando of hired assassins working for drug traffickers rolled five "impeccably" severed heads, still bleeding, onto the dance floor of the Luz y Sombra nightclub in the small city of Uruapan in the Mexican state of Michoacan. The message that accompanied the heads was: "the family does not assassinate women or children." It was said that the event caused panic among the patrons-turned-witnesses, that it was a revenge killing between drug gangs in response to the alleged assassination of the wife and children of a local kingpin by a rival cartel, and that the assassins might have been *maras salvatruchas* or *kaibiles*.[2] This particular performance has two dimensions. On the one hand, it confirms that below the surface of the much-agitated waters of formal politics there are uncontrollable forces that control broad geographic territories and that are able to operate beyond the law. On the other hand, it delivers an unquestionable message that "they" are "plaintiff, judge, and executioner" in a trinity that instead of challenging juridical norms or laws—which are not taken as parameters or units of measurement—establishes its own frameworks of operation and meaning.

If we add to the twenty-five beheaded bodies that "appeared" in different parts of the country in 2006—thus inaugurating a new phase of the *violencias* linked to the drug cartels—if we add to them the available data on all such activities, it is possible to affirm that we are currently facing a large-scale operation on the part of organized crime without control or limits.[3] Given these circumstances, it no longer seems possible to appeal to the irruption of an anomaly or to the state of exception as an analytical recourse. And although, to a great extent, distance and exceptionality have served as the symbolic mechanisms through which these *violencias* have been processed, recent events themselves have rendered the deterioration of these interpretive ruses evident. *Violencias* are not circumscribable to an "other" space, to a savage and far-removed heterotopia linked to a barbarism that is the opposite of civilization.[4] They are here, in the present, located in a complex space in which the distinctions drawn by the old dichotomies are no longer tenable.[5] Furthermore, there is no doubt that their characteristics and their recurrence reveal, at the very least, the fallacy of understanding them as exceptional outbreaks that on occasion disturb the otherwise peaceful and harmonious landscape of "normality."[6] Perhaps it is also important to add, at this juncture, that neither Foucault nor Agamben articulates epistemological coordinates capable of fully assimilating and incorporating such an excess of anomaly and exceptionality.

Yet if it is, in fact, the normal, the ordinary, and the everyday that are the expression and the site of the spectacular performances of violence (I think here of the bodies of so many women assassinated in Ciudad Juarez, in Guatemala, and elsewhere), then what follows should be an examination of the place of legality as that space where the fractures of the present order become most clearly visible.

Legality represents a social contract constituted by norms and agreements which draw their supports from the law and juridical discourse. But perhaps what is most important for our discussion is that legality constitutes a limit, a wall that separates and that in the act of separating distinguishes, qualifies, sanctions, and erects hierarchies. What is more, its pretense of universality leaves little room for doubt or gaps, and clearly establishes an inside (of legality) and an outside (in illegality). Legality is the history of delimitations and of the efforts and struggles to make these delimitations prescriptive fields capable of incorporating inequalities and differences, as well as local, national, and global logics. International legality (called international law) is continuously confronting interpretations that are incompatible with local spaces. Conversely, the local is continually defied by supranational delimitations.

In this context, it is difficult to claim that the *violencias* unleashed by the drug trade and organized crime are situated within the space of illegality. By all accounts, such analysis would be simplistic and insufficient. Thus, I propose a third analytic space—that of paralegality. Paralegality emerges precisely on that border zone inaugurated by *violencias*, generating an order that is not illegal, but one that is parallel and that generates its own codes, norms, and rituals that by ignoring institutions and the social contract present, paradoxically, a challenge greater than the one posed by illegality. Using a childhood metaphor, we might say that the game of cops and robbers has lost its attraction and that the new game consists of the dispute among thieves, in their own separate world, in which the police play the role of accessory. The notion of paralegality thus names an order that challenges state power not through the breach of its established and intelligible codes, although this may certainly be part of its challenge, but through the audacity to create a separate, parallel order with its own protocols and modes of intelligibility.

And in order to confirm this parallel power, or this second state as Rita Segato (2004) would call it, there are two moments upon which our analysis must be brought to bear.

1   The first is the rise of expressive violence to the detriment of utilitarian violence.[7] These are *violencias* that do not seek an "instrumental end" (such as war between states, kidnapping, and theft), but that constitute themselves as a language that seeks to affirm, dominate, and exhibit the symbols of its total power.

2   The second is the almost absolute control that the great kingpins exercise even from prison, which ceases to be a "total" institution in Goffman's (2001) terms, in order to organize, dissolve, and produce important arenas of social life that may be relevant to their interests. Thus, Hobsbawm's figure of "the bandit" (2000), which emerged for the first time in the context of the drug trade with the figure of Pablo Escobar (whom Mexican kingpins like Osiel Cárdenas have attempted to emulate), is displaced by the figure of a powerful entrepreneur-prince who is magnanimous with those at his unconditional service and brutally cruel with his adversaries. This entrepreneur-prince is lord and owner of a vast social territory that is not hidden in the woods or ensconced in the high mountain.

Expressive violence and geopolitical control have thus become the key mechanisms in the production of the growing power of an expanding paralegality that, resting on its enormous capacity for action, mobilizes what Bourdieu and Passeron (1977) called *symbolic violence*. This violence is capable of imposing legitimacy upon multiple codes and meanings through its inscription onto the social fabric. But, as both authors warned early on, symbolic violence requires an identification with the vessels of meaning in order to constitute the signs of its legitimacy.

Not long ago, Cristian Alarcón, a journalist for the Argentine newspaper *Página 12* who recently received an important award from *NACLA Report on the Americas*, pointed out to me that the Mexican press covers narco-executions with the same astonishing tranquility that the Argentine media reports on variation of the "country-risk" index or on the alarming indices of contamination in large urban centers: narco—315 dead; narco—515 executed; narco—3 more decapitations. And in Colombia, when one inquires about a particular person, people often respond "he had to go" to say without saying that the person in question has become one more victim of violence. In Mexico, the word "executed" has come to signify the deaths and daily tolls of the drug trade.

Perhaps the rise of paralegality is precisely this: the normalization of a particular mode of conflict in a border zone or an intermediate space.

In the summer of 2003, with early effects this interventionist war in Iraq still fresh and the stale scent of blood and gunpowder from the struggle against global terrorism in the air, Danny Boyle's film *28 Days Later* opened in movie theaters. In Spanish, the film was titled *Exterminio*. Beyond its many cinematographic merits, Boyle's film dramatizes to the extreme one of the greatest contemporary social fears: deadly violence (exercised by others) that is uncontainable, unleashed, and without form, like a virus that spreads without sparing women, children, priests, and respectable heads of households now turned into agents of violence. The virus is inoculated, and thus in the face of its enormous power the only alternative is violence itself. In Boyle's allegory, no institution remains standing, there are no spaces capable of containing the irrationality of the destruction. When it appears that the Army might offer an alternative, the very characteristics of the institution— extreme obedience, arrogance, excessive power and, especially, a masculinist order—turn it into a germ even more virulent than the violence itself. In the "society of extermination" staged by Boyle, there is no escape possible, and the protagonists are forced to face up to uncontestable evidence that the only possibility for surviving the violence is through violence.

Violence has indeed become the robust narrative of contemporary times, which means that its presence, its data, its images, are at the center of a public space that finds in violence a narrative that, much like Scheherazade in *The Book of One Thousand and One Nights*, is capable sustaining the suspense and of "reenchanting" the world each day through a narrative ruse that is perpetuated in a story without end.

The data are certainly terrifying, yet beyond the epidemiology of *violencias*, what fails to appear or what appears in a very weak manner, is a reflexive analysis of what the message of these *violencias* might be signifying. Much like Boyle's narrative, society appears to relate to violence as if it were a virus that accidentally escaped a laboratory, an unconquerable and fatal germ, but one that is always exterior.

Rhetorics of Security: The Political Use of Fear (of *Violencias*)

This now well-established "atmosphere" of fatality in the face of *violencias* is the space that imbues them with their capacity to reproduce themselves limitlessly. Within this imaginary, there is no institution capable of protecting us against this mortal virus. The alternative, then, is to confront them with the tools we have at hand: solitary prayer, the private stockpiling of weapons, a retreat toward what is intimate and individual, the establishment of increasingly harsher borders and customs checkpoints, an everyday life on the cusp of self-vigilance, and the political production of "zero risk zones"—security at all costs.

Up to now, I have attempted to think about *violencias* from a particular point of view, from a specific place (legality defied). Now I will attempt a countermaneuver, one that involves a detachment from a specific place, and a displacement that might allow us to calibrate the sociopolitical impact of their presence in society.

It already seems clichéd to appeal to the events of September 11, 2001, as a "foundational date" for the global reordering that that has redefined the security-freedom relation, but I am convinced that these events, which took place in the United States, represent a dramatic turn for global society. This terrorist attack has dramatically brought to the fore a rethinking of the classical security-freedom binary (Bauman, 2003) inaugurated during the formation of nation-states—giving up freedoms in order to achieve a minimum of security.

In complex and problematic ways, this terrorist attack brought with it a "return of the state," and not only in the United States, which has relied on emotional appeals to an outdated nationalism and has simultaneously exhibited, before a strange geometry of global coresponsibility that it has itself interpellated, its ugliest and most feared visage—that of the policing repressor.[8] In Latin America, this face of the state, which had been "subdued" with relative success by incipient democracies throughout the region, has found in this event and its political and juridical interpretations new vigor with which to deploy its repressive apparatus.

A second characteristic has been the exacerbation of suspicion not only in the relationship between the authorities and citizens but also in the narrative of daily and horizontal interactions within society itself. The linking of terrorism with local processes, zones, landscapes and identities whose vocabularies previously operated within other logics has (d)evolved into an agenda of and a concern about so-called national security. The criminalization of poverty, the ethnic stigmatization of particular social groups (or the racialization of crime), the intensification of mechanisms of vigilance, and the tense debate around human rights as a space that protects "criminals" have configured an atmosphere in which the notion of security is substantially overvalued.

These characteristics or tendencies do not, of course, exhaust the explanation of an imaginary that has undergone a process of normalization since September 11, and which has itself been fed by processes of violence and the growth of organized and common criminality in the region. But they do allow us to organize, analytically that is, both the macro and micro—the structural and the anthropological—dimension of the rhetorics of security, which I understand as *that set of eloquent arguments that seeks to persuade and provoke emotive responses through tropes (reasonings and judgments) anchored in a principle of generalized insecurity.*

When we analyze the set of signifying chains that are circulating profusely through public space in the region, it is possible to confirm the growing weight of "security" as discourse for the ordering of social dynamics. Numerous polls conducted in the past few years in a number of Latin American countries reveal that the issue that most concerns the citizenry, along with unemployment, is the question of security. And beyond the local circumstances that breed the hypersensitivity toward the issue (the growth of the drug trade, the rise in criminality, the structural deterioration of societies, for example), there is little doubt that both the perception of and the action in response to security-related issues are profoundly influenced by a geopolitics of fear. This geopolitics, moreover, is not only explicable as a result of the powerful influx of the United States—the self-appointed paladin in the struggle against insecurity—but also by the articulation of transnational spaces and processes that tend to unify the modalities through which security is perceived and through which public policies and concrete measures are taken to confront it. I can cite as an example the infamous "Anti-Maras Summit" that took place in June 2005 and was attended by the presidents of Mexico and Central American nations. What are known as "iron hand" and "super iron hand" laws, which are of Salvadorian origin,[9] are extending to other countries, and the frameworks for understanding the security-insecurity binary are showing a tendency toward stabilization and (self-)legitimation. Simultaneously, most attempts to question these punitive logics are unable to achieve a minimum level of efficacy or visibility.

Today, all factors conspire to strengthen sites of enunciation that are linked to "security," and that operate as an efficient machinery for the production of visibility, credibility, and most importantly, of the agenda for debate.[10] The securitization of spaces, practices, and discourses has brought with it new syntaxes, aesthetics, and valuations—all of which coalesce around the production of a disciplinary narrative that allows no refutations.

Image One: The Expert System?

And thus, millions of travelers comply without protest with the so-called security measures and willingly submit themselves to the scrutiny of a highly fallible but enormously powerful system. Because they constitute a priori motives for suspicion, travel and displacement produce a perverse effect, disidentification, or in other words, the need to distance oneself from and/or remove any possible indicator of suspicion. This makes travelers enter a territory of continuous self-vigilance with respect to any traces or indices that may raise suspicions. A valid passport and a legal visa are no longer enough if brown skin, kinky hair, any movement, a book, a gesture or an absence of gesture appear suspicious to the security guard on duty.

What is most powerful about the effects of these dynamics, which are sustained by the rhetorics of security, is precisely that they depend on the subjective and contingent interpretation of the "transit police." In other words, there is an irresolvable disjuncture between the expert system of airport security and its moment of operationalization.[11] People do not only confront machines and procedures, but other people, infused with fears, prejudices, preconceptions, and perhaps most important, attributions.

In whose hands does security rest? How do we reconcile the abstract norm with its empirical application?

Image Two: The Importance of Being Named Samuel

Harry Pross tells us that "the dark image of the enemy unites the State and its subjects. . . . The figure of the enemy enables the symbolization of all the darkness and baseness necessary for internal constitution to be strengthened." (1989: 63). This citation lucidly articulates two key concerns with respect to rhetorics of security: The first is the notion of a border and the second is the image of the intruder.

In both cases, I have been unable to find a better interpretant than what I call the "Huntington effect." In 2004, the Harvard professor returned to the public debate with his controversial hypothesis about "American identity." Intruders and the border play a central role in his well-oiled analysis. The issue here is not that I believe it worthwhile to refute the fallacies, gaps, vices, and manipulations of the arguments of this metropolitan professor, but rather that he, along with the immigrant-hunting militias known as the Minuteman Project, represent the most deteriorated discourses with respect to rhetorics of security. In Huntington's neoconservative prophesy, which is positioned in vigorous tension with neoliberalism, "others"—those different, those recently arrived—"are without doubt evolving, assisted by the diffusion of evangelical Protestantism, [but] it is unlikely that that (cultural) revolution will reach its conclusion any time soon." Professor Huntington continues by adding that "the high levels of immigration from Mexico sustain and reinforce among Mexican-Americans the Mexican values that are the primary source of their stunted educational and economic progress and of their assimilation into American society" (2004: 295).[12]

Arrearage and assimilation, backwardness and progress, good and evil reemerge within the horizons of the neoliberal order as uncomfortable categories within a civilizing matrix that is unable to break with its ethnocentric vocation of distributing labels that double back upon the systems of classification that establish the difference between civilization and barbarism.

If nervous authoritarianisms and their strategies of enunciation—so in vogue following the rupture that the terrorist events of 2001 represent—configure a knowledge that is sustained by power, there is an interesting question that emerges, in my opinion, about the complex and contradictory relationship between neoconservatism and neoliberalism in the United States (and the world). How, I would ask, are these two regimes reconcilable when the second appeals to the individual, to deregulation and the delocalization of identities, while the first appeals robustly to a community and to essentialization, both territorial and symbolic? The paradox and the questions installed by rhetorics of security are multiple and they do not spare those who attempt to turn "security" into a creed, into a formulaic catechism that offers salvation.

The Bush administration's border wall between Mexico and the United States has been widely praised by the militias of the Minuteman Project, which is currently the most visible anti-immigrant organization in the United States.[13]

In 2007, on the Univision network's talk show *Cristina*, there were heated debates about the effects of Latin American migration to the United States, the problem of "illegals," and the defense of North American borders. Raymond Herrera, the Minuteman Project's Spanish-language spokesperson, appeared on the show (the mostly widely seen program on the network, with an estimated daily audience of 14 million viewers) declaring with great conviction that Mexican migration to the United States must be stopped at all costs because it is "destroying our great nation."[14] Speaking Spanish with an accent similar to that of George W. Bush, Herrera (a Mexican-American) spent his air time denigrating Mexicans, Hispanics, and Latin Americans, along with their values, their culture, and their stubborn resistance to living "the life of Anglos." Herrera also took the liberty of affirming that "people from Mexico are like little headless chickens imbued with machismo," and that he was glad they would all be "going back."

Huntington's arguments and the fascist militias deployed on one of the most heavily policed border in the world enable us to give our question about the effects of the rhetorics of security a greater scope and importance, and to affirm that the values, the ideas, and the ideologies associated with them—repeated endlessly and disingenuously—have effects on social organization and on the substance of the "contract" that emerges from the geopolitical reordering of the world.

Image Three: A President in Search of a Project

Finally, propaganda and advertising also generate political symbols, modes of recognition, and categorizations. In the face of the growing discredit of politics, the crisis of representation, and a challenged legitimacy, recourse to rhetorics of security as way of robustly fortifying the image of an individual or a regime appears to be a sure strategy.

In the Mexico of the crisis that followed the 2006 presidential elections, with a recently named and much weakened president fraught by powerful conflicts and intense social polarization, the first measure following the inauguration could be none other than a signal against the drug cartels and one "in favor" of national security.

And so it was. The new president, Felipe Calderón, announced a reduction in federal spending on education, science, and culture; an increase in the budget for security forces; and the creation a new umbrella agency of national security. His first act as chief executive in December 2006 was the incorporation of 10,000 army troops into the Federal Preventive Police and the Federal Intelligence Agency. In January 2007, and with great media fanfare, he launched a "frontal attack" against the Michoacán and Baja California cartels—yet not without warning that "in this war, lives will be lost."

Yet in what is not an insignificant development, 2006 ended with ten *narco* "executions" in a single day in the states of Mexico and Guerrero, despite the military operation to seal state borders in order to prevent drug traffickers from escaping. At the same time, it was also confirmed that at least since 2003, a number of drug traffickers and their families had been receiving "agricultural" subsidies along with others for animal husbandry and the production of cattle feed. These stories were received with silence on the part of the government and neither taken up nor problematized by the mainstream media commentators favorable to the iron hand of the new president.

Guarding the Invisible?

What these three images allow us to see is that the principal effect of the rhetorics of security is to exacerbate preexisting tensions, on the one hand, and to promote the emergence of new categories under suspicion that sow the seeds for a "zone free of human rights," as Donald Rumsfeld once referred to Guantanamo.

At such a juncture, it is useful to turn to the old philosophers. In his theory of the passions (fear, hope, hate, love), David Hume argued for the need to distinguish between causes and objects. The "cause" would be that idea that inflames the passions, whereas the "object" would be that toward which passions are directed once they have been inflamed (Hume 1990: 23–27).[15]

I am interested in highlighting the notion of the "object of attribution" here, insofar as it is always produced by someone's own passion, thus allowing for the destabilization of the positive idea that the motive (cause) and object of passion—in this case fear (of insecurity, of *violencias*)—are the one and the same. Hume's notion of the "object of attribution" is fundamental for understanding the mechanisms that intervene in the diffusion of rhetorics of security and their effect on the emergence of "objects of attribution."

My interest is precisely to calibrate the impact upon the dynamics of everyday life, on the processes of sociality and sociability, each time I encounter a direct interpellation of passions (or "affections" in Hume's vocabulary) in these rhetorics. According to the philosopher,

> nothing excites an affection with greater force than the occlusion of part of its object behind shadows. While simultaneously revealing enough of the object to dispose us in its favor [*or against it, I would add*], some work is also left for the imagination. Along with the fact that an uncertainty always accompanies darkness, the effort of the imagination to complete the idea awakens the spirits and imbues passion with an additional force. (Hume 1990: 149).

It is my argument that rhetorics of security operate upon the tension between reality and imagination. They make visible and occlude, and in this sense, the role that Hume ascribes to the uncertainty produced by this tension comes into its full magnitude in this citation. Even if the fear (of insecurity), the hope (for a solution), the hatred (of those presumed guilty) and the love (for the charismatic leader who eliminates fear) promoted by discourses of security are a subjectively experienced passion, its rhythms and tones may be modulated as the space of its indefinition is expanded.

(In)visibility as a Strategy

One of the principal characteristics of the rhetorics being constructed around security is their rejection of any form of dissent with respect to the truths that it erects. Authoritarian in nature, these "truths" tend to be self-erected as universal proclamations beyond the reach of critique or empirical refutation. They acquire the status of "prophesies," and as they conquer common sense, they bring with them heavy doses of social disciplining, to such an extent that in ambiguous ways, the territory in which they operate forbids argumentation altogether.

In this context, the protection of their own (in)visibility that characterizes *violencias* is the key to the maintenance of a collapsed order; their visibility or lack thereof serves as a mechanism that ensures the perpetuation of a deteriorated and anachronic order that has been overwhelmed. This mechanism, moreover, plays the all-important role of making invisible the growing emergence and empowerment of a paralegal order.

Despite the dramatic character of their effects, rhetorics of security never cease to function as a "lament," an "incantation," or an "amulet" against the evident effects of a paralegality that is perpetually announcing a world in which known "contracts" and agreements have hit rock bottom. In this light, Norbert Elias's argument (rehearsed in his critique of Kant) that the search for personal causes (the culpability of persons) characterized the period before modernity is indeed paradoxical. "The question 'Who destroyed my house with a ray of lightening?' precedes the question 'What destroyed my house?'" (Elias 1994:43). Following Elias, we could affirm that the historical stage in which we are living resurrects the question about the responsibility of "living persons," and eludes the question about social configurations and change. While the operators of paralegality "modernize," advance, and reconfigure, the rhetorics of security appeal to the primordial sources of pre-Hobbesian fears—the efficient cause, the example at hand, the exemplary enemy.

Thus it appears that the geopolitics of fear, the complex collaboration between expressive violence and compensation for a lack (of order), and the rhetorics of security bring to the table the need for a very serious rethinking of the notion of modernity that we have created for ourselves.

Without certainties, I would adventure to argue that the paralegality inaugurated by organized crime constitutes a first response to the decline of institutionality and its accelerating disaffiliation. For this reason, I would like to ask myself, with Elias, about the changes that explain the configuration of the contemporary world.

Notes

This chapter was translated from Spanish by Marcial Godoy-Anativia.

1   I use the term *violencias* (in the plural) to emphasize that violence is not a uniform continuum in time and in space. Based on my research, I posit the existence of four forms of social violence whose specificities configure distinct domains. These are structural violence, which alludes to those forms linked to the economic and sociopolitical system (poverty, marginality); historic violence, which is exercised on persons or groups because of their belonging or affiliation to an ethnic or political group from a presumption of superiority; disciplinary violence, which seeks to send "corrective" messages through the exercise of violence on particular bodies or social categories (women, youth); and diffuse violence, whose ends and perpetrators are difficult to isolate or identify. This is not a "pure" model, as these forms are intertwined, but for analytical purposes, the use of the plural enables, in my opinion, sharper analysis.

2   *Mara* is the term used to refer to Central American and North American immigrant gangs, whose violent methods and cruelty have intensified in recent years. *Kaibiles* are elite units of the Guatemalan armed forces, who gained an unfortunate visibility during the years of the dirty war in the nation. There are several reports that indicate that both *maras* and *kaibiles* have become the new operative forces of Mexican drug cartels. See Reguillo 2005.

3   Reports from different security companies indicate that in Mexico there are approximately 130 organizations linked to drug trafficking, with an infrastructure and weaponry that is superior to that of local police forces. The most recent report from the attorney general's office states that of the approximately 100,000 federal crimes committed in 2006, 51 percent were related to the production, transport, commercialization, provision, and possession of drugs.

4   I develop this concept, which allows for an anthropological analysis of the specialization of social fears, in Reguillo 2006.

5   The execution of Saddam Hussein by hanging serves as a good metaphor for the collapse of the civilization-barbarism binary.

6   A casual perusal of the Latin American news media on any given day would be sufficient to destabilize this notion of "exceptionality."

7   I borrow this categorization from Segato, who utilizes it to refer to the assassinations of women in Ciudad Juarez.

8   I think a telling example of emotional interpellations disguised as science are the intrepid "arguments" rendered by Samuel Huntington in his most recent work

about US-American identity and the Mexican plague; see Huntington 2004. The simplistic ordering of global geopolitics into an "axis of evil" and an "axis of goodness" provides an example of the thesis of global responsibility.

9   See the "Ley para el combate de las actividades delincuenciales de grupos o asociaciones ilícitas especiales," of the Supreme Court of Justice of El Salvador, officially published in *El Diario Oficial 65*, vol. 383. Or "Operación Mano Dura y la ley antimaras," proposed by the president of El Salvador Francisco Flores, and transmitted live through a mandatory radio and television broadcast on July 23, 2003.

10 In order to understand these mechanisms, it is essential to establish the political difference between an "issue" and an "agenda." All agendas are sustained by issues, but not all issues become agendas.

11 It was Giddens (1993) who introduced the important category of "expert systems" to refer to the "blind" system constituted by depersonalized decisions and operations that are systemic and invisible. Although I have shared his view for quite some time, I now have serious doubts that the system is as "blind" and as "expert" as Giddens and advance technologies presuppose.

12 Huntington considers the fact that in 1998, "José replaced the name Michael as the most common name given to newborns both in California and Texas" to be sufficient evidence of this "backwardness." Thus the title of this section, "The Importance of Being Named Samuel."

13 To visualize the Minuteman Project, cf. http://minutemanhq.com.

14 A synopsis of this episode was available at the time of writing at the website http://www.minutemanproject.com/default.asp?contentID=99, but is no longer accessible. Raymond Herrara now has his own organization called "We the People." One can acquire a sense of the ideology at work in his line of thought in the videotaped interview available at http://www.youtube.com/watch?v=05AStdM3uFs.

15 See the interesting introduction by José Luis Tasset Carmona to Hume (1990).

References

Arendt, Hannah. 2005. *La condición humana*. Barcelona: Paidós.

Bauman, Zygmunt. 2003. *Comunidad. En busca de seguridad en un mundo hostil*. Madrid: Siglo XXI.

Bourdieu, Pierre, and Jean-Claude Passeron. 1977. *La reproducción: Elementos para una teoría del sistema de enseñanza*. Barcelona: LAIA.

Elias, Norbert. 1994. *Teoría del símbolo: Un ensayo de antropología cultural*. Barcelona: Península.

Giddens, Anthony. 1993. *Consecuencias de la modernidad*. Madrid: Alianza Universidad.

Goffman, Erving. 2001. *Internados: Eensayos sobre la situación social de los enfermos mentales*. Buenos Aires: Amorrortu.

Hobsbawm, Eric. 2000. *Bandits*. New York: New Press.

Huntington, Samuel. 2004. *¿Quiénes somos? Los desafíos a la identidad estadounidense*. Mexico City: Paidós.

Hume, David, 1990. *Disertación sobre las pasiones y otros ensayos morales*. Barcelona. Anthropos/Ministerio de Educación y Ciencia.

Löwy, Michael. 2003. "Las formas modernas de la barbarie." *Metapolítica* (Mexico City) 7(28) (March-April):38–46.

Mongin, Oliver. 1993. *El miedo al vacío: Ensayo sobre las pasiones democráticas*. Buenos Aires: FCE.

Pross, Harry 1989: *La violencia de los símbolos sociales*. Barcelona: Anthropos.

Reguillo, Rossana. 2005. "La mara: contingencia y afiliación con el exceso." *Nueva Sociedad* (Caracas) 200 (November):70–84.

———. 2006. "Los miedos: Sus laberintos, sus monstruos, sus conjuros. Una lectura antropológica." *Etnografías contemporáneas* (Buenos Aires) 2 (April):45–74.

Segato, Rita Laura. 2004. "Territorio, soberanía y crímenes de segundo Estado: La escritura en el cuerpo de las mujeres asesinadas en Ciudad Juárez." In *Ciudad Juárez: De este lado del puente*. Mexico City: Instituto Nacional de las Mujeres / Epikeia / Nuestras Hijas de Regreso a Casa. http://www.unb.br/ics/dan/Serie362empdf.pdf; and *Labrys, estudos feministas* 6 (August-December), http://www.unb.br/ih/his/gefem.

CHAPTER NINE

The Securitarian Society of the Spectacle

Nicholas De Genova

In a society that really has been turned on its head, truth is a moment of falsehood.
—Guy Debord, Thesis 9, *The Society of the Spectacle*

The simple fact of being without reply has given to the false an entirely new quality. At a stroke it is truth which has almost everywhere ceased to exist or, at best, has been reduced to the status of pure hypothesis that can never be demonstrated.
—Guy Debord, Thesis V, *Comments on the Society of the Spectacle*

This perfect democracy fabricates its own inconceivable enemy, terrorism. It wants, actually, to be judged by its enemies rather than by its results. The history of terrorism is written by the State and it is thus instructive. The spectating populations must certainly never know everything about terrorism, but they must always know enough to convince them that, compared with terrorism, everything else seems rather acceptable, in any case more rational and democratic.
—Guy Debord, Thesis IX, *Comments on the Society of the Spectacle*

Uncertainty, ambiguity, equivocation, dissimulation, intransigent secrecy, inconceivable enemies, falsehoods without reply, truths that cannot be verified, hypotheses that can never be demonstrated—these have truly become the hallmarks of our (global) political present.[1] An audacious confrontation with this same constellation of epistemic enigmas distinguishes the unique imaginative force of the social critique of Guy Debord (1967; 1988). Although it emerged as the articulation of a radical political project during the 1960s, and despite contemporary efforts to domesticate it by safely consigning it to the mausoleum of the past, Debord's work, like that of his Situationist cothinker Raoul Vaneigem, remains "part of a subversive current of which the last has not yet been heard" (Vaneigem 1967/1994: 18).[2] This persistent pertinence of Debord's thought in the wake of the so-called war on terror is especially evident in light of his bold and arresting proposition that the society which fashions itself as a "perfect democracy fabricates its own inconceivable enemy, terrorism" (Thesis IX, 1988/2005).[3] Thus, our present and unrelenting moment of crisis summons forth a reanimated consideration of the enduring explanatory power of Debord's austere theoretical formulation of spectacle.[4] Debord himself stringently cautions against quotation as recourse to "a theoretical authority invariably tainted if only because it has become quotable, because it is now a fragment torn away from its context, from its own movement" (1967/1995: 145–46). Nevertheless, he endorses plagiarism in the service of genuine subversion (154). With the aspiration of frankly confronting the terror of the spectacle of security, and thus with precisely strategic purposes (cf. Agamben 1996/2000: 73), I hope for this essay to incite Debord's specter to contemporary purposes.

In his *Comments on the Society of the Spectacle* (1988), Debord retrospectively provides a concise summation of the society of the spectacle, as he had originally depicted it in 1967: "the autocratic reign of the market economy, which had acceded to an irresponsible sovereignty, and the totality of new techniques of government that accompanied this reign" (Thesis II; 1988/2005). Significantly elaborating upon and extending Marx's critique of the fetishism of the commodity under capitalism (1867/1976: 163–77), Debord identified the overwhelming and unprecedented hegemony of image and appearance mediating all social relations, by which "the whole of life . . . presents itself as an immense accumulation of *spectacles*," ensuring that "all that once was directly lived has become mere representation" and tending to reduce all social life from its already estranged and atomized condition to the sheer passivity of spectatorship (1967/1995: 12; emphasis in original), "a generalized autism" (153). In his subsequent reformulation, Debord further elaborates "five principal features: incessant technological renewal; fusion of State and economy; generalized secrecy; forgeries without reply; a perpetual present" (Thesis V; 1988/ 2005).[5] Whereas the spectacle may be quintessentially characterized by an incessant monological tyranny and garrulous redundancy—"a sort of eternity of non-importance that speaks loudly" (Thesis VI; 1988/2005; cf. 1967/1995: 17, 19)—Debord's subsequent reflections nonetheless concentrate more pointedly on the "generalized secrecy" that "stands behind the spectacle, as the decisive complement of all it displays and, in the last analysis, as its most important operation" (Thesis V; 1988/2005). Hence, the brazenness of the spectacle—its reliance on unrelenting mass mediation and exuberant display to manifest itself as a specious unity, "an enormous positivity, out of reach and beyond dispute" (1967/1995: 15)—remains, as in Marx's classic account (1867) of the thing-like reification of relations between people, inevitably accompanied by the invisibility of the real social relations of (alienated, exploited, and subjugated) life. What, then, might the concept of the society of the spectacle, with its emphatic interest in the cynical mobilization of appearances over and against lived social relations, have to offer a history of our securitarian present?

Catastrophe and History

The end of history, being itself a catastrophe, can only be fueled by catastrophe. Managing the end therefore becomes synonymous with the management of catastrophe.
—Jean Baudrillard, *The Illusion of the End*

In his concluding remarks in *Comments*, Debord notably acknowledged that the subjugated, and even some of those who are directly implicated in the management of the spectacle's domination, are "made to believe that, essentially, they are still living in a world which in fact disappeared." Furthermore, he predicted that a change that would "decisively complete" the work of the spectacle was "imminent and ineluctable," but would ultimately appear "like lightning, which we know only when it strikes" (Thesis XXXII; 1988/2005).

Not long thereafter, in 1992, several key personnel in the highest echelons of the United States government elaborated a post–Cold War military doctrine for which the "first objective is to prevent the re-emergence of a new rival" and, more specifically, "to prevent any hostile power from dominating a region whose resources would, under consolidated control, be sufficient to generate global power," in the interest of upholding and promoting the supremacy of "the sense that the world order is ultimately backed by the U.S."[6] During the ensuing years, these same figures then collaborated in the formation of the Project for the New American Century (PNAC) and were signatories to its founding programmatic documents (1997; 2000), which unabashedly called for a robust expansion of the United States' military capabilities and a dramatically more aggressive agenda for actively and deliberately reshaping global geopolitical realities according to what the Project deemed to be the United States' strategic interests. The Project was not at all reticent about its proposal for "preserving and extending an international order friendly to our security, our prosperity, and our principles" (1997). Memorably, the authors of the Project's most important position paper acknowledged that financing such militarism would require popular justification, and explicitly and wistfully remarked upon the likely need for "some catastrophic and catalyzing event" reminiscent of the Japanese bombing of Pearl Harbor in 1941 (2000: 51). Then, "like lightening, which we know only when it strikes," as if fortuitously, on September 11, 2001, this "new Pearl Harbor" came to pass, in a spectacle of fiery death and mangled limbs and the thunderous redoubled collapse of the monumental twin towers of the World Trade Center. Leaving all the world paralyzed in front of their (our) television screens, watching the incessant coverage and inescapable repetition of the grisly scene, the events of September 11, 2001— in the eloquent words of Jean Baudrillard—presented themselves as "the brutal irruption of death live, in real time" (2001/2002a: 408; 2001/2002b: 16–17). Yet, as if miraculously, we the global multitude of televisual witnesses were seemingly rendered invulnerable in our isolated spectatorship as virtual "all-seeing survivor[s]" of the calamity-as-image, free "to remain indefinitely the same," in exactly the same place (Weber 2002: 454–555; cf. Lefebvre 1961/2002: 76).

Conveniently, PNAC stalwarts (Dick Cheney, Donald Rumsfeld, Paul Wolfowitz, Lewis Libby, Stephen Cambone, and others) were, by this time, strategically (re-)positioned at the helm of the US state.[7] That is to say, they were prepared to husband and reap the harvest of the seemingly cataclysmic events, which President George W. Bush, in a nationally televised address to a joint session of Congress, promptly and predictably analogized to "one Sunday in 1941" as the purportedly singular previous exception to a narrative wherein "Americans have known wars—but . . . they have been wars on foreign soil" (September 20, 2001). Then, on the anniversary of that earlier catalytic exception, Bush demonstratively identified the events of September 11, 2001, as this generation's Pearl Harbor, in response to which, he affirmed accordingly, "Now your calling has come" (December 7, 2001).

The rest, as they say, is history, or rather, more precisely, the rest is what they call the end of history.

The function of the spectacle, as Debord so presciently and emphatically contends, is "to bury history in culture," affirming "the eternal presence of a system that was never created and will never disappear" (1967/1995: 137). Indeed, in spite of the overt recourse to invoking an historical event (the Japanese bombardment of Pearl Harbor), such ritual evocations of the past operate less as a cogent reflection on history and rather more as a kind of mythmaking. This is made abundantly evident inasmuch as the Pearl Harbor comparison was deployed to authorize the enunciation of an extravagantly metaphysical discourse in which, according to Bush, "each of you is commissioned by history to face freedom's enemies" (December 7, 2001). The principal work of such mythification is aimed to recast contemporary militarism as the (implicitly masculine) generational duty of "the children and grandchildren of the generation that fought and won the Second World War" (ibid.). Indeed, this sort of ideological short-circuit is all the more crucial for contemporary war making because it pretends to suture the unfathomable rupture imposed by the US defeat in Vietnam. The humiliation of US military power and imperial prestige by the Vietnamese people's anticolonial aspirations for self-determination, as Linda Boose (1993) argues persuasively, represented "a traumatic break between the men of one generation and those of another," in effect, between fathers and sons. By seeking to dress that open wound in imperial-patriarchal intergenerational connectivity, the mythological evocation of World War II as a precedent for contemporary militarism is thus conscripted to restore the hallowed heritage of a "regeneration through violence" (Slotkin 1973).

The "first priority" of the spectacle, in Debord's account, is precisely "to make historical knowledge in general disappear," for "the end of history gives current-day power a pleasant break" (Thesis VI; 1988/2005). Inevitably assisted by Hollywood's seemingly fortuitous delivery earlier in 2001 of the feature film *Pearl Harbor*, this sort of spectacular effort to "bury history in culture" is well demonstrated in the ideological operation by which the ostensible "suicide bombing" of the World Trade Center and the Pentagon were pressed to evoke the spectral memory of Japanese kamikaze pilots. This analogy nonetheless resonated even in commentary that presented itself in the guise of critique, as in Baudrillard's discussion of the events of September 11, 2001, where he makes repeated reference to the presumed hijackers as "the kamikazes" (2001/2002a: 405, 411).[8] Such historical allusions, however, are strictly anachronistic. Indeed, the historically inaccurate elision of the Pearl Harbor attack (in 1941) with kamikaze suicide bombing (which was first deployed in late 1944; see Dower 1986: 52), is a perfect instantiation of what Michael Rogin incisively depicts as spectacular historical/political amnesia, upholding "an identity that persists over time and that preserves a false center by burying the actual past" (1993: 508). Suspending history by smothering it in a mythified culture of catastrophe, the spectacle of terror thereby served to hint at not only the much-celebrated "end of history" but also a quasi-eschatological end of time.

The Perpetual Present

That the so-called war on terror does not properly belong to historical time was reinforced in Bush's originary discourse by a still more grandiose and equally metaphysical gesture:

> There is a great divide in our time—not between religions or cultures, but between civilization and barbarism. People of all cultures wish to live in safety and dignity. The hope of justice and mercy and better lives are common to all humanity. Our enemies reject these values—and by doing so, they set themselves not against the West, but against the entire world. (December 7, 2001).

By disqualifying the "terrorist" enemy from civilization itself, and thereby from humanity as a whole, the ostensible "great divide in our time" is in fact shadowed by a preposterously implausible unity of humankind as such, under the aegis of "America" as "freedom's defender" (December 7, 2001). Thus, whereas "the bitterness . . . of our war in the Pacific now belongs to history"—and as such, by implication, may be consigned to a remote and domesticated (already "known" but effectively unknowable) past—the United States' present commitment to global war was refigured as "civilization's fight," in which even Japan, "one of our former enemies," may be counted as a junior partner (ibid.). At least in its ideological intent, these mystical fashionings of the United States' "mission" and "great calling" (ibid.) enact Debord's depiction of the spectacle as "essentially tautological" (1967/1995: 15) and the expression of a "ruling order [that] discourses endlessly upon itself in an uninterrupted monologue of self-praise" (19).

The events of September 11, 2001, were almost immediately codified (and commodified) as the quasi-hieroglyphic ideogram, "9/11" (Heller 2005: 3; cf. Simpson 2006), and as we have already seen, ideologically figured as a rupture in time that altogether severed those events from any prior history and enshrouded the perpetual spectacular present in the timelessness of a war without end (Trimarco and Depret 2005). True to the mandates of the society of the spectacle, the originary "shock and awe" of the attacks on the World Trade towers almost instantaneously became, in Wyatt Mason's words, "the most exhaustively imaged disaster in human history" (2004), and has retained the character of what Dana Heller aptly calls "a kind of memory that is not a recollection but a repetition" (2005: 24). Indeed, beginning exactly from the literal void left by the collapsed towers, tellingly designated "Ground Zero," there was initiated, through persistent insistence and astounding repetitiveness, a spectacular void in time itself, after which, by implication, there could be no past, no history that might illuminate, but only the "social organization of a paralyzed history, of a paralyzed memory" (another of Debord's formulations of the spectacle; 1967/1995: 114). Already by the following day, the script was fixed in place: "We're facing a different enemy than we have ever faced. . . . This will be a monumental struggle of good versus evil" (Bush, September 12, 2001). A few days later, Bush's handlers had consolidated their discourse further: "This will be a different kind of conflict against a different kind of enemy" (Bush, September 15, 2001). The following day, this "new kind of enemy" was further glossed as "a new kind of evil," which would be met with a "crusade" (Bush, September 16, 2001). Four days thereafter, it was nothing less than "a different world" (Bush, September 20, 2001).

The self-evident anti-Muslim overtones of Bush's invocation of a "crusade"—an apparently fleeting yet flagrant ideological gesture (notably made on a Sunday, which Bush explicitly hailed as "the Lord's Day" when "millions of Americans mourned and prayed," accompanied by nine mentions of the word "faith")—met almost immediately with vociferous opprobrium. The "scandal" conveniently allowed Bush to cynically disavow such allegations in a classic instance of what Slavoj Žižek (1997: 31–33) describes as a momentary revelation of the obscene, which enables power to retroactively engage in self-censorship in order to enhance the efficiency of its own discourse. The day before, Bush had already dutifully conscripted an emphatically ecumenical multiculturalism into the service of reanimating US nationalism, promulgating that "Americans of every faith" were committed to "eradicate[ing] the evil of terrorism" (September 15, 2001). Earlier still, in a televised phone call with the mayor of New York City and the governor of New York state, Bush had already declared, "our nation must be mindful that there are thousands of Arab Americans . . . who love their flag just as much as the three of us do. And we must be mindful that as we seek to win the war that we treat Arab Americans and Muslims with the respect they deserve" (September 13, 2001). Thus, he had already implicitly instituted the notion that there were some Arabs and other Muslims who—because they might in some manner demonstrably perform their "love" for the US flag and thus confirm that they are "good Americans"—could thereby be verified to be deserving of respect. Then, upon delivering his ultimatum to the Taliban regime as the prelude to war against the people of Afghanistan, Bush explicitly addressed himself to "Muslims throughout the world," avowing "We respect your faith. . . . Its teachings are good. . . . The enemy of America is not our many Muslim friends; it is not our many Arab friends," and thus made explicit the capricious distinction between "good" Muslims and "evil" ones, enemies who "hate us."

Notably, in the truest spirit of the society of the spectacle, Bush speci- fied among the Taliban's most reprehensible crimes the charge that "you can be jailed for owning a television" (September 20, 2001). All religious creeds, however "diverse," may be interchangeably "good," or are at least universally tolerable, insofar as they interchangeably refract the universal estrangement of human productive powers and creative capacities. But then television's spec- tacle too must be venerated, or at least granted its due toleration, alongside all the other proverbial opiates of the mass of humanity. What is decisive in Bush's magnanimously "multiculturalist" discourse of US power is the more fundamental friend/enemy distinction (De Genova 2010). Such imperial multiculturalism is inevitably premised upon submission and conformity to the global regime of capital accumulation which enforces such alienation—a "world order . . . ultimately backed by the U.S."[9] Thus, the ultimatum to the Taliban also notoriously provided the occasion for an ultimatum to the world: "Either you are with us, or you are with the terrorists" (Bush, September 20, 2001).

If this was a discourse that sought to interrupt and suspend history, there- fore, it was also one that aspired to fix the future, matching retrospective recon- structions with century-long projections. Precisely in the posthistorical spirit of divining and conjuring into existence a "new American century" (and honoring the sheer inconceivability of such an epoch not being predicated upon warfare),

Bush had promptly nominated his so-called war on terror as "the war of the twenty-first century" (Bush, September 13, 2001). Thus, this discourse aimed to preempt the possibility that there could be even a plausible future within the scope of any living person's life span that might be different from the regime of the present moment. In a peculiar turn of events, however, the mass media widely reported Bush's formulation of an implicit hundred years' war as "the first war of the twenty-first century," thereby parochializing this war as just one more in a presumably never-ending prosaic succession and also implicitly limiting its temporal horizon. A notoriously ineloquent (and therefore all the more congenially populist) mouthpiece, Bush very probably misspoke in the first instance; hence, his oratory may have been subsequently rectified by those who superintend his cue cards and speech teleprompters. Or perhaps his rhetoric was simply subjected to the stringent discipline of the spectacle itself, and had to be brought in line with a phrase that had already become inflated by its almost instantaneously global circulation. In any case, the slogan was accordingly revised in Bush's own rhetoric (e.g., September 16, 2001). Later, however, in an effort to promote the notion of a necessary and overdue "revolution" in "the American way of war," Bush did nonetheless rekindle another variant of this millenarian century–speak, referring to "the terrorists" definitively as "the enemies of the 21st century" (December 11, 2001).[10]

Thus, everything is new, nothing will ever be the same again, but henceforth, nothing will change, ever again.

In the wake of the election of Barack Obama as Bush's successor to the US presidency, the facile illusion that the most pernicious aspects of the Bush administration would now be simply finished, or promptly rectified by a new regime in the White House, has had to be tempered by a sober and intrepid assessment of the deeply consequential institutionalization of antiterrorism (De Genova 2010). One need only note that in his speech on the evening of the election, Obama found it imperative to proclaim to the world: "And to all those watching tonight from beyond our shores, from parliaments and palaces to those who are huddled around radios in the forgotten corners of our world . . . a new dawn of American leadership is at hand. To those who would tear this world down—we will defeat you" (November 4, 2008). Even as Obama gestured toward a "new" (and by implication, different) style of "leadership," here was the requisite signal and the belligerent affirmation of a pronouncedly "American" imperial will to overpower those who might dare to set themselves up as the enemies of "this world," which is to say, after all, this global regime of capital accumulation and its regnant sociopolitical order. In his speech on "national security," delivered on the eve of the Memorial Day (militarist) holiday weekend during the first months of his presidency in 2009, Obama reasserted the entrenched idiom of the Bush administration's rationalizations for its overseas military adventures, vowing to "take the fight to the extremists who attacked us on 9/11." Indeed, he invoked yet again the dominant ideological message of historical rupture—"After 9/11, we knew that we had entered *a new era*"—while he likewise reaffirmed the well-worn theme that could situate his own devout commitment to war making within a larger national-family narrative of perpetual renewal: "Now this generation faces a great test in the specter of terrorism" (May 21, 2009; emphasis added). Remarkably though, if only inadvertently, Obama designated the defining enemy of the era—"terrorism"— to be but a "specter," a haunting metaphysical fixture virtually indispensable to the ongoing project of US empire and militarism as a way of life.

Under Obama, furthermore, Bush's "state of emergency" has been normalized and routinized, now articulable in a rather more prosaic language. Instead of incendiary alarm or millenarian urgency, Obama recites his antiterrorist articles of faith in the manner of a somnambulist: "We know that al Qaeda is actively planning to attack us again. We know that this threat will be with us for a long time . . ." (May 21, 2009). Most revealingly, upon the assassination of Osama bin Laden in 2011, Obama's presumed triumph was distinctly understated and somber. In place of trumpeting the bravado of assault squad commandos, he quietly praised the "tireless" and "painstaking" work of "counter-terrorism professionals" and "our intelligence community." While unequivocally characterizing the event as "the most significant achievement to date in our nation's effort to defeat al Qaeda," Obama nonetheless insisted, "[bin Laden's] death does not mark the end of our effort. There's no doubt that al Qaeda will continue to pursue attacks against us. We must—and we will—remain vigilant at home and abroad" (May 2, 2011). Thus, the resounding message was that, in effect, nothing had changed— that perpetual warfare as well as the "vigilance" of a veritably global security state would remain the banal fact of a by now relentlessly tedious "new era."

Rupture and Continuity

In terms that Debord surely must have appreciated for their obscene piety toward the spectacle, the end of the Cold War had occasioned Francis

Fukuyama's precipitous (and precisely, spectacular) proclamation of the End of History in 1989, with a crypto-Hegelian neoliberal anticipation of "the universal homogeneous state" tersely characterized as "liberal democracy in the political sphere combined with easy access to VCRs and stereos in the economic" (1989: 6; cf. 1992). Exactly one month after September 11, 2001, Fukuyama found it proper to reiterate his position. Perfectly enacting Debord's contention that "the spectacle is the self-portrait of power" (1967/1995: 19), Fukuyama announced: "We remain at the end of history because there is only one system that will continue to dominate world politics, that of the liberal-democratic West" (2001; see also De Genova 2010).

Within this resounding echo chamber of triumphalism, much of contemporary social and political criticism is itself a merely "spectacular critique of the spectacle" (Debord, Thesis III; 1988/2005), recapitulating as many of its conceits as not. Perhaps the most telling example of such spectacular criticism, precisely because of its flagrant combination of at times astonishing lucidity with casual and abject cynicism, is that of Jean Baudrillard. The enduring salience of Debord's thought may indeed be detected in the analogies with it suggested by Baudrillard's work. Although, in his later works, Baudrillard is fairly circumspect about his theoretical debts to Debord, evidences are ample, nonetheless, as in his audacious gesture: "The spectacle of terrorism imposes the terrorism of the spectacle" (2001/2002a: 414; 2001/2002b: 30).[11] Because of the distinct affinities between Baudrillard and Debord, therefore, my critique aspires to engage Baudrillard in a manner both more generous and more interested than might be viable from the vantage point of more polemically anti-"postmodern" treatments (e.g., Norris 1992).[12] After all, Baudrillard had the critical acumen to respond almost instantaneously to the events of September 11, 2001, by declaring unsentimentally that "free-market globalization is in the process of actualizing itself . . . [as] a globalized police state of total control, with a security terror" (2001/2002a: 414; 2001/2002b: 32).

For discrepant reasons theoretically, and with the apparently opposite political conclusion, Baudrillard nonetheless concurs with Fukuyama's prognosis: against those who "believed in a resurrection of history beyond its well-advertised end," Baudrillard affirms with regard to the events of September 11, 2001, "this terrorist violence is neither a reality backlash nor a history backlash" (2001/2002a 413; 2001/2002b: 28–29). Thus, Baudrillard effectively replaces Fukuyama's cheerful neoliberal triumphalism with predictions of an inexorable apocalyptic doom. Interlaced with eulogies for "the West" and "the white world" as "the waste-product of its own history" (1992/1994: 67), Baudrillard forecasts "the slow extermination of the rest [*sic*] of the world" (66) and ultimately humanity's "death as a species" (71). It is, however, a distinctly "retrospective apocalypse" (22). Elsewhere, moreover, he is emphatic about his particular objection to the notion of an "end" of history, as such: "We have to get used to the idea that *there is no end any longer, there will no longer be any end*, that history itself has become interminable. . . . This attempt to escape the apocalypse of the virtual is a utopian desire, the last of our utopian desires" (116–117); emphasis in original). The apocalypse that Baudrillard announces, then, is expressly not real but rather "virtual" (119)—not so much an "end" of history as a veritable reversal (10–13), and thus history's nullification through perpetual recycling (27), "a catastrophic process of recurrence" (11). If it is catastrophic, then, it is only so in a more or less predictable—hence, strictly manageable (66)—way, because it is never genuinely new but rather a mere repetition and virtual recapitulation of history in a state of suspended animation. Fukuyama's "end of history" thus presents itself in Baudrillard's interpretation as something more akin to an incessant barrage of reruns, engulfing us in virtuality and evacuating all events of any meaning. From the same perspective, but referring to "the spirit of terrorism" and the aftermath of the events of September 11, 2001, Baudrillard detects merely "a repetitive and déjà vu type of pseudo-event" (2001/2002: 415; 2001/2002b: 34). Hence, for Baudrillard, "we no longer make history. We have become reconciled with it and protect it like an endangered masterpiece" (1992/1994: 23), and "in this way, we enter, beyond history, upon pure fiction, upon the illusion of the world" (122). Like Fukuyama, nevertheless, Baudrillard (even in the guise of criticism) merely exalts the futility of resistance, and what is ultimately the smug conceit of an unabashedly solipsistic Eurocentrism in his philosophical standpoint is tantamount to a grand injunction to paralysis and, precisely, specular passivity.[13] Baudrillard's critique of the notion of the "end of history" amounts to little more than the countercontention that nothing has changed and, indeed, nothing can change.

The compulsive proclamation that "everything changed," on the other hand, is indisputably one of the more blatant if no less nefarious ideological operations of the hegemonic discourse of antiterrorism in the aftermath of the events of September 11, 2001. As for Bush, so also for Obama: "After 9/11, we knew that we had entered a new era . . ." (Obama, May 21, 2009). Critical social inquiry would of course be well-advised to shun such apocalyptic rhetoric, as if we were truly the bewildered inhabitants now of the end of time. "Discontinuity," Walter Benjamin aptly suggests, "is the regulative idea of the tradition of the ruling classes" (1927–40/1999: 364). Hence, the poignancy of Baudrillard's suggestion of a management of catastrophe, its superintendence, and all the finely calibrated orchestration and choreography thereby implied. If one may speak of cataclysmic and catalytic events, however, it is useful to recall a still more fundamental critical insight derived from Marx's analysis of capital's voracious appetite for surplus value as its defining feature. Insofar as surplus value can only be extracted from living labor (so-called variable capital), the cyclical crises of undervalorization compel a process whereby unprofitable investments in physical capital must occasionally be sacrificed in favor of new investments that can put living labor to work and thus generate new sources of surplus—what, since Schumpeter, has been known as the "creative destruction" of fixed capital (Schumpeter 1950: 83; see also Sewell 2012). We are therefore left to confront what becomes, in Amadeo Bordiga's memorable elaboration of Marx's crucial thesis, nothing less than a "ravenous hunger for catastrophe and ruin" in "an economy based on disasters" (1951; see also Klein 2007). Furthermore, it is instructive to guard a deep and abiding sense of Benjamin's parallel theoretical concern: "that things are 'status quo' *is* the catastrophe" (1927–40/1999: 473; emphasis in original); "The tradition of the oppressed teaches us that the 'state of emergency' in which we live is not the exception but the rule" (1940/1968: 257).

Nevertheless, as Debord sagely recognizes, "To analyze the spectacle means talking its language to some degree" (1967/1995: 15). In other words, to dissect and interrogate the spectacle's semblance of unity, one must become practically entangled with a unity that the spectacle itself projects. The specious unity of the spectacle is "merely the official language of generalized separation"—the separation occasioned by the systemic and universal detachment of fractured images from every aspect of what may formerly have been cognizable as the totality of social life (12). Reality then becomes apprehensible, if at all, only in always-already partial and fragmented shards, so innumerable that the only semblance of a unity is that grand inversion presented by the spectacle itself. In his reflections on the Bonapartist despotism of the French Second Empire, Benjamin memorably offers a prescient remark: "In times of terror, when everyone is something of a conspirator, everybody will be in a situation where he has to play detective" (1938/1973: 40). Like a detective, indeed, one must gather apparently disconnected clues from the many shattered and scattered fragments, and reconstruct a negative image of the spurious totality that the spectacle bombastically and gratuitously supplies in the course of its own narcissistic exhibition.

Confronted with the diversionary tactics of this ubiquitous fragmentation, spectacular criticism of the spectacle, in contrast, can merely ironize "the unfolding of events which are themselves also without meaning and consequences and in which . . . there are no longer any causes, *but only effects*" (Baudrillard 1992/1994: 121; emphasis in original). This sort of nihilistic disillusionment, reduced to rhetorical contrivance, which we may detect in one such as Baudrillard, provides an exemplary instance of what Giorgio Agamben (following Debord) identifies as one of the defining features of the spectacle itself as "our epochal condition": "What prevents communication is communicability itself; human beings are kept separate by what unites them. . . . Language not only constitutes itself as an autonomous sphere, but also no longer reveals anything at all—or, better yet, it reveals the nothingness of all things" (1990[1996/2000]: 85; cf. Lefebvre 1961/2002: 76). In contrast to the garrulous irony of spectacular criticism, as Agamben incisively notes with regard to the creative paralysis of the satirist Karl Krauss in the face of the "indescribable" rise of German fascism, "Debord's discourse begins precisely where satire becomes speechless" (76).

Where Satire Becomes Speechless

Amid the cacophony of heightened security alerts and the proclamations that everything had changed, that we were living now in an altogether different world, there were also immediately discernable calls summoning ordinary US citizens to demonstrably enact with patriotic fervor the "the steel of American resolve" to not allow those "despicable" terrorist bullies to intimidate "a great nation" (Bush, September 11, 2001). What was the precise content of this relentless flattery of "American resolve"? Anything less than a dazzling display of collective will to "be open for business" would be tantamount to conceding that the enemy had succeeded in their mission of depriving "Americans" of "our way of life, our very freedom" (ibid.). The day after September 11, 2001, when Bush appeared for a media photo opportunity with his National Security "team" to announce that the prior day's events were indeed "more than acts of terror. They were acts of war," he assured the public that the state was indeed there to protect "the nation" and deliver it from darkness, that the federal government was fully operative, that all of its agencies were indeed "conducting business." "But," he continued, "it is not business as usual" (September 12, 2001). Evidently in a spirit of magnanimity that inadvertently confirmed that "our way of life, our very freedom" was not, in fact, to be confused with free time, however, when Bush officially proclaimed Friday, September 14, 2001, to be a "National Day of Prayer and Remembrance for the Victims of the Terrorist Attacks on September 11, 2001," he "encourage[d] employers to permit their workers time off *during the lunch hour* to attend noontime services to pray for our land" (September 13, 2001; emphasis added).

Five days after the events, on the same occasion when Bush notoriously announced that the so-called war on terror was a "crusade" in which "we will rid the world of evil-doers," the complementary and truly emphatic message of his prepared remarks was nonetheless that it was time to "go back to work" and "work hard like you always have" (September 16, 2001). Indeed, in this brief outdoor press conference, for which the prepared opening statement consisted of only five short paragraphs, Bush remarkably uttered the words "work" or "job" fifteen times. In a subsequent media event, staged in an airport to shore up confidence in the ailing airline industry, Bush ventriloquized the air travelers in attendance by proclaiming "their" clear message to the "American public": "get about the business of America" . . . "we must stand against terror by going back to work" (September 27, 2001). In the face of increasing evidence of an economic recession, these ham-fisted injunctions to collectively shake off the proverbial posttraumatic stress syndrome and return to productive labor were also coupled with tinny bids to go shopping. However uncannily, Bush even declared it "one of the great goals of this nation's war . . . to restore public confidence in the airline industry . . . to tell the traveling public: Get on board . . . Fly and enjoy America's great destination spots. Get down to Disney World in Florida. Take your families and enjoy life, the way we want it to be enjoyed." One could scarcely miss the spectacular code-switching between the commander-in-chief's millenarian scenarios of "a new type of war" against an elusive network of "evildoers" "who know no borders," intent to "terrorize America" (ibid.), on the one hand, and the chief executive cheerleader's feeble pleas for what Dana Heller has called "the promise of closure through consumption" (2005: 20) and "America-as-cure marketing" (21), on the other, luridly strung together in absurd dissonance, alternating currents within the same speech. Hence, the message: Be scared, be very, very scared . . . but don't neglect your patriotic duty in the war against terrorism to "get on board . . . and enjoy life"; just be mindful to do so "the way we want it to be enjoyed." As if to verify that his own incessant labor "to rout out and destroy global terrorism" was enough to work up a beastly appetite, furthermore, Bush opened his remarks (September 27, 2001) with mention that Chicago's mayor, who was on hand, had reportedly promised to buy him lunch; Bush predictably pandered to what Benjamin DeMott (1990) has called "the imperial middle": "I like my cheeseburger medium."

It should suffice to say nothing else of Bush's mediocrity than that it supplied only the most perverse instance which cynically confirms, indeed displays, nothing so much as the veritable status of all US presidents, precisely, as puppets. Here is a revealing instance, however, of just what kind of theatrical work is required of those who come to serve as such prominent devices in the larger spectacle. "The self-movement of the spectacle consists in this," Debord clarifies, "it arrogates to itself everything that in human activity exists in a fluid state so as to possess it in a congealed form—as things that, being the negative expression of living value, have become exclusively abstract value. In these signs we recognize our old enemy the commodity, which appears at first sight"—very much like the cheeseburger that the mayor is going to *buy* for the president— "a very trivial thing, and easily understood, yet which is in reality a very queer thing, abounding in metaphysical subtleties" (1967/1995: 26). Prefiguring the spectacle indeed, as Agamben notes in his reflections on Debord, the "secret" of the commodity was one that capital sought to most effectively conceal "by exposing it in full view" (Agamben 1990 [1996/2000]: 74]).

Bush's seemingly trite and ephemeral remark about an apparently trifling cheeseburger, which he was so performatively eager to consume, abounds in the sort of metaphysical subtleties that command immanent critique. Indeed, the gesture recalls Andy Warhol's famous observation about the metonymic relation between "America," the illusory egalitarianism of the market, and the absolute supremacy of the commodity:

> You can be watching TV and see Coca-Cola, and you know the President drinks Coke, Liz Taylor drinks Coke, and just think, you can drink Coke too. A Coke is a Coke and no amount of money can get you a better Coke than the one the bum on the corner is drinking. All the Cokes are the same and all the Cokes are good. Liz Taylor knows it, the President knows it, the bum knows it, and you know it.[14]

Bush's cheeseburger thus signaled his fatuous equality (his primacy among equals, we might say) with the citizens and denizens alike who comprise the US populace and are routinely interpellated into varying degrees of subjection by his discourse. The cheeseburger's prospective consumption promised to consummate what would be, by implication, the well-deserved but emphatically humble reward for Bush's tireless labor of protecting "the American people" by waging and winning the so-called war on terror. Earlier, in an awkward effort to strike a measured balance between the potentially competing demands of compassion and "resolve," tragedy and opportunity, mourning and war making, Bush had remarked: "I am a loving guy, and I am also someone, however, who has got a job to do—and I intend to do it" (September 13, 2001). The middle-brow, "Middle America," and compulsively "middle-class" (reactionary) populism of US politics aside, and its egalitarian ethos of wholesome and unpretentious sameness notwithstanding, the message was clear. The president was simply and dutifully doing *his* job, just as he urged everyone else to get back to work and do theirs: "And we have got a job to do—just like the farmers and ranchers and business owners and factory workers have a job to do. My administration has a job to do, and we're going to do it. We will rid the world of evil-doers" (ibid.). The just reward for each and every hardworking drone (as patriotic citizen-bystanders in the larger passion play of "America" versus evil) would also be "at first sight an extremely obvious, trivial thing," which upon closer inspection is revealed to be "a very strange thing, abounding in . . . theological niceties" (Marx 1867/1976: 163)— the commodity—in this instance, dressed down in the homely and diminutive garb of so many unassuming cheeseburgers, all the same, and all good.

Or, at least, as good as anyone should have any right to expect.

Securitizing Everyday Life

The demand for a dutiful and docile (and now, patriotic, even heroic) submission to the terrifyingly mundane business-as-usual of alienated labor and joyless consumption has to be recognized as the covert yet resplendently overt "truth" of the regime of the spectacle and its official "state of emergency" (Bush, September 14, 2001). While Bush persistently reiterated the litany, which he had enunciated in his very first "Address to the Nation" on the evening of the events, that "the terrorists" were obsessed with "America" and targeted it because it is "the brightest beacon for freedom and opportunity in the world" (September 11, 2001)—later embellishing the claim with the contention that "these people can't stand freedom; they hate our values; they hate what America stands for" (September 13, 2001)—his injunctions to the citizenry in this monumental struggle against evil itself were consistently and remarkably quotidian. "Americans are asking: What is expected of us?" Bush ventriloquized, with the immediate reply, "I ask you to live your lives, and hug your children" (September 20, 2001). He went on to list a series of other modest, even pedestrian, requests: do not single out anyone for "unfair treatment or unkind words because of their ethnic background or religious faith"; make charitable donations for the victims of the attacks; cooperate with the FBI; be patient with delays and inconveniences caused by more stringent security measures, for a very long time to come; continue to "participate" confidently in the US economy; and pray for the victims, for the military, and "for our great country" (ibid.). In short, leave the war in the hands of the experts (including the prosecution/persecution of suspected enemies; cf. De Genova 2007), submit to the authority of the security state, combine religious devotion with nationalist and militaristic acquiescence, work hard, spend money without inhibitions, and above all, just "live your lives"—which is to say, conform to the dreary lifeless conventions of an already alienated everyday life.

The spectacle of "terrorism," however, electrified the overall sense that the everyday—if consistently disappointing, universally dissatisfying, and in general, excruciatingly boring—was now to be both equated with a nostalgia for a putatively "lost" sense of safety and comfort, and permanently if ineluctably imperiled by an elusive menace. Baudrillard notes incisively:

> [The terrorists] have even—and this is the height of cunning—used the banality of American everyday life as cover and camouflage. Sleeping in their suburbs, reading and studying with their families, before activating themselves suddenly like time bombs. The faultless mastery of this clandestine style of operation is almost as terroristic as the spectacular act of September 11, since it casts suspicion on any and every individual. Might not any inoffensive person be a potential terrorist? . . . So the event ramifies down to the smallest detail—the source of an even more subtle mental terrorism. (2001/2002b: 19–20; cf. 2001/2002a: 409–410)

Furthermore, Baudrillard adds, "If they could pass unnoticed, then each of us is a criminal going unnoticed . . . and, in the end, this is no doubt true"

(2001/2002b: 20; cf. 2001/2002a: 410).[15] Here, indeed, is the most profound possible meaning to Baudrillard's contention that "a globalized police state of total control" is being actualized through "a security terror" (2001/2002a: 414; 2001/2002b: 32). This subtle terrorizing that apparently disrupts and destabilizes the somnolence of the everyday, which Baudrillard attributes to the cunning of "the terrorists," is figured however as an effect of a larger "vertiginous cycle" in which the suicidal death of the terrorist is "an infinitesimal point," a kind of miniscule puncture "that provokes a suction, a vacuum, a gigantic convection" around which power "becomes denser, tetanizes itself, contracts and collapses in its own superefficiency" (2001/2002a: 409; cf. 2001/2002b: 18). He goes on to claim that "all the visible and real power of the system" is virtually helpless against the merciless and irreducible potency of the minute but symbolically supercharged suicides of a few individuals—exactly because their deaths challenge power to match their exorbitant audacity and determination by doing what it could never do (destroy itself), thus leaving it with no possibility of a symbolically adequate reply (ibid.). Yet, in all of this, Baudrillard never parts company with the official story, by which we are instructed to believe—based on the "intelligence" of the police and secret police, the veracity of which may strictly never be demonstrated and is therefore never strictly verifiable—the unquestionable and irrefutable "truth" of what is finally a conspiracy theory *par excellence* about a handful of fanatics.

The "shock and awe" publicity campaign for the obscenely asymmetrical and ruthlessly indiscriminate aerial bombardment of Iraq (to say nothing of the less trumpeted assault on an already prostrate Afghanistan before it, and then again subsequently under Obama) surely never matched the palpable symbolic momentousness of the collapse of the World Trade Center's twin towers. Nevertheless, that spectacular "originary" moment indubitably did provide the ensuing onslaught of global militarism with the necessary (and arguably adequate, if not sufficiently persuasive) symbolic "cause." And if these spectacular events have indeed ensured that we are all now suspects (De Genova 2007), each a potential "criminal going unnoticed" (Baudrillard 2001/2002b: 20; cf. 2001/2002a: 410), then the securitization of everyday life that has ensued from the gigantic convection generated by those events may itself be their supreme achievement. For, the "terrorist" menace is the state's pronouncedly evil changeling, its most perfect and ideal enemy, whose banal anonymity and phantasmagorical ubiquity prefigure and summon forth the irradiation of the everyday by the security state as our savior and redeemer.

The ascendancy of the reanimated security state may even be an expression of the would-be superefficiency of the system of power. In contrast to Baudrillard's sense of its impending doom, this securitarianism has precisely not gone reeling from a symbolically mortal assault and careening toward an implosive collapse, but rather has refortified its foundations by seeking to meticulously secure and perpetuate what Vaneigem called "the everyday eternity of life" (19911994: 7), with all its "abundant and bitter consolations" (8).

By now, we are overdue to revisit some of the critical insights of the critique of everyday life postulated by Henri Lefebvre (1947; 1961; 1968; 1981; 1992), who was, after all, a major intellectual precursor and interlocutor for Debord, Vaneigem, and their Situationist collaborators. Indeed, in *Everyday Life in the Modern World* (1968), his boldest reformulation of that critical itinerary, which he ultimately continued to elaborate and refine over the greater part of a long and remarkably prolific intellectual lifetime, Lefebvre arrives at an arresting conclusion: the outcome of an excessively bureaucratitized capitalist society of controlled consumption and regimented everyday life is, precisely, *terrorism* (1968/1971: 148). More specifically, Lefebvre interrogates a kind of terrorism predicated upon a repressive social order "that, in order to avoid overt conflicts, adopts a language . . . that deadens or even annuls opposition . . . a certain type of (liberal) democracy where compulsions are neither perceived nor experienced as such," which "holds violence in reserve . . . [and] relies more on the self-repression inherent in organized everyday life" (146). In *a terrorist society* (in emphatic contradistinction with the reign of political terror and its extravagant recourse to outright violence to terrorize a polity), Lefebvre continues, "compulsion and the illusion of freedom converge . . . terror is diffuse, violence is always latent, pressure is exerted from all sides." The putative "values" of such a society "need no explaining, they are accepted, they are compelling, and any desire to understand or question them savours of sacrilege" (147). In a terrorist society, "each individual trembles lest he ignore the Law . . . everyone feels guilty and is guilty—guilty of possessing a narrow margin of freedom and adaptability and making use of it by stealth in a shallow underground darkness, alas, too easily pierced" (159). Hence, "moral discipline [is] the insignia of terrorist societies . . . the façade exhibited for the benefit of a well-governed everyday life" (161). This sort of terror defines for itself a pure, formal, abstract, unified societal space of everyday life as the arena of its power, from which time—and thus, history and historicity—must be unrelentingly evicted. Rather than a space of "false consciousness," therefore, it is one of a true but crippled consciousness of reality, severed from the sheer open-endedness of radical possibility and unscripted creativity, which renders terror *normal* (179). Thus, we may say that securitarianism is the spectacular face of what Lefebvre calls a "terrorist society." Securitarianism is indeed a form of rule enacted through the spectacle of terror.

The spectacle of security then recalls again Marx's more elemental depiction of capital (dead labor), sucking life from the wakeful death of the living, ensconced as we are in the routinized subordination of our work and the subordinated routinization of our everyday life. Indeed, as Marx incisively notes, "Security is the supreme social concept of civil society; the concept of the police. . . . Security is . . . the *assurance* of its egotism" (1843/1978: 43; emphasis in original). The egotism of the global capitalist sociopolitical order, of course, operates both as the unencumbered reign of private property and private aggrandizement, but also as the atomizing individuation that ubiquitously accompanies an alienated everyday life, where privacy is haunted always by privation (cf. Lefebvre 1947/1991: 149; 1961/2002: 70–74). If security is the assurance of the generalized poverty, tedium, and humiliation that together comprise the most elementary preconditions of capitalist social relations of both production and consumption, then the spectacle of security, like all propaganda, necessarily takes everyday life as its premier object and entails a strategic struggle to possess it by tactical calculation (Lefebvre 1961/2002: 73), to "[smother] it under the spurious glamour of ideologies," and to perpetrate and perpetuate "a passive awareness of disaster and gloom" (Lefebvre 1968/1971: 33).

Their Terror, or Ours?

It is safe to say, in conclusion—and without at all compromising the requisite methodological agnosticism about "conspiracy theories"—that, to paraphrase Sartre, were there no terrorists, the US nation-state, in its ongoing bid for hegemony over the global empire of capital accumulation, would have to invent them. The terrorist menace has simply been altogether too enormously profitable and frighteningly (indeed, terrifyingly) enabling, politically. The self-anointed most perfect democracy fabricates its own inconceivable enemy, terrorism. It wants, actually, to be judged against the inconceivable (phantasmatic) ghoulishness of its spectral enemies, rather than by any of the measurable results of its actual endeavors. The authoritative account of the ahistorical timelessness of terrorism is written by the imperial state in its ever-agonistic plea for genuinely global sovereignty, and it is thus instructive. We, the spectating populations, must certainly never know everything about terrorism, but we must always know enough to be convinced that, compared with terrorism, everything else seems rather acceptable, in any case more rational and democratic. Their terror, or ours? Pick your poison—in the end, they may just as well be indistinguishable.

Notes

1   Acknowledgments: I am grateful to Marcial Godoy for his vision as the organizer of the workshop, "Citizenship, Securitization and Vernacular Violence," sponsored by the Social Science Research Council, and held at Bogaziçi University in Istanbul (January 2007), for which this essay was first commissioned. I also owe a note of profound appreciation to Ayça Çubukçu, Zeynep Gambetti, and Magdalena Rodríguez for their intellectual engagement during its original formulation and revision. Some portions of this essay were included in my chapter, "Spectacle of Terror, Spectacle of Security," in Shelley Feldman, Charles Geisler, and Gayatri Menon, eds., *Accumulating Insecurity: Violence and Dispossession in the Making of Everyday Life* (Athens: University of Georgia Press, 2011).

2   Remarkably, the French state authorized an injunction on January 29, 2009, signed by the minister of culture, Christine Albanel, to prevent the selling of Debord's archive to Yale University, officially declaring it to be "a national treasure" with "a great importance for the history of the ideas of the second half of the twentieth century and for knowledge of the still-controversial work of one of the last great French intellectuals of the period" (Gilman-Opalsky 2011: 23, 31–32n.16).

3   Debord would indubitably have had as his principal frame of reference the state repression of "terrorism" associated with the left-wing "armed struggle" movements that emerged in Europe during the 1970s, as well as the various military formations associated with separatist movements demanding national self-determination in Europe, such as in Northern Ireland or the Basque country. Writing in the late 1980s, during the waning years of the Cold War, when anti-imperialist national liberation struggles throughout the so-called Third World were routinely branded as "terrorist," and in the aftermath of various sensational airline highjackings, however, Debord would already have recognized the increasing salience of the figure of "international" terrorism. Thus, in retrospect, we may appreciate his insights with

regard to the contemporary (post-2001) discourse of antiterrorism, not merely as a commentary on the devolution of the social and political struggles of the 1960s but also as a remarkably prescient anticipation of post–Cold War geopolitical realignments.

4   For more extended elaborations of Debord's conception of the society of the spectacle, see De Genova 2011. For other recent engagements with Debord, see, for example, Agamben 1990; cf. 1995/1998: 6, 10–11; Gilman-Opalsky 2011; Giroux 2006; Hussey 2001; Jappe 1993; Merrifield 2004 and 2005; Retort 2004, 2005, 2008; Rogin 1993; Weber 2002. For critical engagements with Retort 2005, see Balakrishnan 2005; Campbell 2008; Katz 2008; Mitchell 2008; Stallabrass 2006; Tuathail/ Toal 2008. For more general invocations of the significance of spectacle, see also the contributions to Garber, Matlock, and Walkowitz, eds. 1993; for a discussion of "the banality of images" for a consolidation of global power through visuality, see Mirzoeff 2005: 67–115.

5   The more prosaic of these themes have already been remarkably prominent in critical scholarship regarding the antiterrorist security state. For work addressing the intersection of "incessant technological renewal" with the operations of state power, see Monahan 2006 and Webb 2007. For work on the fetishization of technology, see Campbell 2006, Goff 2004; Johar Schueller 2007, and Parenti 2007. For work on the "fusion of state and economy," see Fernandes 2007; Hughes 2007, Martin 2007, and Wolin 2008.

6   I. Lewis Libby, Paul Wolfowitz, and Zalmay Khalilzad, draft of "Defense Planning Guidance" (1992), a classified document prepared for Secretary of Defense Dick Cheney, later leaked to the *New York Times* and the *Washington Post*, at which point public controversy required that it be rewritten; excerpts available at: www.pbs.org/wgbh/pages/frontline/shows/iraq/etc/wolf.html. See also "Excerpts from Pentagon's Plan: 'Preventing the Re-Emergence of a New Rival'," *New York Times*, March 8, 1992; "Keeping the U.S. First," *Washington Post*, March 11, 1992.

7   Notably, in addition to his vice president, secretary of defense, and other top-ranking officials in his war cabinet, George W. Bush could likewise count his own brother, Jeb Bush (governor of Florida) as yet another PNAC signatory. Especially in light of the state of Florida's pivotal role in securing the presidency for George W. Bush in the 2000 election, and with regard more generally to the beleaguered status of his accession to the office, many have posited that the whole constellation begins to bear the hallmarks of a palace coup, albeit one of a peculiarly "democratic" and ultimately "legal" sort. This, of course, is merely one of several conceivable conspiracy theories, of which I am inclined to be a purveyor of none, and about which,

following Debord's preoccupation with the woefully agonistic character of any quest for "truth" under the regime of the spectacle, I find it prudent (and productive) to remain agnostic, as these matters are finally uncertain and probably genuinely unknowable. Methodologically, however, the more pertinent challenge is not to engage in conspiratorial guessing games, and even more important, to remain averse to any still more dubious endeavors to evaluate good faith or bad intentions on the parts of the personnel who administer the spectacle's domination, which can only be tantamount to apologetics. Instead, the task of critical social inquiry has to be to scrutinize and soberly assess the real effects.

8   Notably, in the translation by Chris Turner (Baudrillard 2001/2002b), published in book form by Verso, the term *kamikaze* is studiously avoided.

9   See note 6, above.

10   For a critique of the strategic reorientation known as "the revolution in military affairs" and its ideology of "full-spectrum dominance," prominently championed by Bush's first secretary of defense, Donald Rumsfeld, see Goff 2004 and Parenti 2007.

11   Much earlier, and at a crucial point of departure in his intellectual trajectory, Baudrillard (1973/1975: 120) paid modest homage to the singularity of the Situationist conception of the society of the spectacle as one of his own theoretical antecedents, and in an interview in 2000 remarked that Debord should be read as "one of the most important thinkers of the twentieth century, precisely because he is not a postmodernist thinker, nor a prophet nor a precursor of the post-modern condition. He is the opposite: a suicide" (Hussey 2001: 7in. 6). For their part, the Situationists also acknowledged the superficial affinities of Baudrillard's thought with their own critique, disparaging him in their characteristically polemical style as a "decrepit modernist-institutionalist" (quoted in Knabb 1981: 211).

12   For a useful critique of Norris's critical strategy of "attacking a soft target of [Baudrillard's] own invention," see Patton 1995:17.

13   For a thoughtful reading that seeks to recuperate the critical potential of Baudrillard's concepts of "simulation" and "the simulacrum," notably posited explicitly in relation to Debord, see Hussey 2001.

14   The Andy Warhol Museum, "Andy Warhol: Life and Art," www.warhol.org/education/pdfs/art_and_life.pdf.

15   Although I have relied upon the Valentin translation (2001/2002a) in citations above and hereafter, I have opted in favor of the Turner translation (2001/2002b) here as a matter of preference for the suggestiveness of his choice of language in this instance.

References

Agamben, Giorgio. 1990 [1996/2000]. "Marginal Notes on Comments on the Society of the Spectacle." In Agamben, *Means without End: Notes on Politics*, 73–90. Minneapolis: University of Minnesota Press.

———. 1995/1998. *Homo Sacer: Sovereign Power and Bare Life*. Stanford: Stanford University Press.

———. 1996/2000. *Means without End: Notes on Politics*. Translated by Vincenzo Binetti and Cesare Casarino. Minneapolis: University of Minnesota Press.

Balakrishnan, Gopal. 2005. "States of War." *New Left Review* 36: 5–32.

Baudrillard, Jean. 1973/1975. *The Mirror of Production*. Translated by Mark Poster. St. Louis: Telos Press.

———. 1992/1994. *The Illusion of the End*. Translated by Chris Turner. Cambridge: Polity Press/Blackwell.

———. 2001/2002a "L'Esprit du Terrorisme." Translated by Michel Valentin. *South Atlantic Quarterly* 101(2): 403–415.

———. 2001/2002b *The Spirit of Terrorism, and Requiem for the Twin Towers*. Translated by Chris Turner. New York: Verso.

Benjamin, Walter. 1927–40/1999. *The Arcades Project*. Translated by Howard Eiland and Kevin McLaughlin. Cambridge: Harvard University Press.

———. 1938/1973. *Charles Baudelaire: A Lyric Poet in the Era of High Capitalism*. Translated by Harry Zohn. New York: Verso.

———. 1940/1968. "Theses on the Philosophy of History." In Benjamin, *Illuminations: Essays and Reflections*, 253–264. Translated by Harry Zohn. New York: Schocken Books.

Boose, Lynda. 1993. "Techno-Muscularity and the 'Boy Eternal': From the Quagmire to the Gulf." In Amy Kaplan and Donald Pease, eds., *Cultures of United States Imperialism*, 581–616. Durham: Duke University Press.

Bordiga, Amadeo. 1951. "Murder of the Dead." First published in *Battaglia Comunista* 24, www.marxists.org/archive/bordiga/works/1951/murder.htm.

Bush, George W. 2001 (September 11). "Statement by the President in His Address to the Nation." White House Office of the Press Secretary, http://georgewbush-whitehouse.archives.gov/news/releases/2001/09/20010911-16.html.

———. 2001 (September 12). "Remarks in Photo Opportunity with the National Security Team." White House Office of the Press

Secretary, http://georgewbush-whitehouse.archives.gov/news/
releases/2001/09/20010912-4.html.

———. 2001 (September 13). "President Pledges Assistance for New York
in Phone Call with Pataki, Giuliani." White House Office of the
Press Secretary, http://georgewbush-whitehouse.archives.gov/news/
releases/2001/09/20010913-4.html.

———. 2001 (September 14). "Declaration of National Emergency by
Reason of Certain Terrorist Attacks." White House Office of the
Press Secretary, http://georgewbush-whitehouse.archives.gov/news/
releases/2001/09/20010914-4.html.

———. 2001 (September 15). "Radio Address to the Nation." White House
Office of the Press Secretary, http://georgewbush-whitehouse.archives.
gov/news/releases/2001/09/20010915.html.

———. 2001 (September 16). "Today We Mourned, Tomorrow We Work."
Remarks by the President upon Arrival, the South Lawn. White House
Office of the Press Secretary, http://georgewbush-whitehouse.archives.
gov/news/releases/2001/09/20010916-2.html.

———. 2001 (September 20). "Address to a Joint Session of Congress and the American People." White House Office of the Press
Secretary, http://georgewbush-whitehouse.archives.gov/news/
releases/2001/09/20010920-8.html.

———. 2001 (September 27). "Get On Board!" Remarks to Airline
Employees at O'Hare International Airport, Chicago, Illinois. White
House Office of the Press Secretary, http://georgewbush-whitehouse.
archives.gov/news/releases/2001/09/20010927-1.html.

———. 2001 (December 7). "We're Fighting to Win—And Win We
Will." Remarks by the President at USS Enterprise Naval Station,
Norfolk, Virginia on Pearl Harbor Day. White House Office of the
Press Secretary, http://georgewbush-whitehouse.archives.gov/news/
releases/2001/12/20011207.html.

———. 2001 (December 11). "President Speaks on War Effort to Citadel
Cadets." White House Office of the Press Secretary, http://georgewbush-
whitehouse.archives.gov/news/releases/2001/12/20011211-6.html.

Campbell, David. 2006. "The Biopolitics of Security: Oil, Empire, and
the Sports Utility Vehicle." In Mary L. Dudziak and Leti Volpp, eds.,
Legal Borderlands: Law and the Construction of American Borders, 351–380.
Baltimore: Johns Hopkins University Press.

———. 2008. "Beyond Image and Reality: Critique and Resistance in the Age of Spectacle." *Public Culture* 20(3):539–549.

Debord, Guy. 1967/1995. *The Society of the Spectacle*. Translated by Donald Nicholson-Smith. New York: Zone Books.

———. 1988/2005. *Comments on the Society of the Spectacle*. Translated by NOT BORED!, www.notbored.org/commentaires.html.

De Genova, Nicholas. 2007. "The Production of Culprits: From Deportability to Detainability in the Aftermath of 'Homeland Security'." *Citizenship Studies* 11(5): 421–448.

———. 2010. "Antiterrorism, Race, and the New Frontier: American Exceptionalism, Imperial Multiculturalism, and the Global Security State." *Identities* 17(6): 613–640.

———. 2011. "Alien Powers: Deportable Labor and the Spectacle of Security." In Vicki Squire, ed., *The Contested Politics of Mobility: Borderzones and Irregularity*, 91–115. London: Routledge.

DeMott, Benjamin. 1990. *The Imperial Middle: Why Americans Can't Think Straight about Class*. New York: William Morrow.

Dower, John W. 1986. *War without Mercy: Race and Power in the Pacific War*. New York: Pantheon Books/ Random House.

Fernandes, Deepa. 2007. *Targeted: Homeland Security and the Business of Immigration*. New York: Seven Stories Press.

Fukuyama, Francis. 1989. "The End of History?" *National Interest* 16 (Summer):3–18.

———. 1992. *The End of History and the Last Man*. New York: Free Press.

———. 2001. "History Is Still Going Our Way." *Wall Street Journal*, October 5, 2001.

Garber, Marjorie B., Jann Matlock, and Rebecca L. Walkowitz, eds. 1993. *Media Spectacles*. New York: Routledge.

Gilman-Opalsky, Richard. 2011. *Spectacular Capitalism: Guy Debord and the Practice of Radical Philosophy*. London: Minor Compositions,

Giroux, Henry A. 2006. *Beyond the Spectacle of Terrorism: Global Uncertainty and the Challenge of the New Media*. Boulder, Colo.: Paradigm Publishers.

Goff, Stan. 2004. *Full-Spectrum Disorder: The Military in the New American Century*. Brooklyn, N.Y.: Soft Skull Press.

Heller, Dana. 2005. "Introduction: Consuming 9/11." In Dana Heller, ed., *The Selling of 9/11: How a National Tragedy Became a Commodity*, 1–26. New York: Palgrave Macmillan.

Hughes, Solomon. 2007. *War on Terror, Inc.: Corporate Profiteering from the Politics of Fear.* New York: Verso.

Hussey, Andrew. 2001. "Spectacle, Simulation, and Spectre: Debord, Baudrillard, and the Ghost of Marx." *Parallax* 7(3):63–72.

Jappe, Anselm. 1993. *Guy Debord.* Berkeley: University of California Press.

Johar Schueler, Malini. 2007. "Techno-Dominance and Torturegate: The Making of U.S. Imperialism." In Ashley Dawson and Malini Johar Schueler, eds., *Exceptional State: Contemporary U.S. Culture and the New Imperialism*, 162–190. Durham: Duke University Press.

Katz, Cindi. 2008. "The Death Wish of Modernity and the Politics of Mimesis. *Public Culture* 20(3):551–560.

Klein, Naomi. 2007. *The Shock Doctrine: The Rise of Disaster Capitalism.* New York: Picador.

Knabb, Ken, ed. 1981. *Situationist International Anthology.* Translated by Ken Knabb. Berkeley, Cal.: Bureau of Public Secrets.

Lefebvre, Henri. 1947/1991. *The Critique of Everyday Life*, vol. 1: *Introduction.* Translated by John Moore. New York: Verso.

———. 1961/2002. *The Critique of Everyday Life*, vol. 2: *Foundations for a Sociology of the Everyday.* Translated by John Moore. New York: Verso.

———. 1968/1971. *Everyday Life in the Modern World.* Translated by Sacha Rabinovitch. London: Allen Lane/ Penguin.

———. 1981. *Critique de la vie quotidienne*, vol.3: *De la modernité au modernisme (Pour une métaphilosophie du quotidien).* Paris: L'Arche.

———. 1992/2004. *Rhythmanalysis: Space, Time, and Everyday Life.* New York: Continuum.

Martin, Randy. 2007. *An Empire of Indifference: American War and the Financial Logic of Risk Management.* Durham: Duke University Press.

Marx, Karl. 1843/1978. "On the Jewish Question." In Robert C. Tucker, ed., *The Marx-Engles Reader*, 26–52. 2nd ed. New York: W.W. Norton.

———. 1867/1976. *Capital: A Critique of Political Economy*, vol. 1. Translated by Ben Fowkes. New York: Penguin.

Mason, Wyatt. 2004. "The Holes in His Head." Review of *In the Shadow of No Towers*, by Art Spiegelman. *New Republic on Line*, posted September 21, www.tnr.com/docprint.mhtml?i=20040927&s=mason092704.

Merrifield, Andy. 2004. "Debord's World." *Environment and Planning D: Society and Space* 22(3):325–328.

———. 2005. *Guy Debord.* London: Reaktion Books.

Mirzoeff, Nicholas. 2005. *Watching Babylon: The War in Iraq and Global Visual Culture*. NewYork: Routledge.

Mitchell, W.J.T. 2008. "The Spectacle Today: A Response to RETORT." *Public Culture* 20(3): 573–581.

Monahan, Torin, ed. 2006. *Surveillance and Security: Technological Politics and Power in Everyday Life*. New York: Routledge.

Norris, Christopher. 1992. *Uncritical Theory: Postmodernism, Intellectuals, and the Gulf War*. Amherst: University of Massachusetts Press.

Obama, Barack. 2008 (November 4). "Remarks of President-Elect Barack Obama: Election Night." Chicago, www.barackobama.com/2008/11/04/remarks_of_presidentelect_bara.php.

———. 2009 (May 21). "Text: Obama's Speech on National Security." *New York Times*, www.nytimes.com/2009/05/21/us/politics/21obama.text.html?ref=politics.

———. 2011 (May 2). "Remarks by the President on Osama Bin Laden." White House Office of the Press Secretary, www.whitehouse.gov/the-press-office/2011/05/02/remarks-president-osama-bin-laden.

Parenti, Cristian. 2007 "Planet America: The Revolution in Military Affairs as Fantasy and Fetish." In Ashley Dawson and Malini Johar Schueler, eds., *Exceptional State: Contemporary U.S. Culture and the New Imperialism*, 88–104. Durham: Duke University Press.

Patton, Paul. 1995. "Introduction." In Jean Baudrillard, *The Gulf War Did Not Take Place*, 1–21. Translated by Paul Patton. Bloomington: Indiana University Press.

Project for the New American Century (PNAC). 1997. "Statement of Principles" (June 3), www.newamericancentury.org/statementofprinciples.htm.

———. 2000. "Rebuilding America's Defenses: Strategy, Forces and Resources for a New Century" (September), www.newamericancentury.org/defensenationalsecurity.htm.

Retort (Iain Boal, T. J. Clark, Joseph Matthews, and Michael Watts). 2004. "Afflicted Powers: The State, Spectacle, and September 11." *New Left Review* 27:5–21.

———. 2005. *Afflicted Powers: Capital and Spectacle in a New Age of War*. New York: Verso.

———. 2008. "The Totality for Grownups." *Public Culture* 20(3):583–593.

Rogin, Michael. 1993. "'Make My Day!' Spectacle as Amnesia in Imperial Politics." In Amy Kaplan and Donald Pease, eds., *Cultures of United States Imperialism*, 499–534. Durham: Duke University Press.

Schumpeter, Joseph A. 1950. *Capitalism, Socialism, and Democracy.* 3rd ed. New York: Harper.

Sewell, William H., Jr. 2012. "Economic Crises and the Shape of Modern History." *Public Culture* 24(2): 303–327.

Simpson, David. 2006. *9/11: The Culture of Commemoration.* Chicago: University of Chicago Press.

Slotkin, Richard. 1973. *Regeneration through Violence: The Mythology of the American Frontier, 1600–1860.* Middletown: Wesleyan University Press.

Stallabrass, Julian. 2006. "Spectacle and Terror." *New Left Review* 37:87–106.

Tuathail, Gearóid Ó (Gerard Toal). 2008. "Pleasures of the Polemic." *Public Culture* 20(3):561–571.

Trimarco, James, and Molly Hurley Depret. 2005. "Wounded Nation, Broken Time." In Dana Heller, ed., *The Selling of 9/11: How a National Tragedy Became a Commodity*, 27–53. New York: Palgrave Macmillan.

Vaneigem, Raoul. 1967/1994. *The Revolution of Everyday Life.* Translated by Donald Nicholson-Smith. London: Rebel Press/ Left Bank Books.

———. 1991/1994. "The Everyday Eternity of Life." Preface to the first French paperback edition. In *The Revolution of Everyday Life*, 7–15. Translated by Donald Nicholson-Smith. London: Rebel Press/ Left Bank Books.

Webb, Maureen. 2007. *Illusions of Security: Global Surveillance and Democracy in the Post-9/11 World.* San Francisco: City Lights Books.

Weber, Samuel. 2002. "War, Terrorism, and Spectacle: On Towers and Caves." *South Atlantic Quarterly* 101(3):449–458.

Wolin, Sheldon S. 2008. *Democracy Incorporated: Managed Democracy and the Specter of Inverted Totalitarianism.* Princeton: Princeton University Press.

Žižek, Slavoj. 1997. "Multiculturalism, or, the Cultural Logic of Multinational Capitalism." *New Left Review* 225:28–51.

Contributors

YASEMIN IPEK CAN is a researcher and PhD candidate in both Standford University and Bilkent University. Her work at the Department of Anthropology at Stanford University focuses on nationalism, public space, temporality, and affective publics in Beirut, Lebanon. She also conducts research on the politics of self, memory, and nationalism in the autobiographies and memoirs of leading figures of early Republican Turkey at the Department of Political Science at Bilkent University. She has published articles in peer-reviewed journals (such as *Toplum ve Bilim*) based on her findings from an ethnographic study of civil society organizations in Turkey between 2006 and 2007, where she explored the juxtaposition of modernist-nationalist middle-class discourse with the neoliberal promotion of self-esteem programs for primary school children from poor and marginalized segments in society.

NICHOLAS DE GENOVA is reader in anthropology at Goldsmiths, University of London. He is the author of *Working the Boundaries: Race, Space, and "Illegality" in Mexican Chicago* (2005); coauthor of *Latino Crossings: Mexicans, Puerto Ricans, and the Politics of Race and Citizenship* (2003); editor of *Racial Transformations: Latinos and Asians Remaking the United States* (2006); and coeditor of *The Deportation Regime: Sovereignty, Space, and the Freedom of Movement* (2010). He is completing a new book, entitled *The Migrant Metropolis*.

GEORGI M. DERLUGUIAN is associate professor of social research and public policy at New York University, Abu Dhabi. He has been conducting field research since the 1980s on various guerrilla movements, revolutions, and civil wars in Africa, Central Asia, and the Caucasus. He also studied the social origins of nationalist intellectuals and the politics of market reforms. In 2006, the *Times Literary Supplement* listed among the books of the year his monograph *Bourdieu's Secret Admirer in the Caucasus: A Biography in World-Systems Perspective*.

ZEYNEP GAMBETTI is associate professor of political theory at Bogazici University, Istanbul. Her main academic interests center around the theory and practice of collective agency, social conflict, and democratic ethics. Besides being engaged in theoretical investigations, especially on Hannah Arendt's political thought, she has carried out research and has published extensively on the transformation of the conflict between the Turkish state and the Kurdish movement. Her work has appeared in a number of journals and publications, including the *Journal of Balkan and Near Eastern Studies*, *New Perspectives on Turkey*, and *Rethinking Marxism*. She is currently working on a book that brings Arendt into dialogue with Marx.

PETER GESCHIERE is professor of African anthropology at the University of Amsterdam and coeditor of *Ethnography* (Sage). Since 1971 he has undertaken historical-anthropological fieldwork in various parts of Cameroon and elsewhere in West Africa. His publications include *The Modernity of Witchcraft: Politics and the Occult in Post-colonial Africa* (University of Virginia Press, 1997) and *Perils of Belonging: Autochthony, Citizenship and Exclusion in Africa and Europe* (University of Chicago Press, 2009). His book *Witchcraft, Intimacy, and Trust: Africa in Comparison* is forthcoming from the University of Chicago Press.

MARCIAL GODOY-ANATIVIA is a sociocultural anthropologist and the associate director of the Hemispheric Institute of Performance and Politics at New York University. He is also editor, with Jill Lane, of *e-misférica*, the institute's trilingual online journal. From 2000 to 2007, he worked in the Program on Latin America and the Caribbean and the Program on International Collaboration at the Social Science Research Council. His recent publications include "Between the Hammer and the Anvil: Middle East Studies in the Aftermath of 9/11" (with Seteney Shami); "We Are Living in a Time of Pillage: A Conversation with Carlos Monsiváis"; and *Ciudades Translocales:*

Espacios, flujo, representación—Perspectivas desde las Américas, coedited with Rossana Reguillo. He serves on the Board of Directors of the North American Congress on Latin America (NACLA) and on the Editorial Committee of *NACLA: Report on the Americas*.

STEPHEN JACKSON is currently chief of staff of the United Nations Office in Burundi (BNUB). His chapter in this volume draws on research from his time as associate director of the Conflict Prevention and Peace Forum, a program of the Social Science Research Council in New York, and was contributed in a personal capacity. He holds a PhD in cultural anthropology from Princeton University. His research interests include the political economy of war, global/local conflict linkages, principles and practice in humanitarian affairs, the political manipulation of ethnic identity, politico-ethnic violence, the postcolonial state, and regional conflict formations. His work has appeared in a number of prominent journals and publications, including *Politique Africaine*, the *Review of African Political Economy*, and *African Studies Review*. He is the coeditor, with Anne-Maria Makhulu and Beth Buggenhagen, of *Hard Work, Hard Times: Global Volatility and African Subjectivities* (University of California Press, 2010).

ROSSANA REGUILLO CRUZ is a research professor in the Department of Sociocultural Studies at the Instituto de Estudios Superiores de Occidente, ITESO, in Guadalajara, Mexico, where she coordinates the program of research in sociocultural studies. Her current areas of study include youth and urban culture, the social construction of fear, and cultural aspects of the relationship between communication and violence. She has been a visiting professor at several Latin American universities and in Europe and the United States. Her publications include *La construcción simbólica de la ciudad: Sociedad, desastre, comunicación* (Guadalajara: Universidad Iberoamericana/ ITESO, 1996); *Ciudadano N: Crónicas de la diversidad*, with an introduction by Carlos Monsiváis and a preface by Jean Franco (Guadalajara: ITESO, 1999); *Horizontes fragmentados: Comunicación, cultura, pospolítica. El (des) orden global y sus figuras* (Guadalajara: ITESO, 2005); and *Culturas juveniles: Formas políticas del desencanto* (Buenos Aires: Siglo XXI).

NANDINI SUNDAR is professor of sociology at the Delhi School of Economics, Delhi University. Her publications include *Subalterns and Sovereigns:*

An Anthropological History of Bastar (2nd ed. 2007); and *Branching Out: Joint Forest Management in India* (2001); as well as several edited volumes. From 2007 to 2011, Sundar coedited *Contributions to Indian Sociology*, and she currently serves on the boards of several journals, including *American Anthropologist* and *International Review of the Red Cross*. In 2010, she was awarded the Infosys Prize for Social Sciences–Social Anthropology. Her current interests relate to citizenship, war, and counterinsurgency in South Asia, indigenous identity and politics in India, the sociology of law, and inequality. Her public writings are available at http://nandinisundar.blogspot.com.

ANNA LOWENHAUPT TSING is professor of anthropology at the University of California, Santa Cruz. She is the author of *Friction: An Ethnography of Global Connection* (Princeton University Press, 2005) and *In the Realm of the Diamond Queen: Marginality in an Out-of-the-Way Place* (Princeton University Press, 1994). She has coedited a number of volumes, including *Words in Motion* (Duke University Press, 2010, with Carol Gluck) and *Nature in the Global South* (Duke University Press, 2003, with Paul Greenough).

Index

Advani, L. K., 158

Agamben, Giorgio, 16, 169, 170, 226, 228

Ahidjo, President, 45

Akindès, Francis, 79–80

Alarcón, Cristian, 201

Algeria, 177, 179

allogène and *allochtone*, 40, 42, 47, 48, 50–52, 55, 60, 77. *See also* autochthony

al-Qaeda, 178, 222

American plutocracy, 177, 191

Amoore, Louise, et al., 5

Andhra Pradesh Civil Liberties Committee (APCLC, India), 166

"Anti-Maras Summit," 204

anti-Semitism, 192

Armenians in Turkey, 132, 139

autochthony: 2006 DRC elections, 75, 77–82, 86; 2011 DRC elections, 87, 90n18; in Cameroon, 12–13, 43, 45–48, 49–51, 63n12; classical Athenian origins, 55–58, 64n25, 64n29; democratization and, 40–41, 44, 47, 61n2; and denial of history, 57–58; in French colonial

Africa, 58–60 insecurity/security, 12–13, 41, 42–43, 61, 62n4; Ivory Coast policies, 60–61, 63n13; nationalism and, 45, 62n7, 62n9; in Netherlands, 51–55; terminology, 42, 71, 77, 78; violence and fear associated with, 41, 43. *See also* citizenship; *Congolité;* identity

Babri Masjid demolition, 156, 158–160, 168

Barkawi, Tarak, 10

Baruah, Sanjib, 167

Baudrillard, Jean, 215, 216, 217–218, 223–226, 230, 236n11

BBP (Great Union Party, Turkey), 139

BDP (Peace and Democracy Party, Turkey), 132, 133, 143, 148n16, 148n23

Beck, E. M., and Stewart E. Tolnay, 142

Bédié, Henri Konan, 79–80

Bemba, Jean-Pierre, 69–70, 73–77, 78, 82–84, 86–87

Benjamin, Walter, 10, 225

Bharatiya Janata Party (BJP, India), 155–156, 158–159, 162, 168, 169

bin Laden, Osama, 190, 222
Biya, Paul, 44–45, 47
Boose, Linda, 217
Bordiga, Amadeo, 225
Bosi, Umberto, 42
Bourdieu, Pierre, 176, 179, 180–181, 183
Bourdieu, Pierre, and Jean-Claude
    Passeron, 201
Boyle, Danny: *28 Days Later/Exterminio*,
    201–202
Brass, Paul, 153
Brown, Wendy, 7
bureaucracy, ruling, 180–181, 184–186
Burkina Faso, 60
Burt, Jo-Marie, 125
Bush, George W., 216, 217, 218–222, 226–
    229, 229–230, 235n7
Butler, Judith, 17
Buzan, Barry, 1, 9–10, 18n2

Calderón, Felipe, 207
California, 22
Cambodian refugees. *See* mushroom
    picking, commercial; Southeast Asian
    refugees
Cameroon: Banyangi, 46; Buea, 47;
    funerals and autochthony, 12–13, 43,
    45–48, 63n12; historical context, 44–45;
    Iwa, 50; Maka, 50; Mamfe, 45–48; new
    forest laws, 48–51
camouflage clothing in mushroom
    picking, 23, 32
Campbell, Bruce, 155
Canon van Nederland, 53–55, 64n24
capitalism: bootleg wars (North
    Caucasus), 189; cultural-linked niches,
    35; disaster capitalism, 6; expectations

post-USSR, 187; fetishism of the
    commodity, 214; supply-chain, 14, 21–22,
    35; of USSR, 180–181. *See also* market
    economy (neoliberal)
Cárdenas, Osiel, 198
Caucasus, 177, 183–184, 186, 189, 190
Chatterjee, Partha, 118n9
Chechens and Chechnya, 177, 179, 189
Chhattisgarh (India), 162–164, 168
CHP (Republican People's Party, Turkey),
    143
citizenship: anxiety over right of, 85;
    autochthony and, 45, 47, 56, 58, 62n9;
    civic responsibilities, 96–98, 102, 120n15;
    education by volunteers, 109–110;
    education for, 108; enemy and stranger
    distinction, 131; entrepreneurial/
    risk taking, 2, 35, 36; modern versus
    premodern, 115; national canons and,
    53–55; rational-legal basis of, 2–3;
    and state response to dissent, 135–136,
    149n29, 160. *See also* autochthony
civil society: autonomy of, 2–3, 146;
    boundaries of legitimate violence,
    140; and Kurdish question in Turkey,
    125–126, 128, 138–139; manufacturing
    social change, 116; neoliberal return
    of, 145; volunteerism and, 14 (*see also*
    volunteerism)
civil society organizations (CSOs):
    civic responsibilities, 96–98, 118n6;
    civic responsibilities versus state
    responsibilities, 101–102, 120n15;
    depoliticization of public sector, 100, 116–
    117; empowerment rhetoric, 105; security
    against social evils, 94–96, 112–115, 118n6;
    terminology, 117n1. *See also* TEGV

development discourse, 156, 160–161, 163, 177, 163. *See also* market economy (neoliberal)

de Villers, Gauthier, 80

Dink, Hrant, 139

disaster capitalism, 6, 225. *See also* market economy (neoliberal)

drug cartels (Latin America): displays of *violencias*, 198–199, 200; humanitarian aid from, 197–198; *maras* and *kaibiles*, 198, 204, 210n2; media reports of, 201; Mexican state policy, 207

Dudayev, General, 178

Duffield, M, 153–154

Eastern Europe, 179, 182, 183–184

Eboua, Samuel, 46–47

economic shock therapy, 182

education: citizenship through, 109–110; Gülen schools, 107, 120n19; problematized (Turkey), 108; to secure security, 113–115; of self, 108 (*see also* empowerment discourse); as solution to social ills, 112–113; in Soviet collapse, 184–185. *See also* TEGV

Elias, Norbert, 209

El Salvador, 204, 211n9

employment/unemployment: blaming the unemployed, 111; hazelnut market, 142; post–September 11, 2001, 227–229; standard employment expectations, 35 (*see also* mushroom picking, commercial); structural unemployment, 114, 179

empowerment discourse, 104–105, 108–109, 111–115, 116

entrepreneurship: to contain urban unrest, 111–112, 113–115; entrepreneur-prince of

drug cartels, 200; of post–Soviet era, 183, 188, 192; in supply-chain capitalism, 21–22, 35–36 (*see also* mushroom picking, commercial)

Erdoğan, Tayyip, 135, 141, 143–144, 149n29

Escobar, Pablo, 200

ethnic violence: in former USSR, 177, 186, 188–191; globalization cause of, 191–193; role of class in, 179, 190–191. *See also* race and racism

EUFOR (European Union force), 82, 84, 86, 89n17

Euripedes: "Erechtheus," 56–57

Eurocentrism, 224

European Union: Orhan Pamuk trial, 139–140; Turkish nationalism and, 128, 147n6

expert systems, 204–205, 211n11

fear, geopolitics of (globalization of suspicion), 9, 41, 43, 125, 140–146, 202–204, 209

financialization, 6

Fiskobirlik, 142

Flanders, 42

Fortuyn, Pim, 51

Foucault, Michel, 101, 102, 104, 117n2, 118n3, 137

freedom: as an illegitimate ideology, 102; citizenship through endorsing, 35; cultures of, 2, 14, 25, 36; from/of war, 27; political and market, 20, 23, 25, 34; in rhetoric post–September 11, 2001, 217–218, 226–227, 229–230; security-freedom binary, 10, 128, 133, 138–139, 202–203, 232

Fukuyama, Francis, 222–224

funeral ritual in Cameroon, 12–13, 43, 45–48, 63n12

industrialization and deindustrialization, 156, 184, 188, 192–193

insecurity/security binary: after social restructuring, 94–96; autochthony and, 12–13, 41, 42–43, 58, 61, 62n4; in displacements, 161; iron hand laws, 204, 211n9; overview of, 9–11; post 1999 Marmara earthquake, 101; in postconflict elections, 88, 90n19; public-private partnerships, 169–171; role of education, 113–115; rule of law, 2–4, 160; state military power and, 167–168; terrorism discourse, 16, 233–234. *See also* security discourses/rhetorics; violence/*violencias*

International Monetary Fund (IMF): loans to Russian Federation, 187; neoliberalism, 6; in Turkey, 96, 127

Iraq, 231

Islamism as TEGV target concern, 107

Islamists, 139, 149n25, 177

Italy, 42

Ivory Coast: autochthony policies, 60–61, 63n13; *Ivoirité*, 79–80, 82

Jackson, Stephen, 43

Justice and Development Party (AKP, Turkey), 100, 119n11, 125

Kabila, Joseph, 69–70, 72–77, 78, 81–82, 84, 85–86

Kabila, Laurent-Désiré, 69, 72

Kemalist discourse, 106–107, 114–115, 133, 147n10

Kerinçsiz, Kemal, 138–139

Krauss, Karl, 226

Kuanda, Kenneth, 79

Kumar, Ram Narayan, and Amrik Singh, 165

Kurds: lynching attempts by, 149n31; lynching attempts of, 132–134, 141, 146, 148n14, 149n24, 149n29; Mersin incident, 130–131, 147n12; TEGV target concern, 107; Turkey's use of terrorism discourse, 15, 125

Lao refugees. *See* Southeast Asian refugees

Latin America, 104–105, 203, 206. *See also* drug cartels (Latin America)

law, rule of: faith in, 2–3; mimicking criminal violence, 165; paralegalities of *violencias*, 200, 209; role in political liberalism, 3; security as counterpoint to, 9, 160; violence in, 10–12

Lazzarato, Maurizio, 6

Lefebre, Henri: *Everyday Life in the Modern World*, 232–233

Le Pen's Front national (France), 57

liberalism (political), 3, 17, 103

Liberhan report (India), 156, 158–160

Lijphart, A, 52

Loraux, Nicole, 57–58

Löwy, Michel, 196

Lumumba, Patrice, 71, 75, 81

Luning, Sabine, 60

lynching attempts (Turkey): boundaries of state power, 136–138; deaths, 134, 146, 149nn24–25; economic relationship, 141–142; historical context, 126, 128, 147n5; motives, 147n4; specific attempts, 130, 132, 133, 139, 141, 148n23, 148nn13–15,

149n27, 149n31; state response to, 135–136. *See also* vigilantism and securitization

Manipur (India), 167

Maoist guerilla fighters (India). *See* Naxalites (Maoist guerillas, India)

market economy (neoliberal): accumulation by dispossession, 161; disaster capitalism, 6, 225; freedom discourse, 20, 23, 25, 36, 144–145; hazelnut production, 142; role violence, 163; vigilante public-private partnerships, 170–171. *See also* capitalism; development discourse; globalization

Marlovits, John, 22

Marmara earthquake. *See under* Turkey

Marshall-Fratani, Ruth, 79–80

Marxism, 179, 214–215, 225, 233

Mason, Wyatt, 219

matsutake. *See* mushroom picking, commercial

Mayi-Mayi resistance, 89n4, 89n6

McNay, Lois, 6–7

Mersin incident (Turkey), 130–132, 149n23. *See also* lynching attempts (Turkey); Turkey

Mexico: and "American Identity", 205–206; drug cartels, 16, 197–198, 201, 210n3; migration to US, 206; security budget, 207

migration. *See* immigration and migration

Milosevic, Slobodan, 178

Minutemen Project, 205, 206

Misra, Kavita, 104

Mitchell, Timothy, 115

Mobutu, Joseph, 71, 72, 80–81

mob violence, 155–156, 171nn3–5. *See also* vigilantism and securitization

Monga, Celestin, 44

Mongin, Oliver, 196

MONUC (Mission des nations unies en RD Congo), 72–74, 82, 83–84, 86

mosque demolition (India). *See* Babri Masjid demolition

Mossi (Burkina Faso), 60–61

Mouvement pour la libération du Congo (MLC), 72–73, 82, 89

"Multicultural Drama, The" (Scheffer), 52–53, 63n19

multiculturalism, 36, 52–53, 54–55, 63n19, 64n24, 220

multinational capitalism, 145

Murray Li, Tanya, 41

mushroom picking, commercial: business men of, 32; Cambodian refugees' experiences, 27–29; freedom, political and market, 14–15, 20–21, 25, 36; Hmong refugees' experiences, 29–32; Lao refugees' experiences, 32–34, 34–35; Latinos' experiences, 34–35; risks of matsutake harvest, 22–23; specific seasons, 38n5; white veterans' experiences, 25–26

Muslim genocide (Gujarat, 2002), 155

mythmaking, 56, 217–218. *See also* spectacle, society of the

nationalism: American, 226–229; autochthony and, 45, 62n7, 62n9; in collapse of USSR, 185; national canons,

52–55; Turkish, 128–129, 130–131, 147n6, 147n12, 149n26

Naxalites (Maoist guerillas, India), 16, 156, 160–164, 166–167, 168, 171n8, 172n9

neoliberalism: accumulation by dispossession, 36; civil society's role (Turkey), 99–102; definition, 4–9; end of political liberalism, 17; local articulations, 96; new strategies of government, 102–103; politics of fear, 140–146; popular (Tsing), 24, 36; psychological techniques, 104–105; reduction of oppositional space, 126, 127; rule of law, 3–4, 7; social effects of globalization, 127; terminology, 103; war dislocations, 21

neoliberal/neoconservative binary, 2–4, 4–9, 102, 206

neopatrimonialism, 176

Nestlé, 108

Netherlands: autochthony, 42, 51–55, 63n18, 64n24

Ngoy, Théodore, 77

non-governmental organizations (NGOs). *See* civil society organizations (CSOs)

Nurcu movement (Turkey), 120n19

Obama administration, 12, 221–222, 224

Olenghankoy, Joseph, 75, 77, 82–83

Olzak, Suzan, 142

O'Malley, Pat, 103

Ouattara, Alassane, 80

Pamuk, Orhan, 139–140

paralegality, 200–202, 209

Pearl Harbor, 216–218

Peru, 125, 136

Piedras Negras (Mexico), 197–198

pilotless drone surveillance, 84, 89n17

PKK (Kurdistan Workers' Party), 125, 128, 132–135, 138–139, 147n5, 148n14

Plato: "Menexenes" and *Politeia*, 56–57

Polanyi, Karl, 177, 187

police, 162–164, 165

political issues versus agendas, 204, 211n10

political rationality, 94–96, 117n2

Ponty, William, 58–59

Poss, Harry, 205

postconflict election process, 71, 73–77, 81–82, 88, 90n19

post-peace accord violence, 128–129

poverty, 104–105, 108–113, 116–117, 203. *See also* class and socioeconomic divisions

precarity (Butler), 17

primitive accumulation, 6, 16, 161

privatization, 143, 180–181

Project for the New American Century (PNAC), 215–216, 235n7

proletarians, 177–178, 181–182, 184–186; subproletarians, 183–184

prudentialism, 103, 113–114

psychological techniques, 104, 114

public-private partnerships (PPP): government-sponsored vigilantes, 165–168, 170; Rashtriya Swayamsevak Sangh (RSS), 157–160, 171n7; Salwa Judum in Chhattisgarh, 160–164; state-condoned violence, 154–157, 169–171

Purushotham, Sri T., 166

race and racism: in Athenian autochthony, 57; in commercial